"An unmissable insight into the true [...] gangs. You should read this."

"There are some books that stay with you forever and Top Girl will be one of those for me. Vivid, insightful and extremely powerful, I have thought about this book every day since reading it. Danielle has opened my eyes to a world on my doorstep that I have never seen before. And I feel that I am coming away from it a more informed person. It is truly a must-read for everyone." *Jenny Proudfoot, Marie Claire*

"I have a feeling this is going to be one of THE books of 2022."
Linda Hill, Linda's Book Bag

"Whoa! Incredible read… had to remind myself that this isn't crime fiction but crime fact. Harrowing but also inspiring."
Joy Kluver, author of Last Seen, Broken Girls, Left for Dead

"I was in awe of Danielle's strength of character, and that she could make a conscious decision to turn her life round. Top Girl is a powerful story that applies to today's younger generation. I think every school-age child should read this book as it's a lesson in the consequences of making bad choices. Highly recommend." *Lorraine Rugman, The Book Review Café*

"…packs a punch and left me feeling every emotion under the sun. I felt sad, happy, proud and broken but what a journey I went on."
Karen and Her Books

"This searing, moving and, at times, gut wrenching memoir pulls literally no punches.

It is a twenty-first century cautionary tale told with grit, authenticity and a brutal sense of self awareness that honestly humbled me when I read it. This is a woman with integrity... identifying the key periods in her life where she was failed by societal structures.

I had to stop reading several times because it was so very brutal and there is a dignity in how Danielle describes her traumas, it is not exploitative or graphic, which makes what happened to her all the more powerful.

I finished this book in tears and in awe, wanting to applaud this woman for her strength and the way that she continues to use her experiences to contribute to a justice system which is deeply flawed and not fit for purpose." *Rachel Read It, blogger*

5* Reader Reviews, NetGalley

"Beautiful. Poignant. Phenomenal. This was a beautiful read and I learnt so much. I cried and I smiled and there was nothing more that I wanted from this book. Truly a gem."

"I devoured this book in a few days. The tales are at times incomprehensible, and the events 'D' gets involved with are really quite hard to come to terms with. Raw, gritty and so very honest."

"I absolutely loved this book and read it in one day... I just couldn't put it down."

TOP GIRL

DANIELLE MARIN

MARDLE

First published in 2022 by Mardle Books
15 Church Road
London, SW13 9HE
www.mardlebooks.com

Paperback ISBN 9781914451065
eBook ISBN 9781914451133

A CIP catalogue record for this book is available from the British Library.

Every reasonable effort has been made to trace copyright-holders of material
reproduced in this book, but if any have been inadvertently overlooked the
publishers would be glad to hear from them.

Page design and typesetting by Danny Lyle

Printed in the UK

10 9 8 7 6 5 4 3 2 1

The names of some people and places have been changed to protect identities.

*Certain details in this story, including names and locations, have been changed
to protect the identity and privacy of (the author and) those mentioned.*

Cover image:
POSED BY MODEL

For all the lost girls
trying to find their way…

This book contains descriptions
of drug taking and sexual violence.

1

CARNIVAL BABY

I scanned the corner south of the block. All clear – for now. Out front was the green – a patch of coarse, prickly grass and sun-baked dirt – where a few mums chatted over pushchairs. Beyond that, the local park. I was three floors up, above the double deckers, as high as the treetops, peering down on the concrete walkways and steel railings below. From here, I could see it all.

Glancing back to the corner, a police car rolled up. I ducked low, grazing a shoulder on the balcony's rough brick, before daring another look. Chances were, it was just on the prowl, a routine drive-by. But if that car slowed down, well – it was here on business. Perhaps a couple of baby mommas punching it out in the walkway. Maybe a drug deal turned messy in the stairwell. If the car teamed up with a van, the block was getting swept. For real.

Now my heart pounded as the car crawled to a stop. Squatting back down with the balcony for cover, I waved to Ryan three doors down, hissing, "Police!"

He nodded. It was on. We were ready for them.

Ryan darted in his flat where Caribbean music boomed and clattered from the open doorway. My alert rippled along the balcony, bringing more soldiers: Jeremy − usually so quiet and reserved − and Kaiylin, her straggly hair pungent with the smell of incense. Ryan reappeared moments later. We huddled around him as he laid out a carrier bag bristling with pistols.

Fully loaded. Battle ready.

Ryan pressed one − cold and heavy − into my palm, nodding with a wicked grin that said, *you know what to do.* We took up position on the balcony − snipers, sights trained on the two clueless officers below as they made their way towards the block. It was almost too easy. They didn't stand a chance.

She's new, I thought, watching the young, blonde police-woman. Her head bobbed and swivelled like a nodding dog, eyes darting nervously from balcony to balcony as she neared the stairwell. I held my breath. *Almost in range. Almost…*

Then Ryan gave the command: "Now!"

We exploded in whoops and giggles, fingers furiously pumping the sprung plastic triggers of our water pistols. The two cops below tried to dodge the spray. Grinning, they squinted up the tower's concrete walls, trying to spot their assailants. To my surprise, Blondie joined in the game, tucking her chin to her radio to bark, "We're under attack! Send back-up!" I liked her all the more for that.

We howled with laughter, trigger fingers burning.

Just as they folded into the cover of the stairwell, two flashes of colour zipped past me, an inch from my nose. The water balloons, chucked off the balcony above, exploded by the coppers' feet, splattering the hems of their police-issue trousers. Squealing with laughter, we scarpered into the safety of our own flats.

Fair play, the police usually met our water-pistol ambushes with grudging smiles. They weren't so keen on the balloons, but a direct hit scored you some proper kudos. And no seven-year-old was getting locked up for lobbing water bombs. What was the worst that could happen? It wasn't done with malice, or because of some deep-seated hatred of law enforcement. The opposite, in fact. I'd been told to respect the police. Even later – all the bad stuff I got up to – it's not like I was on some massive vendetta.

My mum, Christina, shot a disapproving look at the dripping wet water pistol in my hand as I careered into the kitchen.

"As if those poor police officers don't have enough to do!" she tutted.

I just stood there panting from the thrill of dishing out our latest wet welcome.

"I told you before – they're here to protect us," Mum said. "Let them get on with their job!"

Didn't mean we couldn't be a little bit cheeky with them.

Had to be done. It was practically an unwritten rule.

I jutted my chin at the steaming pot on Mum's stove, and groaned, "Is it ready yet?"

There was no such thing as fast food in Mum's kitchen. Her cooking always took a long time. Slow roasts. Stews. That pot – rich and juicy with meat, lemon and olive oil – could simmer for hours. For me and my little brother, John, it was pure torment.

"It's ready when it's ready," she shrugged indifferently.
She was like that.

Hundred percent – Mum's beef and lamb were cooked so meltingly tender you could cut them with a spoon. But she served her love tough.

You scuffed a knee? Sure, she'd dust you off and make sure you weren't bleeding to death. But if you wanted it kissing better? Well, best bend over and do it yourself. Sometimes, at the school gates, I'd have to squash a pang of jealousy watching mums hugging their kids goodbye. My mum was protective, and I knew she loved me, but she didn't really say it. I don't remember cuddles. The most she'd do was brush my hair.

Perhaps she got that tough streak in the crossing from Cyprus, when the churning sea got her so mad sick that she never set foot on a boat again. Or maybe it was when her carefree Cypriot childhood – long, hot days on the beach, stealing donkeys and galloping them around the olive groves – got blasted to rubble by Turkish bombs.

She'd been in her early teens when my Yai Yai – my grandmother – fled the ruins of their bombed-out village and escaped to the UK. They literally packed a bag and ran, leaving everything behind. Arriving in the 70s, my mum looked every inch the Cypriot refugee, with her dark features, olive skin and brown eyes. "I'm the ugly duckling," Mum would say. "Your auntie Maria – she's the pretty one."

Mum settled in a corner of West London and got a job in the Department of Health. In 1993, she had me. At three years old, she got me baptised in the presence of Our Lord God

Almighty at the Greek Orthodox Cathedral Church of All Saints in Camden. I never knew my dad, nor anything about him. He never came up in conversation, and I never asked. Mum got with Dave not long after I was born and I can't remember a time when he wasn't around. Like the London buses he drove for a living, Dave was solid and dependable. I never asked him for anything, but the unspoken truth was he was there if I needed him. He had this composed, unflappable air about him, like the time my baby brother John put in his first appearance – a week early – on New Year's Eve 1998.

I was just five years old. With Mum ready to pop, there were no grand plans for seeing in the New Year beyond watching Big Ben chime in 1999 on the telly. Her labour took us by surprise late afternoon, too sudden to make it to the maternity ward. Instead, Dave calmly ran her a warm bath, held her steady as she climbed in, then called an ambulance.

Meanwhile, I huddled in the chill of the grey concrete stairwell outside our open front door, where Mum's screams reached me all the way from the bathroom. I was torn – stay out the way or run and comfort her? I rocked back and forth, hugging my knees to my chest, as a couple of paramedics bounded up the stairs. I'd only ever seen them scooping people up off the pavement. I was gripped with panic. *Was Mum going to die?*

Man – having a baby sounded like an ordeal!

Then, all of a sudden, Mum fell silent. There was a pause before Dave came out and reached for my hand. "Come and meet your little brother," he said.

He took me inside where Mum was beaming, lying exhausted in bed, holding this thing – my brother, John.

"I don't like it," I said, grimacing at the pink, damp, wrinkled lump cradled in Mum's elbow. "It looks like a chicken."

That set the tone for years to come.

I'd got used to it being me, Mum and Dave, and even though there was plenty of room for a baby brother in our three-bedroom flat, I just thought John was in the way, a spare part. I'd tease him and wind him up by hiding his favourite toys. It wasn't until years later that I started to gel with him.

But whatever my reservations about the new arrival, Dave still treated me like his own. He'd take us both to gawp at the fossils and the little skeletons in their glass boxes at the Natural History Museum, or the Crown Jewels in the Tower of London. I do remember that about Dave, how proud he was showing us the city, its history, its sights.

Poor Mum, though. She couldn't make sense of it. I think some part of her still longed for the sunshine and olive groves back in Cyprus. She was a square peg in a round hole. "British culture!" she'd sigh. "I get it, but I don't get it. I'm trying, but I don't understand!"

"There's nothing to get, love," Dave would shrug.

Then Mum would cuss in Greek so we kids couldn't understand. "I don't know if I belong here."

Dave would soothe her with a calming word or two in her mother tongue that he'd taken the trouble to pick up, for her sake. She loved how he was on board with her culture – even nailing up those traditional 'evil eye' lucky charms above our bedroom doors – despite her struggling with his.

I thought Dave had a point.

British culture? What even is that?

Our bit of London was Somali, Caribbean, Irish, Greek. I was practically the only white kid in our ends. On summer evenings, front doors hung wide open. Music and kitchen smells from all corners of the world spilled out, and us kids found a welcome at any dinner table. On Monday I could be eating fried chicken and peas round Ryan's, on Tuesday some chickpea hippie food at Kailyn's served up on a tie-dye tablecloth.

Surrounded by all this multiculturalism I should have had a clue there was a big, wide world beyond our postcode. But in my little head, our neighbourhood was *it*.

"Is my headteacher God?" I asked Mum one day. The block, the corner shop, the school, as far as I was concerned, there was nothing else. Didn't *want* anything else.

"Well, no, she's not," she told me. "God created all the world and he's within us all."

"So, my headteacher *is* God, then."

"Here," she said, changing the subject by dragging open the cutlery draw. "Help your mum set the table."

I think it was carnival that really opened my eyes to the fact there were millions more people than just the faces who hung around by the swings, or lived in our tower, or bought Panda Pops from the shop on the corner. Growing up in certain parts of West London, carnival is in your veins. You're a carnival baby. Born to party.

Outsiders – driving up from Devon in their Volvos – think it's just a bank holiday thing. In and out, two days and done. But in our ends, that carnival vibe hung in the air year-round. Parties could blow up any time. All you needed was a sound system and somewhere to plug it in. If that happened to be the high street and the traffic backed up while people danced in the road – tough. Sometimes all it took was a van with a decent stereo cranked up to full volume. No special occasion needed. Just because.

The carnival shop on the main road was busy from early March, as the dressmakers stitched costumes for the local dance schools. Soca music and salsa boomed from its open doors. Lorries unloaded huge rolls of sequin fabric, glitter, head-dresses, coloured feathers, angel wings.

To us kids, it was dazzling, the buzz building all year. By the time August came around, you felt like your heart would explode. Christmas Day thrills served up in late summer.

At first, when I was tiny, I'd stay on the edges of the party, Mum gripping my hand tight. "I'm not letting you out of my sight," she'd say. "You stay right by my side."

This human river bumped and shuffled along Kensal Road, down Ladbroke Grove, dishing out fag burns and trampled feet along the way.

Little kids got swallowed whole, swept away. If you lost your mum at carnival, you'd better know your own way home because you were fucked. Even staying on the fringes, by the time you hit Notting Hill, you were done. Carnival was exhausting.

Of course, I wanted to be in the thick of it, above the crowds, not stuck on the edge staring at bums and backs of legs. So around seven or eight years old, I joined one of the dance schools. It was serious. You had to earn your place on the carnival truck. We practised four nights a week after school. At home, when I had the living room to myself, I'd run through the routines, dancing to music on our little stereo.

One year, when I was maybe 10 years old, we had this routine to S-Club 7. I had it *down*, on automatic. If that tune came on now, I bet I could still do the moves.

Carnival Sunday arrived and I was vibrating with excitement. I felt like I could burst. I was wearing a little, white, sequined bra top – covered in feathers – paired with white shorts. Looking back, for a 10-year-old, it was a bit weird, but there were like 50 of us in the troupe. I guess the costume made sense to someone.

Mum combed my hair into two little braids and we met Kaiylin and the rest of the troupe in a cut-through by Kensal Rise station. It was organised chaos. Chaperones marshalling kids around. Guys loading sound systems onto flatbed trucks. Smoke pluming from charcoal grills. The smell of jerk chicken and charred corn mingled with the sweet funk of weed.

Ah, yeah. That was another feature of life in the ends.

Weed was everywhere. Hard drugs and dealers were part of daily life. They were just there, part of the wallpaper. Back in the day, there was less of this rolling round in cars shotting drugs. The idea of selling Class As by text message was years off – mobile phones were for stockbrokers and big business, not drug addicts.

Instead, deals got done out in the open, bold and brazen, on the street corner. No shame. No real policing.

Walking past with your mum, the dealers didn't even bother hiding what they were up to. No need, they knew you weren't the police. I'd see the boys in the big, shiny cars, one arm slung over the sill, wrist flexing a fat Cuban link bracelet. I wasn't dumb. I knew where they got their money, and I didn't care. True, I didn't know the difference between a Range and a Porsche, but it didn't matter. Even as a little kid, you know what expensive looks like.

At the other end of the transaction – the sharp end – I knew the guy with bad teeth and stinking clothes slumped against the phone box was a crack or smack head.

"Nitties", we called them. And we didn't know any better, so they got singled out for ridicule. One day, playing out on the estate, we stumbled over this desperate soul, drooling down his anorak and missing a shoe. Scabs crusted one corner of his mouth.

"Look at the nitty!" Ryan yelled.

The guy was gone. Skin and bone. Chin nodding into chest. He could have been 18 or 80.

"Hey, nitty!" I joined in.

"Found your shoe, nitty," Ryan mocked, kicking a dumped fried chicken box at the guy. "Come on nitty – put your shoe on!"

Something stirred in him and he tried to fix us with one, wasted eye, fighting the drugs trying to roll it to the back of his head.

We ran, whooping, shouting, "Nitty! Nitty!"

On our block, a kid called Tyrell stalked the darker corners of the alleyways knocking out weed. Tyrell and his little friends, circling the same spot on their bikes every single day, swapping joints, trailing smoke.

"Stay away from them," Mum would warn me. "They're going to cause trouble."

I didn't need no warning. Didn't even look at them. Not that I was scared, but they were like 10 years older than me and I wasn't interested in weed. The only time they spoke to us little kids was to tell us to keep the noise down when it intruded on their music.

They got nicked on a regular basis, the police rolling up in a couple of cars or a team of vans doing their storm-the-block thing. Word soon got around who'd been pinched. More often than not, Tyrell would be back in the same spot the next day, business as usual. One time, they were gone for a couple of weeks, maybe a month.

OK, Tyrell went jail. Cool.

But he was soon back. I had no idea what the police thought they were doing, but to me it looked like a right old waste of effort.

Not for the last time, I thought to myself, *They're not very good at their jobs, are they?*

2

ROUGH DIAMONDS

Tammy snapped a hairband over the end of my pigtail then shuffled round to present the back of her head to me. "You do mine now," she said.

Tammy was half-Moroccan, tiny and gorgeous, with skin the colour of caramel and long, dark hair, reaching almost to her waist. Looks aside, we were like twins – boisterous, cheeky and up for mischief.

"Oh man, you've got mad bed head!" I laughed. "Give me that brush!" I was on a sleepover at her place on a neighbouring estate. 8am, still in our PJs and we'd just woken everyone up blasting out Steps on the stereo. Her mum already had me pegged as a bad influence, so it was another black mark in the naughty book for me. But this was serious business. We had dance moves to learn.

Remember, this was still before the internet and mobiles really took off. I think we were lucky. We made our own fun or played out in the street. Genuinely just kids being kids.

We scoured every corner of our neighbourhood. From an early age, we knew the tube, the buses, Oxford Street, Covent Garden, Hyde Park. As boundaries stretched, our playground grew. Not like today, where everyone's shitting it, and kids are stuck inside all the time staring at their phones. I wish they could have a taste of the freedom we had.

Yet even though we had the city on our doorstep, all roads led back to the ends – to home. To our balcony neighbours and 'the cage' out front, the sandpit and weather-battered playground enclosed by a rectangle of flaking iron fence.

I didn't want or need anything more. But now there was change in the air.

Me and Tammy had been best friends all through primary, but my world was expanding and, with it, a knot of anxiety was tightening in my chest. We sensed the threat to our friendship.

"Are you really going to the grammar school?" Tammy said.

"Still waiting for the results," I told her.

"Edenwood – it's miles away, isn't it? You won't get home until late…"

Yeah. No shit.

I hated talking about what might lay beyond the next summer holiday. Didn't even like thinking about it. OK, a tiny bit of me was excited, curious. Mostly I just felt dread. All my friends were heading to the local comp, but someone – a few people, actually – had decided it'd be a good idea if I tried out for Edenwood Grammar School for Girls. Half-hour train commute each way. Disgusting uniform. I mean, pure embarrassment. Designed by nerds, for nerds. The travel alone would put a serious dent in my after-school social life. And I'd be out of the loop – all the chat and gossip from my friends' classrooms and playgrounds would be lost on me. I knew that even being considered for the grammar was a massive deal, but to me it just felt like the end.

"We'll still hang out though, if you get in? Won't we?" Tammy said.

"Yeah, 'course!" I told her, almost reassured.

This grammar school idea, it wasn't mine, that's for sure. It started with the teachers.

I was good in primary. It was a safe, happy time. The only drama I remember was us daring each other to go in what we called the scary woods in the scrubby patch of green behind the school. Once, we found an abandoned tent hidden among the trees. Even more exciting – there was a knife laying on the dirt nearby. Obviously, someone had been living there. We let our imaginations run wild until we were all screaming and hysterical, convincing each other there were Red Indians holed up in the woods.

"Do we tell the headteacher?" one kid said.

"What about the knife?" said another, bending to pick it up.

"Don't touch it!" I squeaked.

In the end, we kept our find a secret. This was treasure for playground chat and sleepover whispers, when you're both lying there in the dark before sleep. Grown-ups would have spoilt it. We wanted it all to ourselves. The idea that it might in fact be a homeless person living in the woods never entered our eight-year-old heads. Red Indians were far more likely. And more exciting.

It got to Year Five. The teachers used to bang on to me about sitting the 11 Plus exam, because that's how you proved yourself worthy of the great grammar school experience. The way they said it, I knew it was something I was supposed to want. Grammar school was aspirational, a cut above. It was a step up and out of the ends.

But I didn't want out. I loved it right where I was. So I didn't listen.

Instead I set my sights on the well-worn path from local primary to local comp, where I'd have all my little friends at my side. None of them were getting told to try for the grammar. Just me.

"Shall we give you some practice papers to try at home?" my teacher asked.

"Nah, I'm OK thanks," I said, brushing it off.

I thought I'd got away with it, until parents' evening rolled around.

I did the usual thing, sat beside Mum as the teacher told her how great I was.

Then she dropped it.

"We think she's really intelligent," the teacher said. "We think Danielle should sit the 11 Plus and try for Edenwood Grammar School. It's a great opportunity."

Mum looked at me, delighted, mouth open in astonishment. She beamed with pride. "The grammar school! My Danielle..."

She didn't even know what a grammar school was. Nor did I, for that matter. But it sounded posh and that was good enough. They had to explain: it was like some higher level of education for clever kids, but this school was free.

Mum was sold on the idea. It carried on back home. Yeah, she was well keen. "You're clever, it's such a waste if you don't try," she said.

I never really felt like I was clever, but that's what the teachers were saying. Everyone was gassing it up so much, they wore me down. Looking back, I think the teachers were right. I *was* intelligent. I forgot a lot of stuff in the chaos that came later, because winning at crime takes a lot of mental energy. You have to push aside some of what you know to give your brain some wiggle room. They talk about criminals outsmarting the law, and that's bang on. The second you let those smarts slip – that's when you get caught.

OK, I thought. *I suppose I'd better go for it. Maybe I can do it. Maybe the teachers are right. Let's see.*

The teachers gave me the practice papers. While my mates played out, I hit the books, did the tests. They never taught us verbal and non-verbal reasoning in school, and these papers were full of it, so I taught myself. Whatever I'm doing, I'm disciplined about it, and this was no exception. I had the marking scheme, but I never cheated even once, just wrote down my answers and marked the paper.

Tick, tick, tick.

I was hitting 70 to 80 percent without trying too hard.

In the meantime, there were open days at the prospective schools. I got the overland to Edenwood with Mum. The grammar was a couple of minutes' walk from Edenwood High Street station. It was only eight stops down the line, but it felt like a different world.

Shit, I thought. *This is posh. Like − hella posh. No way I'm gonna fit in here.*

I slowed to a halt and rocked on my heels looking up at the fancy gates. Mum was itching to get in there. She was getting different vibes, buzzing that anyone could even think her daughter could slot in a place like this.

"We're just looking. It can't hurt to look!" she told me, snatching up my hand.

Edenwood Grammar is like 300 years old, with archways, imposing Victorian red-brick buildings and tall feature windows. It looked like something from the pages of the *Harry Potter* books in my bedroom. That jump from primary up to big school is a head-wrecker any day of the week, but I just felt overwhelmed.

A prefect showed us around. Everything was so neat, like the whole place had been buffed and polished − even the kids, all pristine and glowing in their spotless uniforms. Those uniforms − ugh! Neon-yellow blouse; blue, knee-length skirt. It was enough to turn your stomach.

You got the same tour at the state schools, but they didn't have the same shine. They were ragged round the edges, a little dishevelled. I knew which I preferred.

Back at home, I tried voicing my misgivings.

"I don't think this school is for me, Mum."

"Oh, come on, just because your friends aren't going! You'll make new friends!"

I looked at Dave. He caught my eye and turned back to his newspaper. He knew who wore the trousers in our house; he wasn't getting involved.

"I don't think I like it," I said.

Mum tutted. "It's lovely! What's not to like? This is going to elevate you, Danielle. You have to try!"

So I did as I was told. Cracked on with the practice papers.

Exam day came, and me and Mum were back on the train. She looked at me over the top of her book. "You're going to try your best, aren't you?"

Maybe she'd read my mind. As I stared out the window, I was secretly wondering whether to fuck it up on purpose and kill this nonsense dead. If I didn't get in because I'd failed the test, she couldn't moan.

"Yeah, course," I said.

By the time I sat down with the test paper in front of me, I'd decided, because part of me wanted to prove myself, to see if there was a place for an estate kid like me in this perfect, shiny world.

OK. Let me just try, I thought. *See what happens.*

It was no stress. I tried, but – honestly – I didn't think I'd got in. Nothing to do with the test and everything to do with the other kids taking it. They were all rich, clever and ambitious. Some wore uniforms for private primary schools. It was written all over their faces – they really, *really* wanted it, like their entire futures rested on the next 90 minutes.

"How was it?" Mum asked expectantly after we'd filed out of the hall.

"Yeah, fine," I shrugged.

We waited.

A couple of months later, a letter dropped through the door, *Edenwood Grammar School for Girls* printed on the front.

"Mum!" I called. "I got the letter!"

She hurried into the hall. "Come here! Give it to me!" She wanted to open it herself. This was *her* dream and she was living it through me. She tore open the envelope and read the letter, a smile bursting on her face as she grabbed me. "You got in! You got in!"

Oh God, I thought. *I should probably go to this school.*

I couldn't let Mum down, kill the dream. And I did feel kinda proud of myself. I'd be lying if I said it wasn't a boost. I'd done it. But – flipside – I wasn't gonna be with my friends.

Through summer, the idea grew on me. I really thought I was ready to take my place in this weird new world of shiny, loaded kids. What is it they say? If you hang around four millionaires long enough, you're gonna be the fifth. I could do it.

But then, that last week of summer hols, realisation dawned as me and Mum did the back-to-school shop.

I got a weird feeling in my belly. This was a bad idea.

While my mates were getting their uniforms in regular shops, I was trying on mine in a dressing room at a bloody John Lewis department store.

John Lewis – that's the only place they sold the damn uniform. Cost a fortune.

'Course, I'd seen this horror on open day and I already knew I hated it. But wearing the thing, I looked a special level of absolute dickhead. Ridiculous long skirt, blue jumper with the school crest and yellow shirt.

"Can I at least get a cool bag?" I pleaded.

I'd had my eye on a little shoulder number with pink lettering. All the girls had them. I even knew what shop to get it from.

But Mum wanted me to fit in.

"I think just get something sensible with plenty of room for your school books," she said, before choosing the ugliest, chunkiest backpack John Lewis had to offer.

The cherry on the dickhead cake. Thanks Mum.

She was keen to come with me that first day, offer me up to the school gates like a sacrifice to progress. I wasn't having it. My credibility was already cancelled; I wasn't gonna make things even worse by having Mum in tow, too. Instead, I braved the train alone, the only kid at my station in an Edenwood Grammar uniform, the carriages rammed with sullen commuters. I stuck out like a sore thumb. Won't lie – it was scary, man.

I'll never forget our first assembly. All the Year Sevens gathered in the hall and, again, I took in the crowd.

Hella posh.

Hella money.

The headmistress got up on stage. She was a stern, dumpy woman with red hair cut like a man's. You could tell she was tough. She fixed the crowd, laser-beaming us with her grammar school vibes.

We are special.

We are better than the rest.

It was contagious. I looked around me. The other kids lapped it up and beamed back.

"My girls," said the head. "You are my diamonds in the rough, you've come to this school, and we're going to polish you up!"

I wanted to puke. First 10 minutes in my new school and the overriding emotion was: *get me the fuck out of here.*

I didn't really make any friends in the first few months. Lunchtimes, I'd sit alone in the playground with my packed lunch and just my stupid big rucksack for company. Hundred percent a dickhead. It was partly my own fault, I was still looking back over my shoulder at Year Six, meeting my old mates after school, clinging on for as long as I could. I was just on a different wavelength to this new crowd. With a passion – I did not want to be like these other girls.

Take Abigail Higgins. White girl with thick, ginger hair and a band of freckles across her nose. We came back to school after the winter break, and everyone was flexing about what they got for Christmas. New make-up. Latest phone. Trainers. The usual.

Then Abigail piped up, "I got a pony."

I looked at her, side eye. "You got a *what*?"

"I got a new horse for Christmas."

I flat out did not believe her. It was ridiculous. Where are you keeping a horse in the middle of Edenwood? Down the end of the garden? I was so confused.

"Let me see your pony then," I said. "Prove to me you got a horse for Christmas."

Abigail shrugged. "OK, you can come to my paddock."

One day I went home with her after school. She lived in a nice semi with bay windows, picket fence, driveway and front garden. Her mum was a GP but she was done for the day and drove us out to this paddock in her BMW X5. I could see her eyeing me up in the rear-view mirror. The estate kid. I got it all the time from the girls at school. *Oh you live in a flat do you? OK…* And then they'd look away, because no one really lived in a flat.

Fair play to Abigail, though – she didn't have just the one horse.

She had three.

"Would you like to ride one," she offered.

"No, but… thanks," I said, peering at the rosettes decorating the stables.

There was no jealousy. Yeah, these kids had cash, but I just thought their lives were weird. Later, when I got invited to the odd birthday party, I felt the same. *Thank God this isn't me.* Some of these girls lived in six-bedroom houses with swimming pools and gyms in the basement. But I felt sorry for them. Their houses were amazing, but there was no corner shop, and everything on the high street shut at 5pm. There were no buses. Their neighbours were strangers to them. Weird.

95 percent of the kids at that school were in it for the win. They wanted the A-stars, the university. It rubbed off on me and I did try with the schoolwork. *If you don't you're gonna look like the stupid one in the class,* I realised. And I didn't want to be that. But when it came to friends, inevitably it was the few naughty kids knocking around that I gravitated to.

I'd seen this one girl, Haina, in the corridor. She literally stuck out – head and shoulders above everyone else – because she was catwalk tall. She was half-Indian, slim and stunning. But it was the way she troubled and back-chatted the teachers that got my attention. She was just plain naughty.

One afternoon, heading home on the train, she got on my carriage with a group of other girls. They headed my way, but got off a couple of stops before me. They seemed more like my kind of people. *These are the girls I need to be friends with,* I realised. Later, walking to the station at home time, we got talking. Sharelle was petite, Asian and always had immaculate nails. There was Alisa – a mixed-race girl, with killer curves and a pretty face. All the boys liked Alisa. And Baduwa, from Ghana, who had dark skin and wore her hair in jumbo braids. I don't know why I was always drawn to people of different ethnicities. I guess because, although I was a little white girl, I never felt like I was from England.

Among these girls, I'd found my place. When I came back to school at the start of Year Eight, it was game over. This rough diamond was gonna take some polishing. From then on, I was all about the 'hood.

3

TREY

Grooming's something you do to a horse, right? It's what Abigail Higgins did to her pony before one of her show-jumping competitions – tie little braids in its mane, plait its tail with ribbons, all that shit. That's how I had it in my 12-year-old head anyway. I wasn't dumb, I knew not to go jumping in Transit vans with grimy old men on the promise of seeing some puppies. But no one told you groomers drove smart cars, too, or that sometimes they wore crisp clothes and nice watches. No one said that they might seem basically cool or could actually be quite fit.

I was out one Saturday in Ealing Broadway, just being on the road. We went park to chill – me, Tammy, a few other girls from the estate. Nearby, a huddle of older boys were passing a spliff around. The coloured bandanas hanging out of their pockets and tied round their wrists were an important detail. They meant 'gang' – and, in this case, a neighbouring postcode with a reputation for extreme violence that was known to have some beef with ours. I wasn't in a gang – I just happened to live in what certain people had decided was gangland.

One guy caught my eye. Dark hair, olive skin. He was slick, Mexican-looking. I smiled, looked away, tugged intently at blades of grass. When I glanced back he was still looking. He flashed me a smile.

"Did you see that?" Tammy said, nudging me. "He's checking you out."

I thought she was probably right, but I played it down all the same. "Nah, shuttup!"

"Oh my God, oh my God, he's coming over!" Tammy said breathlessly.

"Shuttup! He is not!"

For real, he was. And making a beeline for me. His little friends swaggered behind. They sat down with us, all smiles and Mexico offered me the spliff. "I saw you watching. You tryna have some of this?"

I shook my head. "Nah, I don't smoke."

"Oh, you don't smoke, no? We got a little goody two-shoes!"

I felt bold. "I don't have to smoke weed to be bad!"

The boys laughed, loving my burn, as one white guy with frosty, pale green eyes pulled out a bag of green buds.

"It's cool, girls, we'll make one for you, yeah?" he said to the rest of my group.

Like me, they declined.

"You gonna tell me your name then?" said Mexico, shuffling closer.

Not gonna lie – it felt electric. But I played it cool. "What d'you wanna know my name for?"

He laughed. "Relax! We just chattin'!"

"All right then, it's Danielle."

"Danielle!" he said. "Hey, let me get your number, Danielle."

"Oh! It's get my number now? I don't even know who you are."

"Trey Perez," he told me. "Put that in your phone."

The Latin looks did indeed come from Mexico. He was old. Like, not even in education any more. Next to him, I felt – and looked – hella young.

"How old are you?" he grinned, taking a pull on the joint.

"15 innit," I lied. "How old are you then?"

He told me he was 17, then added, "You gonna give me that number?"

Trey and his little friends chilled with us lot for like an hour, and by the time he left, he had my number stored in his phone.

It was a thrill, man. I felt like the best thing since sliced bread. I'd never even kissed a boy, let alone had a boyfriend. Some of the estate girls had had their little things with boys, but not me. When Trey got up to leave and plipped a BMW parked nearby, I thought I was fucking *it*.

"Oh my God, he's so cool! Are you gonna see him then?" Tammy said.

"Ahh, I dunno man. He's *old*, no?"

"I guess. Why d'you tell him you were 15 though?"

I didn't have an answer for that one. And it was only later that I realised what a stupid lie it was. Lies have consequences, and even an innocent little fib like that can come back to bite you. 15 made me 'almost legal'. Yeah – Trey was finished with education, but he could still do the math.

"Dunno," I shrugged. "It just came out."

"Hey," Tammy said, changing the subject. "You gonna skip school with us next week?"

"Nah. Getting back to the ends — it's long, man."

A few of them had started bunking off, and they were always pestering me to chill with them. It didn't make any sense, though. Bare hassle — I still had to sign in the register at school, which meant getting the train all the way out to Edenwood, before coming all the way back again to meet them.

Long.

And for what? Walking round the park in the freezing cold until home time, with the same people I was gonna see after school anyway? At least in lessons it was warm. If I was gonna skip, I needed incentive.

Incentive like, I dunno, a cute boy with Mexican vibes and a BMW.

Trey texted me later that day, weighing in with the soppy stuff for starters.

Hey — so glad I met U. C U l8r? xx

Want to meet up babes? xx

This went on for a couple of weeks before he switched things up, with romantic gems like: *My dick's big — you want some?*

I did not want some, but nonetheless the chat felt exciting and dangerous. At home, I was forever nose-down in my Nokia, thumbs a blur as they punched the keys.

"Who's that you're always texting?" Mum would say.

"Just a friend."

I became the focus of attention in my little circle. I know now that what Trey was doing wasn't cool. But everyone, including me at the time, thought it was. No one else had anything like this going on – it was a buzz. My mates pored over Trey's messages. Sometimes they'd snatch the phone off me, invent some weird sexual shit in reply, then hit send, laughing their heads off.

Let me suk it.

Oh yeh – I can't wait to fuk u. x

Big talk for a 12-year-old. And not even *my* big talk.

I wasn't ready to fuck anyone, and nor were any of my friends. It was all in our heads. I was like some human guinea pig, being offered up to a sex experiment. More lies. Lies with consequences.

I kept this secret from the new friends I'd made at Edenwood Grammar, because on some level, I got that it was a bit wrong and I didn't want them judging me.

In the meantime, Trey's game was getting me to skip school. My inbox was getting more persuasive by the day.

My mum's in work.

We'll have the place to ourselves.

Pick u up at the gates? xx

Incentive. Right there.

I can't even say Trey wore me down, because skipping school with a house to go to made total sense. I wouldn't have to be on the road, in the cold. I left home in my uniform, an extra set of clothes stuffed in my bag – some little leggings or a pair of jeans. I stuck my autograph on the paper register in my form room, and apparently that was the only proof they needed that I'd be spending the rest of the day in school. In the toilets, I got changed and put my big hoops in. And then

I walked out. Brazen. Not even trying to hide it. A train took me to near Trey's place, and when I came out of the station, the BMW was purring on the car park outside.

"Hey," I said to Trey as he popped open the passenger door.

"Everything cool?"

"Everything's cool," I said, sliding in beside him, loving the pop and creak of the leather interior. Rap music bumped and clattered along on the stereo.

"We'll go my place, yeah?"

I nodded. Won't lie, my nerves were jumping a bit. I don't know what I wanted – or what I was expecting – from Trey. Just to chill, I think. In the back of my mind I thought he might try it on a little bit, but I was sure I didn't want to do anything with him. I was too scared.

In any case, that first time, his mum was there. When we walked in, she was sat in the living room. An overflowing ashtray was cupped in the palm of one hand, and in the other she had a cigarette pinched between nicotine-stained fingers. She was tall, and so slim she looked like she'd skipped breakfast. And lunch. For at least a month.

"Did you get my cigarettes?" she said from underneath damp curtains of dirty blonde hair. Trey tossed a packet onto the sofa. She barely looked away from the telly as her very grown-up son led me – a 12-year-old schoolgirl – to his bedroom.

Trey had a double bed pressed against one wall and a little chest of drawers with a TV on top. He stuck *Jeremy Kyle* on, then we got into bed – wearing our clothes – and cuddled up. It put me at ease. I felt super comfortable. While the geeks at Edenwood Grammar were listening to the Literature and

Classics teacher gassing up some dead poet, I was having a little cuddle, watching TV. My head felt heavy. I yawned and followed up with a deep, relaxing sigh.

"You tired babes?" Trey said. "Have a nap if you want. You're safe with me."

"I think I will," I said, closing my eyes and melting into his chest.

It was chill, man. When Trey dropped me off back on the estate at home time, I was already thinking about when I could go again. It got to be a regular thing, a couple of times a week. I still did my homework on time, caught up on stuff I missed in class, and somehow the school never even noticed I wasn't there. The teachers, my mum, Dave – they were oblivious. Did not have a single clue.

Chilling at Trey's one day, his phone lit up with a text. And then a couple more.

"Yo – I gotta go work, do some things. You coming with me?"

"Sure, I'll come," I said.

We got in the BMW. Trey plugged the key in the ignition then pulled a bag of weed out of his pants. I mean a *big* bag, with loads of little bags inside.

"Here, hold this for me, yeah?"

I took the weed. "Yeah, cool."

So, Trey's a drug dealer, I realised.

So what? I'd been around weed since long; it was everywhere. OK, it wasn't my thing, but whatever Trey was doing, I figured he was just providing a service. People smoke weed – they gotta buy it from someone.

But hang on. Let's back up.

So – now we're out on the road, I'm seeing the calls and texts coming in, I'm seeing the shots – the deals – going out the car. I'm clocking the money changing hands, and Trey's billfold getting fatter and fatter.

Only… who's the one holding all the weed?

Who's the one getting nicked for holding all the weed if we get a pull?

Yeah. It's me.

12-year-old kid. Rolling around in a Beamer with a guy who reckons he's 17 but is in fact probably more like 19 or 20.

If that doesn't sound a bit groomy, I don't know what does. Wisdom with the benefit of hindsight. Replaying it back now, it's so clear that the whole situation was more than a little bit fucked up, but I thought it was cool! We drove around, got some snacks. Went back to the house to watch some TV. Little cuddle. Nap. Back on the road. The texts came in steady – not like a crack or heroin line where it just never stops – but maybe three or four an hour. Then, to finish up, Trey parked near a school just before the end of last lesson, to catch the kids at home time.

He knew what he was doing.

The shots flew out. The pocket money rolled in.

We were done for the day, and this time – when Trey dropped me home – he peeled a crisp £50 off his roll. "That's for you – for helping out."

"Really?" I'd never had so much cash to myself. Certainly never seen a £50 note. "Thank you! I mean, it's cool. Any time."

I'd had the hood-girl look – the hair, the tight clothes, the hoops – for a while. Now, thanks to Trey, I was learning the street smarts, and the street had shown me the money. I had no plans to spend my £50, and I wasn't about to start blabbing around the ends about it — I was too scared of someone busting in and robbing me. My whole thing then was: *yeah, let me keep getting money!* Later that night, as I hid the note in my bedroom, I realised: this was a valid way to make cash. Drug dealing was a job. Maybe it could even be my job.

* * *

Trey was my boyfriend now. He gave me cash to fund my constant texting. I wrote his tag name on my pencil case and Nike *Just Do It* bag in Tippex, circled in a love heart. He could have been 15 or 50. No one asked. No one was checking.

Our little weed runs became standard. I should have been learning humanities basics — instead I was getting schooled in drug dealing 101. But while I'd been counting money and dreaming about how to spend it, Trey had been counting down the days to my birthday.

Remember that fib I told him when we first met? He sure had.

It was May 2006 and I was about to turn 13.

"It's your birthday soon," Trey said. "You're gonna be 16."

"Yeah — I can't wait!" I bluffed.

"You're gonna be legal then!" he grinned. He said it in a jokey way, testing the ground and seeing how I'd react. "What we doing? Go park or just chill?"

"Yeah, whatever, I don't mind."

"OK. Come to mine and we'll figure it out."

15 years later, the memory of that Saturday is so razor sharp, it could have been yesterday. And like a razor, it still cuts deep.

Heading to Trey's by train, I tried to settle my nerves by focusing on my iPod. Tune of the day was 'Wifey' by Next, and I played it over and over on loop, miming along to the lyrics. I was wearing a little purple cardigan, tight jeans, and knock-off Chanel sunglasses from Wembley market. I'd smoothed my hair back into a tight ponytail, with baby curls slicked to my forehead at the front. For the first time, I was wearing fake eyelashes. Having sex wasn't part of my plan, but I figured it was Trey's. Hundred percent he was gonna try something. Until now, I'd avoided doing anything with him – and to be fair he was being like some moral guy, waiting until I was 16. I'd been getting away with it for ages, but now my lies had run out of track. It was serious.

Trey invited me in. His mum had vacated the living room but left behind her cigarette stink and a mountain of crushed fag ends. I followed Trey through to his bedroom where the cloying scent of lavender hit my nostrils. It was wafting up from the box of scented tissues beside his bed. To this day I can't stand that smell.

"I got us this," Trey said, picking up a bottle of blue Alizé. "Want some?"

I nodded. "Sure." And Trey went to fix us some drinks.

We were chilling, sipping Alizé, listening to music, when Trey said suddenly, "Take off your jeans."

"Why?" I asked. Delaying tactics. As if I didn't know.

"Just take them off. I just want to cuddle."

"OK cool."

I undid the button, then tried to long it out by fumbling with the zip, making out like it was stuck, before wriggling out of them. My heart was pounding and my stomach was doing flips.

Man, once them jeans were off, it was game over.

He went in for the kill. I didn't even have time to breathe. One minute I was a just-turned-13 virgin, and the next... I wasn't. What I remember above all was that it *hurt*. Pain like I'd never felt before. All I could think was, *What the fuck is going on? This is so painful. I thought it was meant to be a nice thing!*

Trey done what he was doing, and I just lay there, trying to force a smile and acting like I was cool with it. In reality, I was so confused. The only good thing about it was that it was over and done with so quickly. It lasted all of one minute – literally 60 seconds. It was so rapid I still had those blag Chanel shades perched on top of my head.

What the hell was that? I asked myself as Trey got up and walked out of the room. Not what I expected, that was for sure. I acted cool, like I'd done it a million times before. But really, I just wanted to puke. Trey came back and got into bed beside me, cuddled up. "You OK?"

"Yeah, yeah. Cool."

Trey stuck the TV on and we lay there next to each other in uncomfortable silence, both of us acting like nothing had happened. That's what I remember about the rest of the day – an overwhelming feeling of awkwardness. We went to get some food – it was awkward. Trey drove me back to the ends. The journey was awkward. Saying goodbye – more awkward.

Things didn't get any better at home, where Mum was putting the finishing touches to my birthday cake.

"Here she is! The birthday girl," she gushed.

I smiled through clenched teeth, thinking, *Yay! Happy birthday to me!* But I felt different. Wrong. *Unclean.*

Mum was watching me as she licked a blob of icing from one finger and I *swear* she could tell. Like she was looking right through me with X-ray eyes that revealed all my dirty secrets.

I wanted to jump in the shower and scrub myself clean, but I thought any change in my routine would set alarm bells ringing. Instead, I joined in the birthday fun. Smiled as I blew out my candles. Forced down the cake Mum had made for me – when really all I wanted to do was puke in the bin. Bedtime – and showertime – couldn't come soon enough. That night, I lay awake for long, a knot of tangled emotions, as I replayed the day over and over. *Did I do it right?* I asked myself. *Was it meant to be so quick?* How could I know? I had no frame of reference. I scrutinised what happened in minute detail, but missed the most important question of all: should Trey have even done what he done?

* * *

The next day I met up with Tammy. My secret was eating me up. I had to tell someone. "We done it, me and Trey."

"Shuttup! Shuttup! You never!" she said.

"For real," I told her.

Her first instinct, bless her, was concern for me. "Wait, did he use a condom?"

"I don't even know!" I said. "I didn't see anything."

She grabbed me. "Danielle – you need to get the morning-after pill."

"Are you serious?"

Tammy was serious. Only neither of us had any idea where to go. Boots? Superdrug? We walked into town and ended up at a youth service place called Connexions, where they gave me a grilling.

Did I want to call the police?

"No."

Had I wanted this to happen?

"Well, yeah," I said, not even sure if I was telling them the truth.

The youth worker filled out some forms and said, "We'll give you the morning-after pill and we'll send you for a sexual health check."

What? Health check?

I remember thinking, *This is turning into a lot of hassle for one shit little thing.* It knocked some reality into me.

"Did you use a condom?" the lady asked.

I shrugged. "I don't know."

I caught the look on her face: *What is this kid on?*

"You really do need to know," she said.

What could I say? Condom or no condom? I didn't have the answer she wanted. But I knew one thing – I didn't want to do it again. It put me right off.

* * *

Now that shotting weed was part of my routine, I started bagging it up for Trey and his friends, too. And as I got closer to them, I discovered selling drugs wasn't their only grind. We were chilling one day when Trey opened his bedside drawer and pulled out a fold of cash. Glancing in, I saw a couple of Rolexes, a tangle of gold chains and a few rings.

"What's all that?" I asked.

"Robbed this house last night. Got lucky."

"You done a robbery?!"

"Kicked off the back door, in and out. No one was even home, man. It's cool."

Another time, not long after I'd waved goodbye to my virginity and been introduced to the joys of the STI clinic, Trey dropped me home and – as I was about to get out of the car – he handed me a bag. "Hey, can you keep this safe for me?"

I peeked inside. Coils of gold glowed against the black velvet fabric. It was full of jewellery. Indian gold – what we called two-twos. 22 carat. 91.6 percent pure.

"Bring it back next week, yeah?"

"Yeah, cool," I said, stuffing it in a jacket pocket.

Things were moving fast. Too fast. I was being swept along by the current, just about keeping my head above some very murky waters. From ducking school, I'd gone to selling drugs, to receiving stolen goods – and having sex with a man who was old enough to know better.

At the same time, in the ends, vibes were turning bookey. There was a new tension in the air. Juicy stuff going down. Knives pulled here. Fights getting more serious there. Maybe it was just that I was growing older and becoming more alert to the rhythm of hood life, but I sensed an escalation of criminality. The whole place felt flammable, like all it would take was a little spark and… boof! Up in flames.

Meanwhile at home, my mask – the good, little grammar school girl – was starting to slip. Maintaining the pretence all the time, and the stresses of this new life I was spiralling into, were wearing me down. Yeah, I was getting the money. Just like I wanted. But I was skipping school more and more – either to chill with Trey, sell weed or just be on the road with the rest of them.

Alone in my room at home, if I wasn't texting Trey, I'd be writing love letters to him, letters he would never read, because I was too shy to post them. I'd had sex with him – if you can call it that – a couple more times since my birthday, and though I wasn't down with that side of our relationship, I was convinced I loved him. From the texts he sent me in reply, I was convinced he loved me, too. The anxious dead zone between sending him a message and getting a reply was always torture, and the longer he kept me waiting, the more impossible it was to focus on anything else. I'd stare at my phone, willing him to reply, physically aching. Usually it would take just seconds, sometimes minutes and – rarely – hours. But Trey never kept me waiting longer than a day.

Which is why, when Trey's messages stopped all together, I knew something was wrong.

Yeah, Trey's name was on my schoolbooks and pencil case.

But one day, without warning, that boy upped and vanished without a trace.

4

GREEN-EYED DEVIL

Now I knew the hollow ache of a broken teenage heart. My head felt like a block of concrete and sleepless nights made dark smudges bloom below my eyes. Trey's number went straight to voicemail. My texts went unanswered. My tears were met with silence.

Even though Trey was out of the picture, I figured it made sense to stay tight with his lot. By chilling with them, I thought they might drop a clue why he'd vanished – and at least I'd be around when he eventually showed up again. I was desperate for answers, but I knew it wasn't cool to go knocking on his house, bothering his mum. And every time I asked his little friends about him, they slapped me down with the same dismissive reply:

"Man's gone jail innit."

"What jail?" I'd ask. "How long for?"

"What, you gonna get a VO? Want to go visit?"

I felt like an inch tall. And lonely. All I could do was hope they'd got it wrong, or trust he'd be out soon. For the time being, I had to own it: Trey was gone.

His disappearance meant my sales assistant job – rolling round, selling weed – was history. I'd got used to having the cash. I needed another way to make money. 13 years old, I already had 'drug dealer' on my CV, and now I had an idea how to plug that gap in my income stream: by adding 'thief' to my skillset.

I was halfway through geography class when I stuck my hand up. As I caught the teacher's eye, a little sigh escaped her lips, as if to say, *What now?*

"Miss, I need the toilet," I said.

"Make it quick, please, Danielle."

"Thank you, Miss."

The corridor outside, usually busy with the bustle and chatter of kids, was so quiet I could hear my black dolly shoes creak against the floor. I headed for the toilets, but then swerved off towards the sports block. Arriving at the changing rooms, I pushed through the double swing doors. From the sports hall beyond, I could hear a PE lesson going full blast, the netball slapping the floor and twanging off the hoop's metal rim. I did a quick recce of the changing rooms, then ducked my head inside the equipment store. I had the place to myself. Time to go to work.

Clothes and school bags were lined up neatly on rows of tarnished metal pegs above the scarred, wooden benches. I dipped my hand in a blazer pocket, but came up empty. On to the next – where my fingers found a crisp sliver of folded paper. £5 note. I pocketed the cash, then switched to another changing-room bay. It didn't make sense to clean out every blazer on any one row: the kids would soon realise they'd been robbed. But if the odd thing here and there went missing – well, you must have lost it. Be more careful next time.

Moving quickly now, I went down the row, roughly grabbing blazer pockets. I found what I was looking for as my hand closed on a blocky oblong. I reached in the pocket and pulled out a Nokia. Not too shabby. The screen was a bit fucked but it still had all its keys. Another bay over and this time I came up trumps. Blackberry Curve, mint condition, in a case. Then I hurried back to Geography, catching a raised eyebrow from Miss as I slid into my seat and stared diligently up at the board.

Later, I met up with Haina and the others to compare notes. Oh yeah, I didn't have an exclusive on robbing the changing rooms. A few of the girls were at it. It usually came full circle, too. I had my own phone robbed a couple times in school years. It was just a normal part of being a kid that everyone had to go through.

"What d'you get then?" Haina said, as she lit up a cigarette.

I showed her the two phones and the note.

"Nice!" she nodded.

"It'll buy us a bottle of Alizé! You?"

"Nah. Rubbish, man. Couple Oyster cards."

Stupid thing was, we actually got free travel for school, so the Oyster cards weren't really worth anything – unless you got lucky and dropped on one that wasn't registered. Then you could return it to Transport for London and claim the £5 deposit. Sometimes I'd be rolling around with like 10 different Oyster cards in my purse, just because.

Phones, there was always someone in the ends who wanted to buy. I'd pick up around a tenner a time. If they had passwords or were locked to a network, the bossmen in the little shops knew how to crack them. For a while, it got to be a regular thing – phones, cash, Oyster cards and iPods. All fair game. There was never any comeback. No one suspected us. In that school, the teachers put all their focus into the try-hards, the pupils with A-stars popping in their eyes. If you were one of those kids who just cruised along, doing the bare minimum, sometimes being a bit cheeky, you flew so far below the radar you were practically invisible.

Outside of school, I was getting bookey vibes off that friend of Trey's with the mad, green eyes: Jake. The boy had a wild streak and a domineering, unsettling presence. Whenever he was around, the air weighed dense and prickly, like the build-up to a thunderstorm. He had a way of looking at me that turned my blood to ice. Jake walked that bit taller than the rest of the boys, chest puffed out like a boss. I sensed he was in some way the leader of this little gang, but maybe they just fell in line behind him because he was so comfortable with violence – and they were desperate to keep on the right side of it. With boys like Jake, you either did as you were told, or you ran a mile.

So they did violence.

In the space of a few months, I went from driving around, banging out weed with someone I really liked, to experiencing horrors no 13-year-old should ever have to see. Gore movie material, without the special effects. I didn't realise at the time how badly it was fucking with my mental state. Years later, some of the darkest corners of my messed-up head are still crying out for some cleansing light.

Take this one time.

I knew Jake and the rest of his circle all carried knives tucked in their waistbands. They weren't just for show, because – besides the break-ins – they were partial to a bit of street robbery. A blade levelled at your eye socket is a convincing incentive to turn over your watch or wallet.

But it wasn't just knives. These boys liked to improvise.

It was a blazing day and we'd been in the park – me, Jake, four other boys – just chilling in the sunshine, cool grass under our backs, listening to music on our iPods. We left to go grab some drinks, and as we got to the cut-through to the station we came across two guys, about 18 years old.

Soon as they saw us, they broke into a panicked run. Rabbits fleeing a hungry fox.

One of our lot shouted, "That's my man! Grab him!"

I'd never seen these two but when you're in a group and someone says "run", you just run. I kicked into gear, trainers pounding the tarmac, our shouts clattering and echoing off the walls of the cut-through.

One of the boys getting chased down was that bit quicker than his mate. He made it to the end of the alley, punched full flow into the passing traffic and peeled away down the high road. Gone. Didn't even look back.

The other kid – not so lucky.

Nah, if he's still alive, he'll be wishing for the rest of his life his Nikes had carried him that bit quicker.

My lot caught up with him and just grabbed him up. Jake pressed a taser in his neck and – zap! – his legs jellied out under him like a pair of strawberry laces. Then Jake pulled him to his knees and pinned his arms up behind his back in an arrest position.

The boy pleaded, "Let me go! Let me go!"

"Stand up, pussy," said Jake, dragging the boy to his feet and shoving him forward. He motioned to the rest of us to follow.

We did as we were told as Jake marched the boy to some garages nearby, a couple of minutes' walk away. They were deserted, with straggly weeds poking desperately through cracks in the tarmac. I was thinking he was gonna get a beating, but then Jake wrestled out one of his arms and grabbed his fingers. The guy tried to bunch them up in a fist but Jake was too strong for him – he prised them apart like he was splitting a pack of sausages for the frying pan.

Then he nodded to one of the other boys. "Do it. Cut him."

"No! Let me go!" the guy pleaded. He was a black boy, hair freshly trimmed into a neat fade.

One of our lot pulled this gardening tool out of his pocket – those clippers with the curved, stubby blades you use for pruning roses. The guy was begging now. Whites of his eyes massive. A thread of spit hung off one trembling lip.

"Do it!" Jake yelled.

The clipper blades closed on the boy's little finger and – crunch! – it fell to the floor. He'd barely had a chance to scream before the finger beside it got the same treatment. He collapsed to his knees, cradling his ravaged hand, the white bone of his finger stumps glinting bright against red blood and ragged flesh. An inhuman cry welled up from somewhere deep inside him. I'd never heard anything like it in my life.

And his fingers – just lying there on the dirt.

I was like – *This is.*

Fucked.

Up.

Surreal. I didn't want any part of it. Blood rushed in my ears. A voice – seemingly from a long way off, like another dimension even – punched through the white static drone: "Run! Go!"

Somehow, my legs followed orders. I ran until I couldn't breathe, then headed for home where I shut myself away in my bedroom.

There was another incident that still gives me the horrors to this day.

A girl from around – not someone I knew by name – had troubled someone's man. I don't know what it was – she'd ended up in bed with the wrong guy or pissed someone's brother off. Somebody felt they'd been disrespected and only a slap was gonna make it right. Jake's lot wanted to fuck her up.

"OK," Jake said to a couple of us girls. "You're gonna shout her and say come meet in the cemetery."

This lot liked to chill in a little park which was part of a big old West London cemetery. Weird place to hang out and lots of craziness went down in this place. We didn't even bother spinning the girl a line, just sent her a text telling her to come hang out. Sure enough, she turned up, oblivious. She was a mixed-race girl, chubby, with a really pretty face – which soon had the easy and trusting smile wiped off it.

It was an ambush.

She'd barely had time to say "hi" when about 12 boys and girls appeared out of nowhere and swarmed on top of her, a blur of pistoning fists and sharp elbows. In no time, they had her lashed to a bench, hands tied behind her back, tears streaking her make-up as she begged for her life. "Get off me! Let me go!"

"Shut up you stupid bitch!" one of the boys snapped.

Everyone crowded round her, jeering, like she was a peasant locked in the stocks. I thought *hang on – I thought she was just getting a smack?*

Then someone said, "Set fire to her hair! Light her hair!"

Fuck. This was *ridiculous*. I got the same feeling I'd had when the boy had his fingers crunched off. That this was surreal. That it couldn't really be happening. Someone pushed to the front and glugged vodka over the girl's head. The liquid poured down her cheeks and drizzled off her chin.

"No!" she screamed, as a lighter sparked. "I'm sorry! Please!"

The yellow flame sputtered in the breeze. It touched her hair which flared up in a plume of blue, before dying out. I caught the unmistakable, sickly-sweet smell of burnt hair. The lighter went in again, and again, leaving behind each time a singed patch of bald scalp. The girl was screaming, sobbing, terrified, as everyone cackled around her.

All of a sudden it stopped – as quickly as it had begun – and they all took off, laughing. It was just me and her. I felt so bad for the girl. I couldn't leave her with her fucked-up face and burnt hair. Hands shaking, I dialled 999 for an ambulance.

"Help is coming," I told her.

I stood off to one side until I caught the distant wail of sirens, then turned and ran.

* * *

In school, Haina's size had earned her a reputation for being a bully. She wasn't, but her height could be intimidating and she didn't take any shit. Now she'd been given a bad girl label, she figured she might as well start playing up to it. In me, she found an all too willing accomplice.

We were in science together when she leaned in to me. "Did you know they've left the IT room open?"

"For real?" I said.

"Yeah. For real."

"So, what do you wanna do about it?"

Haina had ideas. "Let's go get the laptops."

I didn't give it a second's thought. I was in. "OK, cool," I said.

Haina stuck her hand up and got excused to go toilet. I waited a couple of minutes and did the same, then met Haina outside the IT block. Sure enough, the door was unlocked. The block was empty, and in one classroom was a cabinet with maybe 20 laptops on charge.

"How we gonna get this lot out?" I said.

Haina shrugged. "Just carry them!"

"OK, we'll stick them in our lockers."

"Then what?"

"Sneak them out of school at lunchtime," I said.

Cool.

I piled up a stack of six laptops, thinking I could probably get £50 a piece. Haina did the same, and we walked out of the block, crossing the yard to get back in the main building, stashing our haul of stolen laptops in our lockers.

It got to lunchtime and Haina texted: *meet me by the gates.*

Back at my locker, I stuffed a couple of laptops up my jumper, put the rest in my bag and walked boldly out of the school. Haina was waiting by the gates as arranged and we set off together. We thought we were home free, and in my head I was already spending the £300 I was gonna bank by selling them.

But we hadn't gone far when Haina got a text from one of our friends: *Police at school. U better get back – looking for u + Danielle.*

"What now?" I said.

No question, we had to go back and sort out this bullshit at the school, but we couldn't just walk in there with a pile of laptops.

Haina spotted a bush nearby. "Let's stick them in here and come back for them later."

Back at Harry Potter High, a police car was parked out front. One of the teachers nabbed us before we'd even got in the building and frogmarched us to the headmistress's office. Honestly – I didn't care.

"You are going to return what you have taken," the headmistress began.

"I don't know what you're talking about," I said.

"Haina?" said the headmistress.

She shrugged and looked at the floor.

"Very well. We'll be pressing charges. Obviously, I'll be informing your parents."

"Go on then," I replied. Beside me, Haina was trying hard not to burst out laughing.

The head pursed her lips. "This is disgusting behaviour. You are both suspended from school for two weeks."

A police officer came in and read us our rights, something I'd seen hella times before on the block – it didn't scare me. "Yeah, yeah, shut up!" I said in reply. Then Haina and I were led to separate police cars and driven to the station.

Occasions like this, where emotions can run high, were delegated to Dave to handle. Mum's Mediterranean temperament made her prone to going off the deep end. Dave had always been a quiet dude, a man of few words, so it was him who turned up as my 'appropriate adult'.

"You all right?" he said.

"Yeah, I'm fine."

"What's going on then?"

"Some laptops went missing," I said. "They think me and Haina done it."

Dave sat beside me in the police interview. I'd already decided to front it out. "It wasn't me," I told the officer, as he started with the questions.

"We know it was you," he said. "We have video evidence."

I shook my head. "Wasn't me. I didn't do it."

"I'm showing the suspect an image captured on CCTV cameras located outside the IT block at Edenwood Grammar School," the officer said with an air of exasperation.

He laid a grainy black and white photo on the table. It was a picture of me carrying the stack of laptops across the yard. We'd had no idea the camera was even there.

Fair play – I was bang to rights. Faced with such conclusive evidence, there was nowhere left for me to hide.

"It's not me," I said, without missing a beat.

The officer sighed. "It's clearly you, Danielle!"

"It's not me. Prove it's me!"

"Come on – this *is* proof! That's your bag. That's your face. That is you, carrying the laptops."

"Prove it then!" I said, and folded my arms.

They didn't need a signed confession: the video was enough to charge me and Haina with theft. I believe the laptops were recovered after a search, and we were let out on bail to start our two weeks' holiday. I mean, suspension.

Mum blew her top in a torrent of Greek swearing, but what could she do? I spent the majority of my 'suspension' chatting to my friends on MSN, living my best life. When the day came to attend youth court, it was Dave who came with me, because Mum wouldn't have handled it well.

I hadn't spoken to Haina since the fateful day, and when I saw her in the courtroom, I made a beeline for her – but I was stopped in my tracks by the duty solicitor tasked with representing me and ordered to sit on the far side. As we waited for the magistrate to arrive, I managed to catch Haina's eye and mouthed at her, *Go to the toilet.* I followed a couple of minutes later.

Our little toilet conference was a tense affair. We took up opposing positions on either side of the hand drier and blamed each other for the laptop escapade.

"It was your idea!" I said.

"It wasn't my idea to walk across the yard with them in front of a flippin' camera!"

"I didn't know it was there, did I? What else were we gonna do?"

A silence fell between us, then I said, "Look, let's forget all that. We're here now. What you doing – guilty or not guilty?"

"I'm going guilty," Haina said. "But if I'm going guilty, you've got to too."

"All right," I agreed. "Deal."

We had a pact. Back in the courtroom, the magistrate took his seat on the bench and the charge was read out to us. I was asked first how I wanted to plead. I glanced over at Haina and said confidently, "Guilty."

Then they asked her the same and my jaw hit the floor as she replied, "Not guilty."

The bitch! I thought. *She shegged me!* I couldn't believe it – she'd snaked my whole life.

Whatever.

The end result was the same, because we both got slapped with a reprimand and a little fine. As the sentence was handed down, I battled to hold off a fit of the giggles. The whole thing was a joke. I had no idea what 'reprimand' even meant. We'd tried to rob the school of thousands of pounds of laptops and the punishment was basically nothing. The magistrate and solicitors had said a lot of big words, but nothing had changed in my life. I think Dave even paid my fine for me.

My big takeaway from this episode was that getting nicked and going to court were nothing to fear. Street justice, on the other hand, was scary business. I'd already witnessed some extreme and terrifying examples and now I was about to experience it first-hand. The irony was that – this time – I hadn't even done anything wrong.

Chilling with Sharelle from school one day, she decided she wanted some weed. I'd been avoiding Jake's lot since the flaming hair incident, but now I hollered one girl who rolled with them. "Hey, have you got a ten-draw?"

"Yeah, no problem," she said. "Meet on the high road."

Me and Sharelle set off, but on the way I got a text: *Actually, can you come to the cemetery?*

I should have known, but I just didn't see it.

No problem, I messaged back, oblivious to what was coming.

Soon as I got there, *that's* when I knew.

There were six girls, maybe four boys. The air was heavy and the vibe was off.

For real – I was getting jumped.

One short black girl, Tania, stepped up. I was dressed all in red. Red skinny jeans, red shoes, laces tied around my high ponytail, red case on my phone. Jake's lot were blue. It was a gang thing. The colour of my clothes was an affront.

"Take off your jeans," Tania sneered.

It wasn't happening. She'd have to drag them off my corpse if she wanted them. "I'm not taking off my fucking jeans," I said.

Tania lunged for me. Stubby fingers wrapped around my phone and snatched it from my grasp. She raised it high in the air, then dashed it against the ground, grinding it into the tarmac with the heel of one trainer. A cheer went up from the rest of them as Tania stared me down, waiting for my next move.

"Let's go," I said to Sharelle and went to walk away.

"Hey Danielle?" I heard a voice call behind me, and I turned around to see who it was.

Suddenly my cheek exploded in pain, my legs gave way as I lost consciousness and I hit the floor. When I came to, Sharelle was crouched over me.

"Give me your hand," she said, helping me to my feet.

I ran my tongue over my teeth, then gingerly touched my face. My nose was still in one piece, but my cheek felt like it had sprouted a grapefruit.

"Don't look at your face!" Sharelle said.

"Is it that bad?" I said.

"Just, don't look."

The girls had fled, taking my Oyster card and the few quid I'd had in my pocket. The boys were still hanging around and one came over. "Come in my car," he said. "We'll go to my mum's and get some ice for your face."

I nodded and followed after him, with two other boys and Sharelle tagging along behind.

By the time we got to his, my cheek was throbbing. I winced as I pressed the ice to it, but after a few minutes it began to take the edge off the pain. I still hadn't seen what the girl had done to me.

"We're gonna go get some chicken," the boy said. "You coming?"

I thought, *just get some food in you and go home.*

"OK," I said.

We drove up to the high road, the boy parked up and we walked on to the shops. The boys disappeared in a corner shop, leaving me and Sharelle on the street outside, me with a bag of ice pressed to my messed-up face. I must have looked a state, because passers-by kept stopping. "Are you sure you're OK?", "Do you need assistance?"

Minutes went by, and there was no sign of the boys. Sharelle went to check in the shop and returned moments later, shaking her head. "They've gone," she said breathlessly.

"Let's check the car," I said. But after walking around the corner to where we'd parked up, we found that was gone, too.

What the fuck is going on? I thought as we walked back to the high road.

Then Sharelle said, "That's them, isn't it?" pointing out a car coming towards us. It parked, and a second car pulled in behind it – and about 10 girls jumped out, started legging it towards us.

"Run!" I screamed, snatching Sharelle's elbow.

She followed my lead and we peeled off with the gang of girls in pursuit. They were gaining on us. I was still feeling wobbly from the beating.

"In here!" I said to Sharelle and dived in a chicken shop. I jumped over the counter and through to the back where there was a staff toilet. "Come!" I said, grabbing Sharelle and pulling her in beside me. I slammed the door and locked it against the commotion kicking off outside – staff arguing with them girls. The girls pounding on the door. "Come the fuck out here! We're not leaving." Sharelle was gulping air, terrified. Girl must have been regretting ever wanting to get high.

"We just wait," I said.

Sharelle nodded, terror-struck.

We waited. And waited. 45 minutes went by and the shouts outside died down.

"It's OK," I heard the boss man saying through the door. "They've gone. It's safe. Come out the back – I'll drive you home."

Tentatively, I slid back the lock and opened the door. Sure enough, the coast was clear. We followed the chicken-shop man to his car out back, and he gave us a lift to a bus stop out of the area.

We limped back to Sharelle's – and found the police waiting to question us on what had happened.

"I texted my mum when we were in the loos," Sharelle admitted.

I gave them nothing. It just wasn't done.

"Who did this?"

"Don't know."

"Where did it happen?"

"Can't remember."

Down at the station, they showed me mugshots of persistent girl offenders.

"Don't recognise them," I said.

Later that night, I woke with a start in bed, dripping with sweat, left eye swollen shut. My stomach lurched and I barely made it to the loo before I puked. Staring into the toilet bowl with my one good eye, I realised – *I can't let this happen to me again.*

Did that mean I was going to mend my ways?

It did not.

It meant I needed to get myself some protection.

5

SHALL WE KILL HER?

"**S**how me what knives you got," I told the corner shop bossman.

He reached under the counter and slapped down a butterfly knife. I rolled it in my palm, feeling its weight, then unfolded the blade from its black metal handle.

"How much?" I asked, folding the blade back again.

"20."

Done.

That £20 was buying me more than a sliver of Chinese steel. It was buying me peace of mind.

I didn't ever want to have to use it. This wasn't about kudos or clout. After that beating, I was just plain scared.

Stop and search wasn't such a big deal back in the day. In any case, this little white girl was still invisible to the local police. I wasn't on their radar – yet. The police were popping up those mobile knife arches here and there, and the black boys knew they were always getting hustled through, guaranteed.

Not me, though. My skin colour meant a free pass.

So that blade went with me everywhere.

School. Down the corner shop. On the road with Haina.

After getting rushed by those girls, I'd shrunk back to the safety of my own area. Me and Haina would get ourselves a bench to chill with a bottle and a few boys from the block for company. Me taking tiny little sips, pretending to drink. Never dropping my guard because I always wanted to know where I was and who was around me.

"That cheek's healing nice," Haina said one evening. It was late summer. Dusk. The pavement still radiating a bit of warmth from the afternoon sun, the air teasing some autumn chill.

I prodded it carefully. "Reckon I'll survive." The Dream Matte Mousse foundation had worked some uncanny magic, but I was still sore, with one crazy-looking eye all bloodshot.

The boys we were with finished up their spliff and started shuffling about, making moves to leave.

"Coming up the flat?" one boy, Marek, said.

"What's going on?"

"We'll go find out, yeah?"

On the next estate over was a nasty ass old house that had been deserted for months. Like a squat. Windows bricked and spider-webbed with cracks. Door booted in, ragged holes punched in the walls. The boys used it for cover to sell drugs from. Evenings, we'd chill there. If we were lucky, someone dragged a sound system down and we'd have a house party.

Instinctively, my hand felt for the reassuring slab of metal sunk deep in my tracksuit pocket.

Peace of mind.

I felt pretty safe on home turf, but if things turned jumpy up at the flat, I was prepared. If some boy got me cornered in the back room where they took girls for sex, I was ready.

We set off walking, passing the bottle between us, smoking cigarettes, laughing. It was the company rather than the alcohol, but I felt relaxed for the first time in weeks.

Just then, my phone pinged in my pocket. I pulled it out to read a message. It was one of the girls with Jake's lot.

If you talk 2 da police, u fucking die. We no where u live.

And just to prove it, they signed off with my actual address.

"Fuck," I gasped.

"D – whats up?" said Haina, catching the look on my face. "You OK?"

I buried the phone back in my pocket. I wasn't a chatty patty. My business was my business. I never really got to the bottom of why I'd been jumped. There was a rumour going round I'd slept with Jake – not true. I think they had me down as a snitch for staying behind with that girl.

"Babes, I'm sorry, I'm gonna cut. Catch you tomorrow. Or Monday in school?"

"Wait, I'll come with you," she said.

I squinted at her through my bad eye. "Nah, I'm just gonna get some sleep. Got a headache coming on. In a bit yeah?"

I span on my heels and headed off, ignoring the boys calling behind.

"D! Where you going, man?"

The text message had rattled me, knife or no knife. Right now, I just wanted the refuge of my own bedroom. I hurried back to the flat – jumping at shadows – and got into bed, tucking my knife inside its hiding place in the slash in my mattress.

I'd soon discover, a little peace of mind can be a very dangerous thing.

* * *

Frozen to the bones. So bitterly cold and numb I couldn't even move. I was wearing just a top and knickers, stood shivering at the top of a fire escape on some estate looking out over the dirty yellow glow of West London.

But that view was the last thing on my mind.

Rain splattered my upturned face as I looked up at the sky and prayed to God I'd make it through this night alive. The chances of that were looking slim.

I heard a voice, and I was shocked to realise it was my own, willing me to run – as fast and as far as I could – until I didn't recognise where I was anymore

Then I picked up another voice, coming from the open window in the bedroom beside me.

"Shall we kill her?"

Wincing, I went back to my prayers. The bruises on my tummy were starting to hurt.

A few hours earlier, I'd had a call – from Jake of all people. "Yo D, it's J. I'm having a house party. What you saying?"

After the thing with them girls, I'd been blanking him. He'd try maybe once in a blue moon to call or send me a text. But running with those boys, it was just stress, man. Too much trouble. Too much violence.

Then I came home from school one day to Mum eyeing me up suspiciously. "The police have been phoning – they want to speak to you," she said. "What have you been doing? Are you in trouble?"

"Chill, Mum. I ain't in no trouble. Gimme that number."

I rang the fed. It turned out they'd rounded up a bunch of them girls over some other crime and seized all their technology in the process. They'd done forensic on their phones – and turned up a load of messages to me.

"We're concerned about the content of some of their texts, Danielle. Making threats to kill is a serious offence – do you want to press charges?" he said.

But the streets hate snitches.

"No. I do not want to press charges."

That was that. My attackers were out of the picture. And the bonus ball – my loyalty, integrity were intact. I wasn't a grass.

A month or so went by and, out of the blue, I got the call from Jake. My scars had healed, the bruises faded – and with them the memory of getting my cheekbone shattered.

So, now there was a party on the cards. It was a school day the next day, but I thought *fuck it, why not?*

"Cool. Give me the address."

I hung up my school uniform and pulled on a new, purple Adidas tracksuit. It matched the purple highlights in my red hair – curled, with extensions. Despite some heavy eyeliner, I still looked every bit the 15-year-old schoolgirl – but nonetheless I felt pretty and confident.

I took a bus, carrying a bottle of Courvoisier for them lot in one hand, and the butterfly knife in my jacket pocket. As I walked to the estate, an uneasy feeling built inside me. It's not like I didn't know these people, but I think sometimes your body and mind send you warning signals in ways you don't understand. I started looking for an explanation for them.

So maybe them girls are gonna show up? I thought. *That's what it is – it's gonna go down. I'm gonna get ambushed.*

Well, cool. Bring it

My hand tightened on the blade.

This time I'm fucking ready.

The council flat was run down as fuck. I knocked on the door and a boy called Danny opened it to a grim-looking stub of dishevelled hallway. Filthy dirty. Absolute dump of a place. At the far end, a door cracked open and an old guy peered out timidly. He looked disabled, Down's Syndrome maybe.

Danny turned on hearing the noise and barked, "What you doing? Get back in your fucking room, man!" Fear flashed on the guy's face before he melted back. "D, come in."

He took me through to a bedroom with just a single bed, a Playstation 2 and a battered wardrobe in the corner. It was dark – with just the light from a little TV throwing dancing splashes of colour on the bare walls. The smell of weed hit my nostrils, battling it out with the sharp tang of men's perfume.

Well, this wasn't looking like no house party. This wasn't the event I'd been sold a few hours earlier. It was just four boys – and little me.

Two of them were glued to the game on the screen. Jake, I knew, obviously. Danny too. I'd chilled with their mums, been to their houses. This Danny boy, he kept a samurai sword under his bed that he was hella proud of. He was very hood.

Marcus I'd seen around couple of times. Mixed race boy, short and stocky. Then there was a tall, slim black guy I'd never met before, Kaleb. He looked uncomfortable somehow, like he didn't really want to be there.

Before I could say *no,* one of the boys peeled off my coat and chucked it on the floor in the corner, well out of my reach.

I knew then I'd fucked up.

In the pocket was my under-16 Oyster card, phone, money. And my butterfly knife.

But OK. Cool. *You know these people,* I thought. *Relax.*

"Man, it's good to see you, D!" said Jake. "I thought you had dropped us out."

"No, we're good," I said. "Just had shit to do, you know? School and that."

"Oh yeah, you started going school now have you?" Jake laughed. "Come here, sit down. Sit down!"

I perched on the edge of the bed, poured out some brandy for them and a little bit for me. We chilled while they hammered this Playstation, and for a while it was fine.

But then I sensed a shift. The vibe turned bad – fast – like it was on a dimmer switch getting dialled all the way down. It all happened in seconds. Someone locked the door and Jake said, "Come lay down with me."

"Err no! What the hell!" I said.

But Jake grabbed me, pulled me across the bed next to him and pushed me down.

The pressure on my body was heavy. I remember someone dragging me so I was half-on, half-off the bed. My trousers were pulled off me so I just had the little top and knickers on.

And then they done what they were doing.

I didn't dare move – just stayed still and did as I was told.

You think if you're ever in that situation you're gonna kick and scream – especially me, being a sassy little person. But no.

Let me just do it, I thought. *Let me just comply. The quicker you can get out of this, the better.*

More than anything, I just felt embarrassed.

These boys – two of whom I thought were my friends – took turns raping me, videoing the whole thing. It was the first time I'd ever had a penis in my mouth and it made me feel physically sick.

I could barely breathe but, weirdly, there was no pain – not that I remember. It was like I was out of my body. Or one of those sex dolls – no feelings, no fight in me at all. I was just made of rubber.

They all finished and Jake said, "OK. You're gonna do a video. You're gonna say you're cool with everything, that no one's harmed you. Got it?"

I nodded. Someone hit record on their phone.

Cowering on the bed, looking messed up and terrified, I followed the script. Told whoever might want to watch, *Yeah, I wanted this. I really did.*

"Now put up the gang sign," Danny said, pulling up his tracksuit bottoms.

For the camera, I bent my fingers into their little sign. They all came round next to me, toward the camera but faces off-screen, and did the gang sign too.

"You can get out of this, D." Jake started. "We just need someone to come here and pick you up. You've got one call.

Make them bring a car, make them bring a phone, make them bring money."

"OK," I said, cautiously.

"But know this – whoever comes for you is getting robbed and stabbed, yeah?"

I had no choice. I had to get someone here. Anything to raise the alarm, any kind of protection was a bonus. I dialled Marek, willing him to answer. Then he picked up, but his voice was faint against a backdrop of booming music and cheering. "What's good, D?"

"Hey! I need you to come pick me up," I began.

"Hello? Hello? I can't hear you, D…"

"I need you to come get me!" I shouted, getting desperate.

"I can't hear you, man. I'm at a party!"

Then the phone was snatched from my hand.

"Bad luck," said Danny.

I'd thought it was over. In fact, this was just a little break. Them boys were only half done with me.

They started again and it went on for hours.

I remember someone pouring brandy over my back and lighting it up. At one point, I was dragged from the bed to the floor. One boy – I couldn't say who – stood over me, and piss poured over my chest, soaking my top and bra. That's what started me crying. Being drenched in piss. I was like – *this is so fucked up. Why would you do that?*

The tears running down my cheeks just mixed in with everything else I was covered in. Then – bam! – my head rocked back from a punch in the temple. I took more blows to my belly, ribs and face.

By four in the morning I was collapsed, curled up on the floor, soaking wet. I couldn't move my arms or legs, and my body was a world of pain. My back was stinging from where they'd tried to set me on fire. Emotionally, I was just numb. I've never felt numbness like it in all my life – the total lack of any emotion. I was finished.

And the worst thing? I didn't care.

Then I felt someone lift me into his arms. I looked up to see who it was – Kaleb, the tall black boy. Somehow, I knew it would be him, that his morals would be the first to kick in. He carried me like a baby to a freezing downstairs toilet, then perched on the edge of the bath, holding me up in his arms.

He turned on the tap in the sink and helped me wash my face, then tied my hair back in a ponytail. "I'm really sorry. It shouldn't have gone this far," he said.

"OK," I replied numbly. I looked at myself in the mirror. My cheeks were streaked with mascara and my extensions were hanging out in lumps.

In that moment, this boy's tiny act of compassion was too much to bear, and I let go and sobbed. We sat there for a while, with me sitting on his lap and him on the edge of the bath, still holding me like a baby. He wiped my nose with a towel, then said, "OK, let's go back upstairs and sort this situation out."

Shivering, bedraggled, I walked back in the bedroom.

"Get out there, man," said Jake, pointing me to the balcony and fire escape. "We're gonna talk about what we do with you."

I did as I was told. Out into the freezing January night air, damp with drizzle. The metal staircase wrapped around the side of the building. I could have legged it down and run away into the night. But I had nothing left. I was paralysed with fear, looking out over the silent estate.

Where I was stood on the balcony was right outside the bedroom window. The curtains were half closed but the window was slightly ajar.

"We're gonna have to kill her – she's fucked up," I heard Jake say.

"Nah man, she's not gonna talk." That was Kaleb.

"Look what we've done to her!" Jake persisted. "We've got to get rid of this girl. She's seen too much!"

I thought – hundred percent – they were going to kill me.

"She ain't gonna tell the police. Let's just let her go," Kaleb pleaded.

Then I heard Danny chip in: "Let's at least stab her or something to scare her."

I looked up at the sky again and prayed. I distinctly remember the stars were very bright.

This is it, I thought.

I'm going to die.

6

UNRELIABLE WITNESS

Running was out of the question – my legs were useless blocks of ice, frozen by fear. Instead I stayed on those stairs, awaiting my fate.

How would they do it? Stab me? Would it hurt? Would it be quick?

The door cracked open and Kaleb poked his head out, motioning me inside. I followed, hugging myself against the cold.

Jake looked me up and down like something he'd dragged in on his shoe. He paced up and down, apparently wrestling with his decision, then stopped, pulled out his phone and dialled a number.

"Bro, who you calling?" Kaleb asked.

"Cab," said Jake, shooting a look at me.

He ordered a taxi and we all stood together on the balcony watching out for it. It was still dark but a bruise of grey light had seeped onto the horizon. The cab pulled up outside about 10 minutes later.

"Let's go," said Jake, dragging a duvet cover from the bed and chucking it at me. "Wrap yourself up."

As they corralled me through the door, I glanced at my jacket lying wrinkled in the corner − containing my phone, money and knife. There was no time to grab them as we bustled down the stairs and out to the waiting cab. No shoes on, still wearing just my knickers and a top. The gritty tarmac and wet paving slabs under my feet barely even registered.

"In the front," Jake snapped, ordering me to take the seat next to the driver, who shot me a what-the-fuck look as I fell in beside him.

Marcus left, while the other three followed me into the taxi, lining up across the back seat. We set off, the cab threading through West London, nudging along vaguely familiar streets. The journey felt aimless, the boys barking random directions from the back.

"Bossman, buck this next left."

"Do a right here."

"Straight over at the lights."

Then Jake tapped me on the shoulder and leant in.

"Rob his phone," he whispered.

The cabbie had what looked like a pristine new mobile, perched in a cradle right in front of me. I shook my head.

"Fucking do it. Grab the phone at the next lights and run."

The cab pulled up at the next red. Jake was so close that the hot, boozy stink of his breath brushed my left ear, stale brandy fumes lighting up my nostrils. "D, I'm telling you…"

No way. If he wanted it so bad, he'd have to do it himself.

"Rob. The fucking. Phone," he hissed.

We drove on. They must have got the message that I wasn't playing ball because Danny suddenly said, "Stop right here, man."

The driver swung sharply into the kerb and came to a sudden halt.

"Get out, just go," said Jake.

I realised then that I'd won.

They knew they couldn't kill me.

Freedom was just a couple of steps away, but as I climbed out, Danny snatched the tail end of the duvet cover and there was a surreal tug of war moment, me half in and half out the car trying to keep hold of this sheet because it was the only thing covering me up.

In the end I thought, *fuck this,* and just let go. *Who cares if I have to walk the streets in my knickers?* I couldn't be any more degraded than I already had been. I was still alive – that was all that mattered.

The taxi pulled away. Finally, they were gone.

OK. Where the fuck are you? How are you getting home?

It was a residential street. I stumbled along, barefoot, trying to get my head together and figure out how the hell I was gonna make it back in just my underwear – with no phone, no money… nothing. All I had was a gnawing hunger to get back to my ends.

An underground station came into view at the end of the road, swiftly followed by the realisation: *You can't get on a train like this.*

Instead, I paced around the station entrance, trying to suss out my next steps, searching for the yellow brick road that would lead me home.

Home.

That word tumbled over and over in my mind. Numbness had crept into every fibre of my body so that thinking or feeling anything else was impossible. My senses had been shredded, or maybe shut down altogether to spare me from more trauma. It was dawn, January, and yet I was now oblivious to the cold.

Home. Home. Home.

There was no other choice. I had to knock on a door.

Approaching the first one, I hovered on the doorstep suddenly aware of how absolutely crazy this was going to look. Who in their right mind was gonna open the door to me? Anyone with any sense would take a peek out the window and decide, *No thanks, not today love.*

I knocked – no answer. Rang the bell – still no answer. Then my right eye caught a curtain twitch and a boy, a few years older than me, blinked back from behind the window. He held up a finger – *one second* – before the door opened. An older woman with a hijab on – his mum, or grandma – was stood there, the boy tucked in her shadow behind her.

"I need help," I said. "Can you call the police? Please?"

"What has happened to you?" she said.

"Please, can you just call the police?"

She shrank back, too wary to let me in her home, and really, who could blame her? "I will call them," she said, then gently shut the front door.

I walked back down her drive and hunched on the pavement outside her house, pulling my knees to my chest and closing my eyes. Waiting. A voice started up in my head, like when you're on a cleaning frenzy and you lock on a few lines of the same song, looping around and around in your brain.

I don't care. I don't care. I don't care.

I kept an ear out for cars but the road was silent for I don't know how many minutes – time had lost any meaning. My senses were feeding back to me in dead, grey tones of nothingness. I was hollow.

I don't care. I don't care.

I didn't even care that Jake and the boys might come back.

Looking back now, how little I cared is actually terrifying.

The lights registered before the car came into view, sparks reflected in the windows of cars parked further up the road. No sirens, just pulsing police-blue lights. The car pulled up directly in front of me – and still, I didn't care. There was no sense of relief. No moment of salvation. Just… nothing.

A female police officer walked over. "What's your name, love?"

"Danielle."

"OK, we're going to take you down the station. Do you need any help getting in the car?"

"I'll be alright."

"Come on then," she said, and hooked one hand under my elbow. I struggled to my feet and got in the back of the car, vaguely aware of the warmth inside. All the way back to Acton police station, the officer chatted with her male colleague, while I stared blankly out the window, seeing nothing.

They led me in through the back, the same way they bring you when you get nicked. I'd been in a police station before over the laptop incident, but never as a victim. We went through the custody suite and then upstairs to the main office, where there were hella police officers getting on with the busy day to day of law enforcement.

And there was me − schoolgirl rape victim, stood there like a dickhead with no clothes on.

I was given the same grey cotton tracksuit you get when you're arrested, and the police confiscate your clothes for evidence. While I put it on, someone made me tea. Another officer took a mouth swab and scraped underneath my fingernails for evidence. Sipping the hot liquid, I pushed my fingers through my hair, teasing out my tattered extensions in bedraggled clumps that looked like something a cat had coughed up.

"Can you throw them away please?" I said to the officer, clumping them together in a pile before twisting my hair into a bun.

She tossed them in a bin, then said, "Danielle, can you tell us exactly what happened last night?"

It was a spur of the moment decision to spin them a story, with the aim of avoiding all the drama of a big aftermath. What happened had happened − and I'd survived. It was time to move on. Plus, telling the truth would mean looking over my shoulder the rest of my life.

"This car pulled up next to me on the high road..."

"Can you remember the make? Or the colour? Can you describe what it looked like inside?"

"It was dark, so, not really."

"OK. Go on."

"It pulled up, these four boys got out and just bundled me in the back."

Lies.

"I didn't see any faces."

"Did you notice any weapons?"

"I think they maybe had knives…"

"OK. What happened next?

"They drove me to an estate," I said.

"Do you know the name of it? Could you find it again?"

"Don't know what it was called. I could probably show you. But, look, I don't want any fuss. I'm fine. I don't need no help. I'm happy to let it go."

The officer looked at me, stunned. "Let it go?"

"I don't want to press any charges. I just want to go home."

"It's not as simple as that, Danielle. We need to arrest whoever was responsible. Let's see if we can find them, OK?"

A couple of hours earlier, I'd been certain I would die on that estate. Now we rolled back to the scene in an unmarked police car, an armed unit following behind for support.

"It's that one," I pointed.

"OK, Danielle. You've done really well," said the officer. She turned to her colleague. "Let's get back to the station."

The armed unit stayed put, presumably to raid the flat. I knew Jake and them lot would be long gone by now – and I was right. They were already in the wind.

Back at the station, I drank more tea and waited for Dave to come pick me up. Then the police sent me on my way with a warning not to wash or shower until they got me into The Haven sexual assault referral centre to take more samples – probably the next day. Yeah, the next day. Looking back, that's almost unbelievable.

The police hadn't told Dave what had gone on, and when we arrived home around 9am it was clear Mum thought I'd been up to no good. Again.

"So, are you going to tell me? What is it this time?" she said, crossing her arms across her chest.

Dave cleared out of the way so we could talk, but my focus was on Returning To Normal, which meant acting like nothing had happened. Far as I was concerned, it was history. Make the breakfast. Boil the kettle. Make the cup of tea. This was a new day.

"What have you done now, mmh?" Mum said.

Furiously scraping margarine across a slice of toast, I tried to ignore her. But Mum stood over me, brooding. Somehow, she even managed to breathe in a way that felt accusing.

"OK," I said finally. "I've been raped."

She snorted. "No, no, no."

"Believe or don't believe. That's the truth."

"I don't know why you would say these things! I don't understand!" she complained, throwing her hands up in the air and muttering Greek curses under her breath. Maybe she was just so shocked that she couldn't comprehend, perhaps she was just in denial, but the way it came across at the time was like she out and out did not believe me.

"I'm serious, Mum. It happened."

She wagged a finger at me. "It's an excuse, isn't it? For you staying out all night. That's what it is."

And that was that. Me and her were done.

You don't believe me? OK, cool. Fuck off.

She wasn't alone. The police didn't believe me either – for totally different reasons – and they were back later that day as my lie unravelled under the scrutiny of technology.

CCTV – again.

Last time I got caught on camera robbing the laptops. This time, the problem was I *hadn't* been caught on camera where I'd told the police I'd been picked up in this car.

"Your story doesn't add up. We know you weren't there, Danielle," they told me.

And yet I still wasn't quite ready to spill my guts. "Oh, yeah. You're right, I got confused…" Giving them another location, I span more lies.

They weren't having it. "Come on Danielle. You really need to tell us what happened. We can arrest these guys for kidnap and rape. We have to. They're dangerous."

The game was up.

Something switched in my head, and it no longer mattered if I got called a snitch, because trying to protect these boys out of some fucked-up sense of loyalty, or because the police were 'The Enemy', was just ridiculous.

These boys needed to go jail. I was sure they would, because that's what happens to rapists, right? Surely they would go to jail. With that in mind, I gave them up, every single one. Names, addresses, the lot. Within a couple of days, the police had them in custody.

My ordeal was wrung out of me over a six-hour interview with a specialist rape officer, a short curvy lady with dirty blonde hair which she wore in a low ponytail. She wore a casual-looking suit with a white top. Man, she was cold. The same questions over and over. It felt like she didn't really care, or that she thought I was just chatting shit. Typical police officer, she just wanted to arrest the bad guy and had lost sight of the victim. She didn't know how to be child-friendly – I was only 15! These days, the police and probation service are trained to use what's called a 'trauma informed approach'. Yeah, of course everyone wants them to catch the criminal, but in situations like mine there has to be some focus on the victim.

I gave diagrams of the layout of the flat, descriptions of all four boys. Yet the more I told her, the less I felt like they believed me. Looking back now, I wish I'd just told the truth that first day.

In the meantime, between hella interviews over the course of the next four days, I went to school like normal – forcing laughter and jokes with my friends, pretending everything was cool, slotting GCSE practice papers and revision around ID parades at the police station. One afternoon, I'd barely finished the final equation in a maths test when the police arrived to collect me from school. At the station, they showed me a video screen with images of various similar-looking guys.

"Do you recognise any of these men?" the officer asked.

They showed me them twice, but I didn't even need to see them all.

"Number 4," I said.

Number 4 in the line-up looked terrifying, and his face still haunts me to this day. Number 4 had cold, green eyes that I'd have recognised anywhere. Even now green eyes give me the creeps.

Number 4 was Jake.

The process was repeated for all four boys. Four boys meant four different defence solicitors, and four different ID parades. Each one, another trip to the station. Plus endless interviews as their lawyers tried to direct the course of the inquiry by pointing fingers at each other's clients. That night was scrutinised in minute detail over and over again because the boys weren't just going to own up. Their line was, the whole thing was consensual. I'd consented to sex with all four of them. I'd consented to being pissed on, slapped and punched. I'd consented to being dumped by the side of the road in my underwear. It sounds ridiculous, right? What jury was gonna believe that garbage?

Jake and the rest were remanded in custody – which meant some breathing space before I'd have to confront them in court. But as we waited for a date, they magicked a damn ace out of their sleeves. A get-out-of-jail-free card which meant a jury would never get to determine their guilt.

The Crown Prosecution Service calls the shots on whether to continue with a case – or drop it. The police phoned and asked me to come in for an update on where they were with their investigation.

"They're not ready to proceed," the officer told me. It was the same moody woman from before. "They've asked us to keep investigating."

"Fine."

"In the meantime, one of the suspects, or, rather, their legal team, has brought a video to our attention…"

"You've found the video they took?" In my mind, this was a result. Anyone with a brain would be able to see I'd been coerced into giving my 'consent'. I would have looked bedraggled, terrified, as I pulled gang signs and mugged for the camera.

"No, something else. Take a look," she said, turning her laptop to face me.

I gasped. This was something from years earlier – recorded unbeknown to me – of me and Trey having sex. Remember, phones back in the day were shit. The video was dim and grainy, you could barely make out my face, but it was me. And it was Trey's bedroom.

"It doesn't look good," the detective said.

"Where's it come from? I've never seen that before."

She said the film had done the rounds on the boys' phones. "Can you explain it?"

"I didn't know I was being filmed. I didn't give permission! Please don't show that to my mum," I begged her.

No one seemed to give a shit that I was under 16 in the clip – which is what's called statutory rape.

I went home. Later that day, family liaison came round to give Mum and Dave the lowdown on the CPS. I was upstairs in my bedroom at the time. Good job because – for reasons best known to them – they decided to show my mum the video.

Afterwards, when she'd done shaming me, the FLO came upstairs to dish out a lecture.

"You're on a very slippery slope," she said, perched on the edge of my bed. "The way you're heading, you're going to end up either dead in a ditch, or a prostitute."

Nice. I'd gone from rape victim to child sex worker in the blink of an eye. All it had taken was one shit video of me having sex with my supposed boyfriend at the time.

That was it for the CPS. The fact I'd started off by lying about what happened to me, plus the video, meant the case was fucked. *No,* they'd decided. It would not be going to court. I was an unreliable witness. Liar and prostitute. It was only a matter of time before Jake and the rest were back on the streets.

7

BABY MAMA

My rage burned and swelled until I couldn't contain it. Anyone and everyone around me felt its blistering heat. The teachers got it worse.

After those boys walked, the police turned up at school and shared their mugshots around the staff. The school was on alert to ring the police if they were spotted lurking anywhere near the gates. Jake and the rest would never answer in court for what they'd done.

And what did I have to show for the hours of interviews, intimate examinations and being outed to my own mum for starring in a non-consensual sex tape?

A big, fat target on my back.

It could have been in my head but, in school, it felt like the teachers were acting funny with me, staring at me. I felt wrong. My emotions teetered on a hair trigger. The slightest thing would set me off, like touching a lit match to a keg of gunpowder.

"Danielle, you're meant to have your book open in front of you."

Ka-boom!

"What did you say?" I replied, jumping to my feet with such force my chair clattered against the desk behind. "Who do you think you're talking to?"

I could feel my classmates' eyes on me.

Oh, here she goes. Danielle's kicking off again.

"Come on, Danielle. Sit down," the teacher said.

"No! Shut up. *You* sit down."

And then I'd spend the rest of the class alone in the corridor, followed by detention after school. The other kids started avoiding me like the plague. Their focus was exams, and I was fucking it all up for them.

The school safeguarding lead, Mr Benson, called me in to see him. Middle-aged guy, stern and always on top. Mr Benson was not the sort of dude a 15-year-old girl wants to sit down and chat with about being raped. Or about anything else, for that matter. Up until then, all my interaction with Mr Benson involved him standing over me in the corridor, wagging his finger and telling me to go babywipe the make-up off my face.

He was concerned now, though.

I wasn't the wild one – the naughty make-up one – now.

I was the one who'd been raped.

"You know, if you need to talk, if anything's bothering you…" he began.

Nah, fuck this, I thought. *I don't need these people.* And I left.

For real, I didn't need the teachers. Nor the annoying, middle-class lady from Child and Adolescent Mental Health

Services – CAMHS for short. She had all the qualifications, but she must have been off sick when they were teaching empathy and dealing with trauma. We met weekly with the goal of 'addressing my aggression'. She just didn't know how to deal with me. Instead, she skirted around asking me questions about the rape, and gave me a pencil and some paper. "Can you draw how you feel?"

What did she think it was? Reception class?

"Shut up! Why do you even care?" I said, then walked out.

Week after week we endured the same routine. She talked for an hour, firing questions at me. I listened, clammed up like I was under siege, shooting back the odd salvo of one-word answers.

"You're a very aggressive teenager," she concluded.

No shit.

Mum got it, too. Yeah, Mum got it bad.

Since the rape, I was barely spending any time at home. I was on the roads, staying with friends, just out. Chilling. The rare times I did come home – not so chilled.

One day, I stormed in for a change of clothes and some food. Mum was in the kitchen, doing some of her slow cooking. We hadn't seen each other for maybe a of couple days. The way I felt at the time, a couple of days was never even long enough.

"Danielle, I need to talk to you," said Mum. She sounded exhausted, like she had nothing left. She was at the end of her tether, hanging on by her fingernails.

"I ain't answering your bullshit questions," I told her bluntly. "You do this every time. Where you been? Who you been with? I've been out. Now I'm back. And then I'm going out again. That's all you need to know."

"It's not about…"

I slammed my mug down on the counter so hard that tea sprayed the worktop.   "What is it then? Come on!"

"We're moving to Cyprus," Mum said.

"Is that the big news?" I scoffed. "Good! I don't give a fuck. Fucking leave, then."

Poor woman. She must have been in turmoil. She couldn't have a conversation with me that didn't end with her dodging missiles. Cutlery, bits of china, whatever happened to be in my hand at the time. All I wanted was to be left alone, and any attempt to communicate with me, however well meaning, was treated like a personal attack. I defended my space with white hot rage and slamming of doors. I was just so angry – through no fault of Mum's.

For Mum, Dave and John, a fresh start in sunny Cyprus was looming on the horizon. No one ever said to me, "you're not coming with us". But it was obvious I wasn't. Which was fine. Didn't want to go anyway. I'd have *asked* to stay there in London. I'm a city girl. The fuck was I gonna do with donkeys and olive groves? As I was still under 18, there must have been a conversation with social services, because while Mum and Dave started packing up the flat – a few weeks before they were due to leave – a social worker turned up.

"Don't worry," she told me, assuming I might be worried. Compared to events of a couple of months earlier, Mum moving to Cyprus was low on the trauma scale. "We're going to place you in a house. You'll have your own room. You're going to be absolutely fine."

Cool. I wasn't scared. Could not have cared less. If anything, I was happy to be going somewhere else.

Packing up my bedroom, I read over the little messages and greetings my friends over the years had graffitied on my walls – scratched into the wallpaper with a Bic biro or smudged on with felt tip, the colours pale and faded with age. Those days were behind me. The rest of the family were loading their belongings into crates and suitcases for the big move. I was off to a new home.

Looking back, I feel like this should have been a huge, pivotal moment, but the truth is, it wasn't. I moved to the foster house – a big semi shared with other foster kids looked after by a well-spoken Italian lady. I had a large room to myself, with a wardrobe and a desk. I really don't remember any grand farewell. The day my family got on the plane, I was out rolling round the ends with my friends. Mum tried to call a couple of times and when I saw her number I didn't pick up. In the end, she sent me a text: "You know where we are, I'm always here for you if you need me."

OK. Whatever.

Maybe, again, it was the trauma that stopped me processing things properly, but that move didn't prick me with emotion in the way it might have someone else.

Despite everything, I did well in my GCSEs and came out with a load of As and Bs. Unbelievably, the school had been keen to keep me on. Mr Benson sat me down one day and said, "You've done really well. Your predicted grades are good. We'd be honoured if you'd consider joining us in sixth form."

Honoured? Really? Come on!

"Nah. Fuck that," I said. "Are we done?"

I left him with his mouth flapping and walked out.

Being out of school, and with Mum gone, my aggression needed new outlets. One night, a fair was visiting a neighbourhood nearby. I made plans to go with Haina and a few others. Around this time, crowds of strangers made me hella anxious. I was already tense and jumpy, but, reaching the edge of the fair, the booming music, shrieking kids and flashing lights flayed my nerves. That hair trigger again.

A little black boy who I vaguely knew came bounding over. He was full-on in my face, chatting shit and kind of grabbing at me. Not in any kind of predatory or sexual way, but it didn't matter. The sensation of a stranger's hands on my body tripped that hair trigger.

"What you touching me for? Move from me!" I snapped.

He backed off. "Woah. Chill sis…"

"Don't sis me! I'm not your sis!" One fist was closed around the neck of a bottle of alcohol and I slammed it on the tarmac, scattering shards of glass.

The boy raised his hands, taking another step back, eyes wide in alarm.

The others laughed.

"She's just playing with you," Haina giggled.

Except I wasn't just playing with him.

The fair was mobbed with police and after clocking me smash the bottle, a pair of them were heading rapidly in my direction.

I wild out on the boy, lunging at him with my jagged weapon, swiping for his head. Luckily – for both of us – he ducked out the way. Then I was on my back, air pressed out of my lungs by the weight of the two officers piled on top of me.

Since the rape, my opinion of the police was rock bottom. I fought like a wild cat, trying to wrestle my tiny frame from underneath them, kicks and punches bouncing pathetically off their stab vests. But I was no match for them – too slow, too weak. They dragged me to my feet and slapped both hands in handcuffs in front of me, then read me my rights. Meanwhile, my friends cussed and shouted for them to let me go.

There was a new *ping* on the police radar – and it was called Danielle Marin. I worked on making it shine.

One night, a few of us headed out to a club in Hounslow called the Tudor Rose. This was one bait club. A couple of boys got shot dead on the dancefloor at a Dizzee Rascal event there in the early 2000s. Ironically it was an anti-gun-crime event. Someone didn't get the memo.

We went up there, maybe five or six of us, for a low-key night, just to get out of the house. There wasn't a whole lot going on so one boy, Bradley, leant in to me and said, "Might as well make some money, yeah?"

What he meant was: *let's rob some phones.*

Bradley was a tall, slim guy, covered in tattoos. There was a lot of fuckery around that boy. His flat was basically a trap house, always full of people smoking weed or just chilling. The whole place was strung with a web of pound-shop extension leads and four-plug adaptors – one plugged into another – because he used to steal his electricity from the block.

Robbing phones in the club was almost as easy as robbing them from the changing rooms at school. Girls in the club are so preoccupied with men, stood there preening with their boobs and bums stuck out, trying to catch some boy's eye, they're not watching their stuff. Plus, too many vodka and Cokes. Their bags are right there, literally an open invite. They're drunk. They're not paying attention.

Phone – thankyou. Cash – even better. I didn't even care if I got caught. This was how it was since I'd been raped.

I don't care, I don't care.

I didn't give a fuck.

Which was just as well, because remember I said *almost* as easy?

I'd lifted like eight iPhones and £50 in cash before someone spotted us and snitched to the management. The dancefloor parted as a couple of square-jawed shaven heads and black nylon bomber jackets zeroed in on me. Two more were steaming over from the bar area. I dashed the phones into the darkness of the dancefloor and made a run for it.

Man, too slow.

The bouncers jumped on me. Each one gripped a limb and lifted me off the ground to carry me to the front of the club. As we reached the door, I managed to wriggle one foot free and booted the one bouncer in the face. There were always police outside these clubs, and the bouncers handed me over to them. This time, once they'd got my name out of me, they pulled my hands back and cuffed me from behind.

"Why are you cuffing me like that?" I said, with a tone of disgust. "I'm just a girl! What am I going to do?"

"We've got you down for violent behaviour towards police officers."

That's how it was from then on. Hands always cuffed behind my back, always too tight so they bit into my wrists, then slammed into the floor of the van. Did I mention? Getting arrested is hella painful, man.

* * *

I knew this one boy, Aidan, from around the ends. He was Marek's friend, and I knew Marek from long. Aidan was very handsome. All the girls wanted to be with him. He was super quiet, never raised his voice and always seemed to be in the background, or on the edge of a conversation – like an observer. Maybe that added to the aura of mystique around him, magnifying his attractiveness. That and the fact he was half Indian, half black – which meant he was exceptionally pretty, with a contoured face and sculpted cheekbones.

"So pretty." That's how the girls always spoke of Aidan.

He didn't do crime. He didn't get mixed up in all the drama and I'd never heard of him getting involved in any bad circles. Aidan was a good boy. Dependable.

I got on a bus one day and climbed to the top deck. As I rounded the top of the stairs, I locked eyes with Aidan, sat at the back. He was wearing a smartly pressed T-shirt, nice trainers and his hair was freshly cut. Typical Aidan. Very clean. Always presentable. We held each other's gaze for a long beat and smiled at each other – just a 'hello' smile, because we'd seen each other around the ends, but it sent me a ripple folding through my tummy and its glow remained long after we'd broken our stare and I'd sat down.

My style at that time was skinny jeans riding low on the hips, with lacy knickers poking out above the waistband, a tight, strappy top and hair tied in plaits or a high bun. The look must have made an impression because when I got home later there was a flirty message waiting for me on MSN.

From Aidan.

Oh. My. God!

Aidan.

I don't know how he'd got my MSN, but he'd got it from someone, somehow and that's how we first spoke.

In the foster home, all us kids had an allocated 45 minutes each per night to use the computer or mess about on MSN. It was a dial-up PC that always wasted a frustrating 10 minutes of semi-audible beeps and screeching while it tried to connect. Straight away, me and Aidan swapped numbers, and from thereon, things moved super quick. We were with each other every single day.

My friends were gobsmacked. Sharelle's jaw hit the floor when I told her. Aidan wasn't known to even talk to any girls, let alone be with one.

And now he was with me.

He lived a bus ride away and sometimes he'd take me home on the bus, before going back to his. In little time, I was around his place almost every single day. He gave me a drawer in his bedroom for all the essentials, and I practically moved in. Even though it was a four-bedroom house, it was still tight with Aidan, his mum, his two brothers and their girlfriends. Plus the dog. Mornings were a noisy chaos of breakfast-making and queues for the bathroom. But downstairs there was a big, open-plan living room/diner, and because there were so many people around there was always a good vibe about the place.

His mum was mostly cool – she was from Mauritius and worked as a carer – but I knew Aidan was her golden child and I always got the sneaking suspicion she thought I wasn't quite good enough for him.

By this time, I'd enrolled in a hair and beauty course at college, with a couple A-levels on the side. Aidan was working as an electrician. All of a sudden, after all the trauma, I felt happy and content.

We'd only been together a few months and we were chilling at his one night when Aidan said, out of the blue :

"I feel like you might be pregnant."

"Why would you think that?" I said.

I had zero symptoms, felt absolutely fine and my belly was super-flat.

"I don't know – I've just got a feeling!"

Aidan wouldn't let up and one day he came home from Sainsbury's with a pregnancy test.

"OK! OK! I'll do the test!" I said.

Triumphant, I showed him the result. "See!" As I'd predicted – it was negative.

A few days later, I was at the foster home, hanging out with Haina and Sharelle. They were pestering me: "Just do another test."

"OK! OK!" I said, giving in, certain it would return the same result.

Only this time, we were all in for a surprise.

Haina and Sharelle erupted in hysterical screams when I showed them the pale blue cross. "Oh my God! Oh my God!"

Meanwhile I burst into tears.

"What the hell are you gonna do?" said Haina.

I mean, I was 17. Still a kid. Hella young. Hella big shock.

My friends assumed, I think, we would get rid of it. But when I caught up with Aidan to break the news later that same day, he had a very different take.

I took a bus to his, bringing the test with me, and sat on the top deck idly watching raindrops trickle down the window, wondering, *What he's going to want to do?*

He'd been saying for a while he thought I was pregnant, so I guessed it wouldn't be a huge surprise, but we'd never talked about next steps if it turned out I really was. Until now, it had just been a bit of banter.

Aidan led me up to his room and put the TV on. "What do you fancy?"

I turned it off again.

"What you doing?!" he said.

"So, you were right, you know?" I told him.

Aidan looked puzzled. "What do you mean? Right about what?"

"About me being pregnant!"

He gasped. "No, you're lying!"

"See for yourself," I said, giving him the test.

"I told you!" he said. "I knew it!"

I waited hesitantly, anticipating an awkward conversation about what we did now – but it wasn't even a discussion.

"So… I guess we're having this baby, then?" said Aidan.

"I guess so!"

This is it, I thought, *I'm gonna marry this person.* I saw a future for us, and in that future was a nice house, couple of kids, a dog. There were parks, parents' evenings and summer BBQs with school gates friends.

This is literally it.

Aidan was amazing while I was pregnant. The first couple months, all I wanted to eat was those Fab ice lollies with the hundreds and thousands crust on the end. I'd destroy a whole box in one go, so Aidan was always running to the shop to buy more. He'd make me ginger tea if I felt sick, and held my hand at the scans as we stared in amazement at our unborn child, tiny heart flickering on the screen.

As part of our preparation for becoming parents, we'd watch the reality show, *One Born Every Minute,* which in hindsight wasn't the best thing to watch when you were pregnant. It was a parade of screaming women giving birth, and when they pushed the baby out it looked horrifying. Half the time, I had to watch through the fingers of one hand while gripping Aidan's thigh with the other.

Money was tight, so we couldn't afford piles of new baby stuff, but we bought a few things and Aidan's sprawling family helped out with hand-me-downs. They were as excited as us, which made up for my lot not being around. Aidan's mum really couldn't do enough.

A few days before my due date, I began feeling really off and kept bursting into tears for no reason. Drop a piece of cutlery – little cry. No milk in the fridge – end of the world. Cry. My head felt as heavy as my bulging tummy and my emotions were like frayed ribbons flapping in the wind. I couldn't snatch hold of them.

One afternoon, stood in the kitchen stirring a simmering pan of bolognese sauce, I suddenly bent over double with excruciating pain. My knuckles stood out white as I gripped the worktop, thinking, *nah, this can't be it.* I didn't want to make a fuss. *Just firm it out,* I thought. *Run yourself a bath.*

I slid into the warm water, willing it to bring some relief, but instead I just soaked the bathroom as I writhed in pain. When Aidan got back from the gym, I told him, "I think I'm in labour."

The house was, as usual, full of people and suddenly it was panic stations. I got my bag together and Aidan's mum drove us to the hospital as I gritted my teeth in the back seat, tears beading in the corners of my eyes. By the time we arrived I was in so much pain I was sure I was going to give birth in reception. But then the midwife checked me over. "OK, you're not in active labour, you're just having a few contractions," she said. "Go home, you'll be fine."

That night. Wow.

I've never felt pain like it, before or since. I was climbing the walls. On fire. Squirming, trying to crawl out of my skin. In the end, I couldn't take any more and we ended up back at the hospital in the early hours of the morning.

OK, I thought, *I've been at this for hours now. We must be ready to go.*

"You're two centimetres dilated," the midwife said.

What?!

From there, my birth experience unravelled exactly like an episode of *One Born Every Minute*. Absolutely horrific, in fact. I was in labour for three-and-a-half days.

"I don't think I can do this," I told the midwife.

"You're going to be fine, love," she said, messing with a face mask. "Let's get you sorted with some gas and air. It might make you feel a little nauseous, but it will help with the pain."

I've had a life-long phobia about being sick to the point I get full-blown panic attacks if I even think I'm going to throw up. That's probably another reason I've never done drugs and don't like getting drunk.

"I can't have it," I said. "I've got a sick phobia. Is there anything else?"

But it was the same deal with the pain-relief drugs. They would probably make me feel queasy, the midwife explained.

"OK," I said. "I can't have any pain relief."

The pain – excruciating though it was – played second fiddle to my fear of vomit. Imagine further down the line, sat in all them trap houses with vomiting drug addicts. Horrific. We'll get to that later.

After two days in hospital with no pain relief, I was still only five centimetres.

"It's because you're so slim!" the midwife told me. Plus, my baby was big. By the third day, I was completely exhausted, drifting in and out of consciousness. As I couldn't take the pain any longer, they gave me an epidural and I finally got some rest. I couldn't move from the waist down, but I managed to sleep a little and even got some food inside me.

Because of the drugs, I was rigged up to monitors. I was snoozing, semi-delirious, when a nurse rushed in.

"Your baby's heart rate is falling. You're going to need an emergency caesarean."

She pressed a buzzer – and everyone burst into action. The surgeon came in briefly to explain what would happen, I groggily added my signature to a disclaimer while Aidan was helped into a surgical gown, and I was taken down for surgery.

There was no pain now, thanks to the epidural, but I felt a sharp tug and pressure on my body as the surgeon sliced me open, and then his slippery, gloved hands rummaging inside me. *He's doing the washing up*, I pondered, drifting on waves of nausea. *He's rearranging my insides.*

Then he lifted my son over the green cotton sheet and said, "Here's your baby."

He was like a hairy little bear. He had more hair on his head than plenty of adults. And to me and Aidan, he was perfect.

I was so completely gone that I couldn't even lift my arms to hold him. Instead, Aidan took him as I lay there thinking, *Is he OK? What about this huge hole in my belly?*

It took me a week to recover from bringing him into the world, and those seven days are a blur of pain-relief meds, breastfeeding and exhaustion. I remember at one point lying there as my baby cried in his cot beside me. I couldn't sit up because my abdominal muscles had been cut, and I didn't even have the strength to reach a buzzer.

When we were ready to leave the hospital, Aidan's mum came to collect us. Our baby – who still hadn't been given a name – was dressed in a little white suit with hat and mittens. "Drive slowly," I pleaded, as Aidan's mum nudged through the traffic or rocked over a speed bump.

Back at the house, a welcoming committee was ready to greet us and a banner with "Baby Boy" was tacked up across the living-room wall. It was sweet, but I just felt overwhelmed by the noise, bustle and sheer number of people fussing over us. What I really needed was a quiet space – for just the three of us – so I could get my head together. No chance of that at Aidan's.

It took us three weeks to find a name for our son. "You can name him," I said to Aidan. But in the end, we chose together and settled on Lloyd.

That first month, I didn't leave the house at all. I cried constantly, felt exhausted and didn't want to see anyone. Where Aidan was amazing during the pregnancy, he struggled with the reality of being such a young dad, and I felt like he wasn't really pulling his weight. When he announced he was off to Vegas on a stag do when Lloyd was just three weeks old, I didn't even have the energy to argue with him.

"Cool. Go to Vegas. Whatever. Have fun."

Finally ready to leave the house, I wrapped up Lloyd for a visit to Sharelle's. Haina was there, and Marek too. Instead of being a welcome change of scene, the whole thing was hella awkward. These people were my friends, but I didn't want anyone touching my son. He was so perfect and smelt like heaven – I couldn't stand the thought of grubby cigarette fingers on him.

At Aidan's, the bustle and vibe that had once been such a buzz, now felt like unbearable torment. I never had a moment away from Lloyd, and I spent almost all that time alone with him in Aidan's bedroom – hiding from the noise and chaos in the rest of the house. I loved looking after him, massaging him, bathing him, rubbing baby lotion into his soft, clean skin. But I began resenting the lack of support from Aidan, and the situation in the house.

One night, I was feeding Lloyd while Aidan started pulling fresh clothes out the wardrobe. He got changed, splashed on some perfume and was lacing up his trainers when I said, "Going somewhere?"

"Meeting some of my boys and then we going to the club. I'll be late – I'll try not to wake you."

"I think I'd prefer it if you stayed in. With us. Me. Our son."

"It's kind of arranged already…"

"Right."

"Are we cool?"

"Yeah. Great. Go have your fun then," I said coldly.

Aidan slunk out. When Lloyd's cries woke me for an early hours' feed, there was a cold, empty space in the bed beside me. No sign of Aidan. It was mid-morning before he showed up, apparently having stayed with a friend. I didn't even care. But I thought, *if this is how it's gonna be, I'd rather just do it alone.*

It wasn't just that incident. We were bickering all the time over stuff that really shouldn't have mattered. One time, as me and Aidan argued, his mum busied into the room and took Lloyd in her arms.

"You can't do this to the little boy!" she said, soothing him. "You two need to sort it out!"

Lloyd was only a few months old, but I realised what me and Aidan had was no longer a relationship. We could try and be friends. But for Lloyd's sake, we couldn't be together.

"We are together, though. You can't just leave," Aidan said.

Except I could.

Aidan's mum was right – we had to sort it out, and I did just that. I went to the council, found myself a housing officer and put in a bid on a flat.

8

FRESH START

In those days it was easy enough getting a council flat. I rolled in the civic centre. Lloyd, cute as hell, a heart-melter in his mini Arsenal kit. I'd tamed his massive afro into plaits and my son was growing more beautiful by the day.

The place reeked of desperation and frayed tempers, with a dash of language barrier thrown in for good measure. Plenty tears wiped from the corners of pleading eyes, fingers jabbed in disinterested faces. A young Somali mum next to me had been waiting a couple of hours while she somehow juggled five kids. Shuffling them from knee to hip, plugging in dummies, failing to soothe their gripes with bits of fruit and tatty toys. We nodded hellos to each other. Her lips tried for a smile but her eyes were full of fear. She was homeless, barely spoke any English and shitting it in case she got kicked out.

My number came up to see the housing adviser, an old white lady with the jaded look of someone who'd heard it all and grown immune to the despair around her. She sounded like she'd been reading the same questions off her screen for about a decade. It was all done by the book.

"Do you have any family?" she asked.

I mean, they've got to try.

"Yeah, I got family. In Cyprus."

"All of them? There's no one…"

"Every aunt, uncle, cousin, pet cat and goldfish, as far as I know."

It was the truth. Lloyd and me were on our own. No private landlord in the whole of West London was gonna chance their £1000 a calendar month on housing benefits and a 17-year-old single mum. We had nowhere to go. So I filled in all the forms, signed on the line and we were dispatched to catch a bus to this flat where a housing officer would be waiting to show us around.

The address was slap bang in the middle of the ends, a couple of minutes from my mum's old place and the sandpit and swings where I'd played and plotted as a kid, palms sticky with one of my homemade chocolate crispy cakes. We found the guy outside a massive, old Victorian house, sectioned into three flats. It's probably worth like three million pounds now. We'd been offered the ground floor. Inside, the high ceilings and airy rooms meant space to breathe, space for Lloyd to grow. We had one bedroom, where Lloyd's cot would fit snug at the end of the bed, with a window looking out onto a messy rectangle of grass – a.k.a. the communal garden. New kitchen, new bathroom. Everything was spotless. A grand fireplace dominated one wall of the front room. In my head, I imagined how it would look done up. *Carpet can go for a start,* I thought.

"Yeah. Like it," I told the guy. "We'll take it."

He handed me the keys there and then. Over the next few days, I set about making the place *ours*. That carpet did indeed go and I had white floorboards fitted in its place. With a few cusses, furniture was wrestled from slabs of Ikea flat pack. Shelves and corners were filled with photos, trinkets and scented candles.

We didn't want for anything. OK, I wasn't hitting the shops every weekend, but it's not like I had a walk-in wardrobe needed filling with new clothes. We had money to eat. I got my child benefits, money from Aidan. I was happy, just cracking on with being a mum.

Years back, over the click-clack of my Yai Yai's knitting needles, and with the aroma of chicken broth and lemon simmering on the hob, I'd had it drilled into me: us girls, we were housewives. That was our role. Didn't matter you could see the square mile skyscrapers from Yai Yai's bedroom window. No point entertaining grand ideas, because our future was all mapped out in two, easy well-worn steps: get a good man, have some kids.

"If you want to find a nice man, you need to go to Green Lane," Yai Yai used to say. What she meant was, "a nice *Cypriot* man". Maybe it was no coincidence that Green Lane and Tottenham is where we used to go shopping almost every weekend.

Yai Yai's path of righteousness was one I was more than happy to follow, all the way up the aisle of the church to wedding vows at the altar. I wasn't bothered about going to uni and getting a degree. And I couldn't see myself mixing with the uptown people in some city office job. I was happy staying home, being a mum. All I wanted was a family. A nice guy, more kids – *four* more kids. If someone wanted to know my occupation, I'd have been proud to tick the box next to 'housewife'.

And I honestly think it would have panned out that way – if it hadn't been for Dajuan.

* * *

I started seeing a guy, nothing serious. Just meals together and chilling. It wasn't going anywhere. Then one day he comes out with, "Hey, my friend says he wants to meet you. Can I give him your number?"

"Depends? Do I know this boy?"

"You know him. It's Dajuan Clarke innit."

For real. Everyone from my area knew Dajuan. I say knew him – knew *of* him, at least. I saw him on the block. I never asked questions, but I knew he and his family were a big deal, and I knew full well he sold drugs.

I don't know why, but I'm like a magnet for drug dealers. I've got a vibe, I think. Like a trap girl. That's a girl who sells drugs. I've had it in the club – "Little trap girl, yeah? What you got? Sniff?"

Truth – I get it even now, men pull up on me, kerbside, all smiles, as they lean on the sill of their open window and look me up and down like they got me sussed.

"Hey pretty! You wanna make some P? Come work with us."

Maybe I'll never shake it.

Maybe that's what Dajuan spotted. I don't know. But I met him and it was like fireworks. I fell in love. Hundred percent in love.

He was dark black, in his 30s, five-eleven and stocky, with these deep, brown eyes. You'd lose yourself in those eyes. You'd drown in them. Everything about that boy was clean. The aftershave. The new season tracksuits. Box-fresh trainers. And of course the chains and watch.

Yeah, he was striking. But what made him really stand out was these cheekbones. Oh my God, he had the bone structure of a catwalk model. You could have plucked him out of West London and dropped him in a fashion show. He'd have slotted right in.

I'd say to him, "D, your cheekbones are so high!"

He'd kiss his teeth and wave me away. "Shut up! Whatever!"

He couldn't take a compliment, but he knew he was striking.

He'd come round. I'd cook. Stew chicken, fried plaintain and dumplings. We'd play card games and watch movies. Sure, I knew who Dajuan was and what he did. But the two of us, in the beginning, before the madness, it felt innocent. Too innocent, perhaps, considering what he was into.

See – it wasn't just anyone got close to Dajuan, not when it came to business. He was friends with the old man in the post office, the dude in the chicken shop – everyone. But there was another side to the softly spoken guy that might hold open the door for you, or ask you how you were feeling today. You don't walk up to a boy like him and start chatting business while he's chilling on the block with his people. The youngers, they didn't get a look in. They didn't even try. Dajuan was like royalty in the ends. Being part of his close circle could put money in your pocket, the latest Louboutins on your feet. It's how the boys looked after their kids and their mums. It got them the Audi, the Hatton Garden Rolex, the gold chains and the diamond grills. If they played the game right, managed to keep two eyes on the prize and 10 steps in front of the feds, it got them *out*, man. Out of the grind, out of London and on to something bigger.

What I had with Dajuan felt real. Outsiders looking in and after the fact often ask if I think I was, maybe, groomed? It's a question I've had chucked at me a lot. Perhaps there was a bit of that, but I don't reckon I was singled out. I think maybe my situation – single, white mum, own flat, not exactly rolling in it – presented a series of opportunities to certain people.

To be fair, they did ask very nicely if they could exploit those opportunities.

I could have said no.

But I was a yes person. I said yes to everything.

They asked. I said yes.

* * *

I was feeding Lloyd when my phone pinged with a text. It was Jordan, one of Dajuan's friends: *Hey D – can I pop round? Wanna chat with you...*

I told him sure, he could knock on my door any time. All the boys could. He called by a couple of hours later.

Jordan had a good 10 years on me. He was light skin with long, kinky hair which he wore in two bunchies. Calm and collected. With age comes experience. You never saw him riled.

"Mind if I use your kitchen for something?" he asked. "Like – an hour tops."

I shrugged, didn't even ask him what for. In the back of my mind, I knew. 'Course I knew. "Yeah, sure."

"I'll pay you."

"OK. Whatever, it's fine."

Couple of days later he turned up with his cousin in tow. He had one of those Asda bags for life swinging at his side.

"You know the way," I said, showing them in. "Make yourselves at home."

"Cool," said Jordan. "We won't make any mess. We'll do our thing, clean up and we're out of here."

"It's all yours."

The boys went through and shut the door. I settled on the bed with Lloyd to watch a film. The little stereo in the kitchen burst into life, masking the racket of clattering pans. The slick, honeyed groove of 90s slow jams came drifting across the hall. Drill wasn't even a thing yet. These boys were old school.

Something else came drifting across the hall, too. An unmistakable smell hit me. I'd never done so much as a bump of cocaine in my whole life, but I'd been around it enough to recognise its chemical tang, catching and scratching in the back of my throat.

Ok, I thought, opening a window. *So, they're cooking drugs. I mean, you knew they weren't stewing no curry goat for their mums.*

They were making cocaine into crack. This basic bit of chemistry turned an expensive, rich-boy drug into something that could be banged out to street addicts in £10 hits.

Maybe an hour passed. The music died suddenly and Jordan knocked at the bedroom door.

"You OK?" I said.

Jordan pushed into the room and said, "D, I'm gone." He handed me a bunch of notes. "Here, this is for you. Treat the little man."

There was like, £250. I'd expected maybe a hundred or something, but not *that* much.

"Oh! Thanks Jordan! I'm around if you need the kitchen again. Any time."

"Be round later to chill yeah?"

"See you in a bit."

£250 to lie around watching films on the iPad? I'll take that. And true to their word, my kitchen was spotless, surfaces freshly bleached. The pots were so clean I couldn't even tell which ones they'd cooked the drugs in. When the boys turned up later to chill, I asked them straight, "What ones did you use? I'm not making dinner in no crack pot."

But Jordan scoffed. "Don't be stupid. We brought our own!"

They'd totally respected me and my space – and paid me properly for it, too. It opened my eyes. The boys wore their money on show, hanging round their necks in gold Cuban link or rope chains and jewelled pendants, but renting out the kitchen brought it home: there was serious cash being made. Dajuan was taking care of everything for me – bills, rent, food – but a little extra in my purse didn't hurt. The very next day, I took Lloyd out shopping and spoilt him. New clothes, new toys, the works.

It became a regular thing over the next few months. I'd get a text, a few of the guys would pull up, Asda bags bulging with a 'box' – that's a kilo – of cocaine, plus their pots, pans and cutlery. I got paid every time, at least a couple of hundred pounds. If they were cooking a big batch, they might be in there four hours. Easy £600 for me. And if Lloyd was napping, I'd sit in with them sometimes, smoking my Mayfairs while Jordan did his thing.

"You gonna teach me, then?" I said one time, watching him cut the coke with a white powder they all called 'madj' or 'magic'. I learned later it was this legal chemical called benzocaine; it made the cocaine go that bit further: more weight, more profit.

Jordan kissed his teeth, looked at me like I was crazy. "D, you're lucky we're even letting you watch!"

"You're forgetting whose kitchen you're in!"

"You're forgetting who's payin' you for it, D!"

He tipped the mixture into a pan, added some water and bicarbonate of soda and set it to heat on the stove.

"Trade secrets pretty girl!"

"Yeah, it's only me, though."

"Need-to-know basis, D," he laughed, stirring as the pan started to bubble. He killed the heat and kept stirring. Creamy lumps formed in the liquid as it cooled.

"That's crack now?" I said.

"I'm giving all my secrets away! You too fast, man! Too fucking fast!"

No doubt the police would have seen it differently, but I didn't feel like I was doing anything wrong. The drugs weren't mine. Never even touched them. Didn't know where they came from or where they went. Most times I stayed out of the boys' way and just let them get on with it. I got paid, and had my kitchen cleaned into the bargain. It was innocent, easy money and it was helping me keep Lloyd clothed and fed. Often, I wasn't even there when the boys were cooking. The kitchen was getting so much use, I gave them all a key and they helped themselves. Sometimes I'd come home from a day out with Lloyd to find my fridge re-stocked with fresh food, or the electricity meter loaded up with credit.

With all the to and fro, for anyone watching, my flat was bait. But the boys always took precautions so as not to make my place too hot. They switched up cars, parked around the corner, made sure they weren't followed. They'd look around for eyes on the flat before they let themselves in. No one wanted the feds kicking my door in while they were cooking drugs. If they came any other time, no problem – so long as they brought a warrant. No warrant, no entry. If they had the paperwork, they'd find the flat clean and tidy with nothing illegal in it.

But as it turned out, an early-morning alarm call from drug squad was the least of our worries. Someone *had* been watching. Or one of our lot had let his mouth run away with him and his secrets had reached the wrong ears.

Because the knock did come – and it wasn't the feds at my door.

9

SHOOTERS

It was around Lloyd's bedtime. We were watching *Pingu* together, stretched out on the bed. Lloyd nestled in the hinge of my elbow while I waited for sleep to steal him away. Next to the bed lay a fold of 20s. Dajuan and Jordan were in the front room. Kitchen cleaned. They were chilling and chatting business. Private business. Where the drugs were going, who was taking them. I just rented out my kitchen. That kind of chat was still way above my pay grade.

"That's it, baby boy," I whispered. Lloyd was giving in, his heavy eyelids drooping. "You go to sleep."

I was on the verge of dozing off myself, but a sharp knock at the door put an end to that. *Fuck's sake*, I thought. *Not now!*

Lloyd stirred as I peeled myself away from him. His face cracked and he sucked in a big breath like he was going to let rip. I put a hand to his chest to settle him, stroked one cheek.

"Sshh now. Mummy'll be right back."

I tiptoed out into the hall, cursing under my breath. Probably just another one of the boys.

Except it wasn't. Because when I opened my front door, the cold, black steel of a gun barrel was pointing at my face.

Four guys, features hidden by black balaclavas. Hyped up, breathing heavy, tensed like coiled springs. Vibrating almost. For a heart-stopping moment, I froze. It was surreal. We stood there facing each other for what felt like ages. Like no one knew what to do next. No one even spoke. My mind raced, trying to make sense of it. *Were they here for me?* It took me a split second to process it all, and I realised it wasn't my couple of hundred quid or my baby they were after. Their target was sat in my front room smoking weed, with a few grands-worth of crack tucked up in Asda bags.

I loved Dajuan, but no way was I putting him, or his drugs, over my little boy. This was a hit. Maybe – if the guys were lucky – it was just a robbery. It didn't matter. Yes, I wanted to come out of it alive. But honestly, they could have shot the place to pieces, put a bullet in my head and everyone else's – as long as they left Lloyd alone.

I was powerless. All I could do was open the door and step aside. The boy with the gun nodded. There was respect in the gesture, as if he was saying, *you done the right thing, girl.* While they walked in, I ran back to the bedroom and scooped up Lloyd.

"Come on, baby," I soothed, cool as anything. "We're just going to play a little game of hide and seek, yeah? Let's get under the bed."

The iPad was still gurgling *Pingu*. I grabbed it, shuffled under the bed with Lloyd and turned the volume up full – just as all hell broke loose.

It sounded like a thunderstorm going off in my hallway. Guns blazed. How many shots, I couldn't tell over the thuds and panicked shouts. Were they kicking the door in? Shooting it down? I hugged Lloyd while his forehead creased in fright at the noise.

"Don't worry, baby," I said. "It's just on the TV." Then I pointed at the screen and cooed in mock surprise, "Look at *Pingu!*" Anything to draw his attention from the mayhem going on the other side of our bedroom wall.

Surely someone's going to call the police, I thought. It seemed to last forever. From under the bed, I watched the crack of light below the bedroom door. I barely dared breathe. I was waiting for a shadow, the door to open, someone sent to tie up loose ends: *Me – the only witness, the only loose end.*

Instead, as suddenly as it began, it was over. The gunfire stopped, there was a stampede in the hall and out into the street. Then – silence.

I waited, making sure, watching that crack under the door. Minutes passed. Still super quiet. *They're dead,* I thought. I expected at least the wail of armed responders. Police swarming to the sound of gunfire. But there was nothing.

"There!" I said to Lloyd. "Let's get you on the bed, shall we? Mummy's gonna take a look…"

He looked kind of confused but soon settled fine with the iPad next to him.

Won't lie – I was terrified.

For Lloyd's sake I tried to stay calm. I pulled open the bedroom door. The hall was empty, the front door open to the evening air. The door to the front room was pretty much disintegrated – a jagged tangle of splintered wood and bullet holes. I took a deep breath and pushed it aside, steeling myself for the sight beyond. Dead bodies. Blood.

Instead, my knees went weak as relief washed through me. The place was empty. It looked like a bomb site, but it was empty. The curtains swayed in the breeze from the open window – *the boys' escape route*. The wall opposite the door was studded with bullet holes. Furniture had been upended. Cushions sent flying.

But they'd got out and the drugs were gone, too.

My way of dealing with a shock like that is to go into cleaning mode. I went through that flat like a whirlwind. First off – I checked the kitchen, made sure the boys had done a proper job of tidying up after themselves. I couldn't hear any sirens right now, but it didn't mean they weren't on the way. They wouldn't send any regular police to a shooting. They met fire with fire – the right and proper response was an armed one. If the feds were tied up with another shooting, you had to wait your turn.

I swept up the splintered wood from the door and the chunks of plaster raked out of my walls. I vacuumed, righted the furniture, put the cushions back on the sofa tidy. Checked the kitchen *again* just to be sure. No drugs. Clean as.

The boys were preying on my mind. I hoped they were safe. I never found so much as a speck of blood – anywhere – so I had to think they'd got clean away, unhurt. I didn't expect a call and knew better than to make one. To the feds, a phone call after an incident like that is more than just a 'hope you're OK…' It's a way-sign. It informs their investigation. It's evidence. So you don't do it. However much it twists and hurts inside, you wait it out. Smoke a cigarette. Wait. Smoke. Wait.

I had time to clean the whole flat and was back on the bed with Lloyd, dozing again, when *another* knock at the door snapped me to. I wasn't expecting such a low-key entrance. Megaphones and battering rams maybe. But this was almost polite.

I opened the door to not one gun this time, but loads. Bare men on my doorstep, bristling with assault rifles. Full-on armed response. Maybe eight feds, more behind. Beyond them were marked cars, plus a van, blocking off the road, their flashing lights rinsing the street in blue.

"Is the shooter still inside?" the lead officer said.

"No," I shrugged. "Come in."

"We're going to have to ask you to step outside and wait here."

"Are you crazy?" I snorted, looking him up and down. "My son's asleep. I'm not going nowhere."

"You've got a child in there?" he said in disbelief.

"In the bedroom."

"I won't ask again. Outside. This is a crime scene."

I knew what was coming. I was getting arrested. "But – my son…" I said.

"One of the officers will look after him."

I looked over my shoulder, sighed. This was only going one way. I walked out the front door and – sure enough – they didn't disappoint.

"All right darling, we're nicking you, sorry about that," said one of the officers.

"The fuck for? I'm the victim!"

He clamped my hands in cuffs, reading me my rights. The charge was a laugh – *possession of a firearm with intent to endanger life.*

"Yeah, I got a disposable lighter, mate, does that count?" I said.

It was bravado. I was in a spin, panicking. Not about the charge, that was just so much bullshit so they could get me down the station and into an interview room. Grill me about who I knew, what had gone down in my flat and why.

No – my worry was Lloyd.

The police were nice about it, if I'm honest. They were just doing their job. Me, and them – we all knew the score, we were playing chess. Making the moves expected of us.

"Look," said this one fed. "We're gonna take you down the station, OK? We'll bring your boy... what d'you say his name is?"

"Lloyd."

"We'll bring Lloyd down there too. He'll be safe, he'll be looked after. Then when you get released, we can take it from there. All right?"

Like I had a fucking choice.

I nodded. "Cool."

They led me to a waiting car.

* * *

It was gone 10pm by the time I got to Belgravia Police Station. Things went downhill quickly. I did the mouth swab. A fresh set of fingerprints unlocked the sorry history of all my previous run-ins with London's finest and spewed it up on screen. I'd had some new tattoos done and because they flagged up 'gang affiliation', the desk sergeant wanted photos. He added them to their portfolio of ink that I'd been collecting since I was 12 years old. Roses on my thigh, a prayer on my neck, my son's name.

Lloyd!

"When can I see my son?" I asked bluntly.

"You're not going home tonight," said sarge. He was a swollen white dude, neck overflowing a too-tight collar and flushed pink and scaly with razor rash. "We need to arrange to take your son somewhere, is there anyone we can call?"

Top of the list was Lloyd's dad. No answer there. We tried and tried. Tried again. No answer. Everyone who I trusted with my son's life got a call. No one picked up. We called Haina's phone, over and over, but it just rang out. All I needed was someone to swing by the station and grab him.

Pick up the frigging phone, I willed. Because with every failed call, my hold on Lloyd slipped a little further, until I was full stretch, just about touching his little fingertips.

Then, just like that, he was gone.

"Sorry," said the swollen fed. "If there's no one to leave him with, we'll have to arrange some emergency care."

"I don't even know why you've got me here. Now you want to put my baby with some stranger?"

"He'll be well taken care of."

"Well taken care of? I'm his mother. Fuck's wrong with you people?"

"This way please."

They herded me to a room with blue lights set in the wall. Any gunshot residue would have showed up under their cold, pale glow. I had none, obviously, having literally never fired a gun in the entirety of my existence. Then I was shown to my cell for the night.

I did my usual: "Extra blankets, and an extra pillow please. Five cups of water, a couple of books or magazines and can you turn off the light?"

People new to cell life think they have to go to sleep with the light on. Not so – just ask nicely and they'll turn it off for you.

I slept until they woke me the next morning with, "Your solicitor's here. Let's go and do your interview."

I had a consultation with the solicitor first. He was a scrawny, unkempt Asian guy who looked like he should still be buying 5p sweets in the corner shop, never mind representing suspected gang members on weapon charges.

This is not great, I thought. *I am actually fucked.*

"Well, this is a very serious accusation," he began. "I have to advise you that you could be looking at 10 years in prison."

Err. Hello? Once more – sing it with me – I'm the victim here. We're saying I shot my own flat up, are we?

"I'll do a prepared statement," I said. "Tell them it'll be a no comment interview."

"Yes. That would, umh, that would be my advice."

See. This kid was earning his keep. He was worth every penny.

We got in the room and I slumped into the chair, arms crossed. My body language screamed 'hostile witness'. My solicitor read the statement to the two women detectives, something along the lines of, "I have no knowledge of this event, I have no knowledge of anyone involved in this event."

Then they started in with the bullshit questions, small stuff that seems irrelevant and inconsequential. But you never know what really matters to them, and what doesn't. So I gave them nothing. And I do mean nothing.

"Can you confirm your name?"

"No comment."

"Do you live at this address?"

"No comment."

"Can you tell us what you were doing yesterday morning?"

You might think it can't hurt to tell a tiny, little truth: went to Asda. Made some food. Watched telly. Standard day.

But no. I stuck to the routine: "No comment."

They start like this, with the bullshit, to try and soften you up. It's a trick. Get you *used* to the idea of chatting with them. You answer a couple of little questions, maybe next time you'll answer a bigger, more important one, and then a bigger one. And before you know it – you're singing like Elton John. You've snitched, and there's a van heading out the police station to nick your people. Didn't work with me, so they moved on to the big stuff.

"How many people were there? Did you see a weapon? What weapon? Why would they want to do this to you?"

It was baking hot in that interview room. I was melting, and this went on for hours. It got to the point where I was like, *I just wish I could fucking say something, I'm so bored.* But you have to fight that urge, cos it'll get you in trouble.

They got to the end – eventually. Interview concluded at… and they turned off the tape.

Finally, I could say something. "Can you tell me where my son is?"

They gathered their papers, looked at each other, then at me, in silence. As if to say, *"No comment."*

Touché, ladies. Touché.

I went for consultation with the lawyer.

"They've got nothing," he said. "There was no weapon found. No witnesses. The only reason you're here is so they can get information from you. You'll be out today or tomorrow at the latest."

Turned out it was early evening. They got me from the cell, gave me my *no further action papers,* told me I was free to go. But not before I asked one last time. I'm like, "Listen, where's my child?"

He looked up my file and said, "He's gone into emergency foster care."

"Well, can I have the details?"

"I wasn't on duty, and they're not down here – I'll have to get them from another officer. We'll email them to you."

I felt then that I might not see Lloyd for a very long time. He was going in the system. How was I ever going to get him back? All my front and bluster drained out of me. I felt like a lump of stone. What could I say? Or do? Lloyd was gone. I wasn't going to be a stay-at-home mum. That was finished. Police made sure of that.

There was a gaping hole in my heart and in my life. In the years to come, I'd throw a lot of shit at it, but I'd never fill it. Not with money, cars, Louis handbags or thousand-pound nightclub tables. Hundred percent – that was the worst moment of my life.

I lit a cigarette as I stepped out into a damp London night. My flat was still a crime scene, dressed up in ribbons of white and blue police tape. There was no going home until forensics had finished, so I called my rock, Haina.

"Babe. Can you come get me? I'm at Belgravia station."

10

EMPTY

It was a couple of days later before I was allowed back home. Shit, that place felt empty without Lloyd. His buggy stood propped in the corner of the hall. I wondered who was wheeling him around now, changing his bum, reading him bedtime stories. There were little reminders all over the place – a sock poking out from under the bed, a stray dummy on a windowsill. They caught me unawares and unprepared every time, a dig in the tummy snatching my breath away.

Haina had sobbed when she picked me up from Belgravia.

"I had bare calls off you last night – what's going on? Who's got Lloyd?"

"That's why I was calling," I said. "I got nicked and they took Lloyd down the station. I couldn't find anyone to grab him. He's gone in care now."

"Oh my days, no! I'm so sorry, babe," she said, breaking down. "If I'd known…"

But it wasn't her fault. "Don't talk shit, man," I said. "I don't blame you for a minute."

She'd taken me back to hers for the full Haina care package. Hot bath, warm PJs and takeaway food. Not to mention a lot of tears on the sofa.

Now I looked at the bullet holes punched in my living-room wall.

It's gonna be OK, I told myself. *Make some calls, speak to the social. He'll be home soon enough.*

I needed snacks, so I went down the corner shop and found Dajuan and Jordan there, smoking weed and chilling with a few of the boys. The spliffs hung loose at their sides, forgotten a moment, as a chorus went up: "Oh my God, D! You're here! You OK?"

"Yeah, yeah, it's all good," I lied, thinking suddenly of Lloyd's empty cot. "You got out? No one hurt?"

"Not a scratch," Jordan said. "They couldn't aim for shit!"

"Where's the little man, D?" Dajuan asked. "You lot good? For real?"

I shook my head. "Social got him. Some emergency foster bullshit. I dunno. I'm waiting to find out where exactly."

"It's gonna be OK, D. Don't worry, yeah?" said Jordan.

"Yeah, I know."

Then Dajuan took me aside. "Babe, I was so worried."

"Yeah, me too. I thought you two were fucking dead!"

"First shot, we just dropped to the floor. The rest went over our heads and we dived out the window." He paused. Looked at me straight. "The feds – what d'you do then? No comment?"

"Yeah, 'course. I didn't tell them anything."

"Cool. They ask anything about us, mention any names?"

"I got you. I'm serious, they NFA'd me."

"All right. Cool. Look, I'm so sorry this happened," he said, taking my hand. "It's fucking mad."

"You're telling me! Any idea who it was?"

"Nah, we're looking into it. You're safe though. I promise you that."

There'd been times before when boys on mopeds had pulled up on the block, brandishing handguns like urban cowboys and beating shots. Dajuan and the rest had dodged their share of bullets, unleashed a few of their own, too. But shooting up a girl's place in broad daylight? That was just fucking crazy. It was so random.

"Are you sure the police are cool?" Dajuan said.

"Hundred percent."

"All right, call them tomorrow, make sure they're done with your place and let's get back to business, yeah?"

"OK babe, like I said, I got you."

* * *

In the meantime, I wanted my son back. But there was a process, and social services were gonna make it long and hard. First off, they wanted me to prove I was Lloyd's actual mum by bringing in a birth certificate. Then they'd need to report this and assessment that. I was in no doubt that it was going to take months.

I called the officer in charge. They were finally seeing me as a victim in this mess.

"So, you're back in the flat then?" the officer asked, with just a hint of that sing-song in his voice that's meant to say *we care*.

"I'm in," I said. "Place is a mess though!"

"Get on to the council, they should take care of that."

I'd already spoken to them. They'd been tipped off about what went down. Now they were reviewing whether I could really be the good little council tenant they wanted.

"Sure thing. Listen, anything you need from me, you're welcome to swing by the flat." I left it open like that, seeing if he'd offer up the info I wanted.

"We're done at your place. We'll let you know if we make any progress in the investigation."

Bingo.

No way they were coming back, and no way they were going to find the shooters. They had no witnesses, no snitches. They had nothing linking me to any of the stuff Dajuan and the boys were into. All they could do was wait and see if justice was served in some other, unofficial way. Meanwhile file under 'unsolved' and move along.

A few weeks later, I was walking home from the shop, cans of KA fruit punch swinging from a carrier bag in one hand. A girl I knew from way back stopped me. She'd heard about the gunmen, the shooting. Hadn't everyone? Talk of the 'hood, man.

"You know who it was don't you?" she told me, giving me some names.

"Fuck – no way? Serious? They're just kids!"

I knew these boys from around. Or thought I did. They were faces on the corner I'd nod a hello to if I was passing. But they were even younger than me. It was a bold move for some youngers, especially in their own ends.

Funny thing was, when I thought about it, I hadn't seen them about for a few weeks.

And you know what? I never, ever saw them again.

* * *

The police didn't want back in my flat, but that didn't mean they were done meddling in my life. The local police Gangs Unit was going to make sure Lloyd stayed in the system.

"She's in a gang," they told social services. "So she shouldn't have her son back."

Gang.

What does that even mean?

Let's clear something up about 'gangs'. This gang thing is something that's been put on us, by the outside, by the media. It's a construct. It's moral panic, man. No one pins up a flyer to convene a gang creation meeting: "Let us now form a gang. Please sign this contract to confirm your membership of the gang."

There's a loose structure, a boss and workers. You don't 'join', and no one from my part of London asks you to prove yourself by shooting, stabbing or robbing someone. Maybe that kind of stuff was someone else's experience, but it certainly wasn't mine. In my area, we were all about the money. If there was to be violence it was meticulously planned and was a means to an end.

Far as I'm concerned, what outsiders call a 'gang' is just a community, usually based on shared street corners, or tower blocks or estates. For me, it was a group of friends doing a common thing, sharing common interests. OK, some of those interests were criminal. Fair. But flipside, plenty of my friends had normal jobs. Were they 'in the gang', even if they weren't doing any crime? I don't know, but they were still getting hassled by the Gangs Unit. And some of the hassle those fine upholders of the law dished out was truly fucked up: "Hey D, wanna get in the van and suck my dick? Maybe I won't arrest you!"

Yeah. For real. More on that later.

So have it how you want. I've never been in a gang – and I've always been in a gang. To me, it was just chilling with my friends, making money and having a good time.

* * *

I was crying out for something, anything, to take my mind off my empty nest of a flat. Dajuan was chilling with me one night. They were cooking drugs the next day. He was getting the jump on proceedings, cutting squares of clingfilm to wrap the rocks.

"Wanna do some of these with me?" he said, handing me the roll of cling.

"Sure," I shrugged.

Harmless, right? The sort of thing you'd see on *Art Attack*. It was just something to do.

"You going away this week?" I asked him. He'd go shotting – selling drugs – for days, maybe weeks at a time. Had to be done. It was work. The boys didn't shit in our own backyard, their drugs went 'out there' – OT. To country. Some of the younger kids might do a bit of local business, shotting to our friendly neighbourhood crackheads. Or they'd hit Soho, Edgware Road, West End with coke, pills, molly. But the smart money was on crack and heroin served up outside of London. Satellite towns and tired seaside resorts. Less heat. Less hassle. No Gang Unit.

"Yeah, hitting the M," Dajuan replied.

"Where you going then?"

"Here and there."

"Let me come with you."

"You don't wanna trap," he chuckled, then touched my temple. "You'll be bored out your likkle mind!"

"I'm bored here!"

"Nah, forget about it. Let's get this cling done."

With time on my hands, over the next few weeks, I went from cutting cling to wrapping drugs. My flat became like the cooking and packaging plant. The work was somehow monotonous and satisfying at the same time. Whatever I'm doing, I properly put my mind to it. And I took this job serious. Which is right, because if you fuck it up you might kill someone.

I had this method: I tripled up the clingfilm, then wrapped and pulled, and wrapped and pulled it again around a 0.2g rock of crack, or a bump of heroin. Then you burn the ends to seal it. It made sense to wear gloves handling the drugs, but they got in the way and I was devoted to the cause of perfect pebs. Pretty soon the skin on my fingers went manky with chemical burns. But I was the expert wrapper, no one else could do it like me. The neatness, the compactness of my pebs was a point of pride. More than that, it kept the boys safe. They knew if they got a pull from the feds and had to swallow their drugs, they weren't gonna bust open inside them. They could wait it out and throw them up when they were safe.

I won't lie, these were relatively happy, carefree times. You've probably got an image in your head of crack dealers – all desperate and dishevelled – working out of some skanky flat with black mould up the walls. In country, maybe. But not in London. I had scented candles on the go, the fluffy rug on the floor. We'd have *Britain's Got Talent* on the telly and fifteen grand's-worth of perfect pebs racked up on my coffee table.

I was wrapping up with Jordan one time when the lunchtime news came on. Prince Charles visiting his subjects. A flutter of plastic Union Jacks on plastic sticks.

"Crassis people," said Jordan, taking a swig of his KA and Magnum. "They not real! How can that even be real?"

"Yeah, it's true. They must be robots!" I said, joining in.

"Lizards, I'm telling you. They're from another planet!"

We loved a conspiracy theory. We could go on for hours like this. The Royal Family. 9-11 (government done it). Even weirdness like the Bermuda triangle.

But it was only ever a temporary distraction. Cos every time I opened my wardrobe – there was Lloyd's Adidas tracksuit. Or the kitchen cupboard – his bottles. The shower – baby shampoo. His photos were all over my walls and the flat felt haunted with bittersweet memories. I needed an escape. I needed to go OT. But every time I asked Dajuan, his answer was the same. "It's not fun, man. You'll hate it!"

"I've got to get out of here. Just take me with you!"

"I'm telling you, it's no fun."

I didn't let up. I wore that poor boy down!

And in the end, he caved in. "All right, all right! We'll sort something out. You'll see what it's all about, and once you know, you won't wanna go ever again!"

I was stepping up. I was going cunch. And if Dajuan thought my first taste of OT was going to put me off for life, he had me figured out all wrong.

11

REHAB TOWN

Drugs are a currency in their own right. Find someone with a deep enough hunger for crack and they'll give you anything you want. They might not have the cash, but they'll trade you a place to stay, or sex, or a stolen phone. Honestly, some of them would sell you their own mothers for a couple rocks.

Me? I marked my first trip to country by getting yet another tattoo, paid for with crack.

Haina had been having man trouble. She was taking a well-deserved break from ducking slaps and fat lips from her heavy-handed boyfriend by chilling in the ends with me. Them times, there were block parties happening regularly. These parties were never anything official, they weren't advertised, and you certainly didn't wait for an invite. That spontaneity was part of the fun. You could go down the shop for a packet of cigarettes and stumble on a street party blowing up into all-night madness.

They usually started as something innocent like a family function with just a handful of guests. Next thing, a sound system gets dragged in the front garden, someone presses *play* and before you know it there's 200 people loitering in the street outside. Everyone's drunk. Everyone's eating food, and no one's going home until the sun comes up. Nine times out of ten, there'd be some angry neighbour screaming at everyone to turn the music off. Usually, the police came by and tried to shut things down, but there was only so much they could do. Come dawn, the street would still be full of people.

This was an escape for Haina. It was like a bubble in the ends, like the world outside didn't exist. I threw myself into it right alongside her. All the stuff with Lloyd, I was trying to numb it out.

Still, I never let up on Dajuan's promise to let me go country. When I'd been begging him for ages, he eventually said, "OK, why don't you shout Andre?"

"You think?" I said.

Andre was a bit older than me, maybe 25. Short. Mixed-race boy. He was super cool, super chilled. He was living down on the south coast at the time – that was his country spot – but he was back in London for the weekend chilling.

"It's up to you, shout him and see what he says," said Dajuan.

I rang Andre and he was keen for the company.

"Come, come, come!" he said. "Go get your stuff, I'll get mine and we'll go!"

The purpose of the trip – to go sell crack and heroin – was irrelevant to me. Far as I was concerned, it was just a nice few days away, a change from London. I threw a couple clothes, pyjamas, make-up and straighteners in a little bag – just enough for a long weekend. Andre had a new sporty little car and, after I'd packed, I found it waiting outside the flat.

That drive south was hella long. We set off around lunchtime, so Andre could catch the evening rush. We killed time listening to music while I quizzed him about Dajuan. Because although me and him were seeing each other, at that point it was still a casual thing. I'd been putting some thought into how I could make that boy mine.

"I really like him," I said to Andre. "Do you think he likes me?"

"Yeah, he likes you," he said, touching the brakes, keeping the car at an inconspicuous 75mph. He swung into the middle lane of the M3 motorway, settled into his seat and started telling me how to get Dajuan.

"See, he likes a good girl, D. You know what I mean?"

"I get you."

"But the thing he likes best, more than anything, is money. Dajuan is money, money, money. So what you need to do is be about the money too, and then he'll like you."

It made sense. I never really saw Dajuan bothering with loads of girls. He didn't have time to be a player, he was too busy hustling. If you weren't doing something for him in some way, I don't think he would have bothered with you. Dajuan was on selling drugs – being the best at selling drugs – and that was it. When I thought about it, it was kinda hard to see a future with the boy. Unless, maybe, I joined in with the selling of the drugs.

We got to this one-bed flat Andre was renting. He loaded the washing machine with his dirty laundry from London and said, "Just chill for a bit, I ain't turned the phone on yet. We got time."

We hung around the flat for a while and, later, went Asda to pick up a couple bits to eat. It was while we were mooching through the aisles getting our little snacks, that Andre turned the phone on. Within the space of two minutes, it was ringing. I'd seen this before with a crack line, I'd been around boys where the phone don't stop ringing. But I'd never seen the next part of it.

Once that phone starts ringing, you're just out. It's all the same faces, faces, faces. The same people coming every day, sometimes coming multiple times a day. The faces who had Andre's number would have been calling it constantly, waiting for him to turn it on and come serve them up some drugs.

I was there for the ride, for the fun-relieving boredom, not the money. None of the drugs were mine. Nonetheless, when that phone started ringing, we went to work. Andre did the phone, I dished out the treats.

Back then, I didn't even see the addicts we were selling drugs to as actual people. With a cocaine phone, you might have a bit more respect for the customer. *All right mate? How's it going?* A bit of banter. A little chit chat while the deal is done. It's a rich man's drug. They're spending decent money.

But these nitties – usually they're not. They're spending maybe £10 a time and they might be paying with a couple of damp, crumpled £5 notes smudged with bloodstains. So, for these people, there was no customer service. The stigma had been drummed into me from an early age, and they got treated like they were subhuman.

Nitty.

Dirty crackhead.

Watch out for them nitties, they'll short you money.

It's horrible to think like that, because they've got an addiction. Later I began to understand – after listening to their stories – there's often trauma behind it, but to dealers, they're an irritation because they take long, or the thing might cost £25 and they come in with £17.23, or they want to pay with a Tesco bag full of coins robbed out of some charity collection box.

That's just annoying. I don't want to sit there counting pennies. Give me the notes! Clean ones!

So our patience was thin with them. They'd get in the car with us and they might have been desperate and broken, but all you could think was, *just get your drugs and come out the fucking car. Nitty.*

I saw that on this trip with Andre, from the get-go.

His patience was *thin*.

We drove down one street to serve up to a customer, turned the corner and the guy was stood there in the middle of the road waiting for us.

Andre kissed his teeth. "State of him." He rolled up on him.

"What you doing in the middle of the road, man? Move out the fucking way! You might as well stick a sign on your head! You're bait!"

He turned to me.

"You don't ever let them have one over on you, because I'm telling you, D, they will stab you for the drugs. They do not care. You need eyes in the back of your head!"

From that day I knew, OK, cool, you can't be too lenient with these nitties. You got to be a bit ruthless.

It was the first time I'd been to this town. It was a very different vibe to home.

"Woah, it's mad nice round here, innit?" I said, gazing up at all the guesthouses, with tall windows and smart paint jobs as we drove around.

"There's parts of this place that are only for millionaires," said Andre. "But you know the other thing about it?"

"What's that?"

"It's rehab town. Hella rehabs here. That's why it's good business for drug dealers. People come down here to clean up. They straighten out for a couple weeks, and we catch them outside the rehab when they're done."

"And then they're hooked again."

"Back on it. There's rehab towns all over the country and they're the good country spots to go if you wanna make quick P."

Other London dealers had already latched on to the big market of rehab cases on the south coast, and we'd see them on the road around town. These other boys were Somalis and whereas most dealers banged out their shots in deals of £10 a go, they sold smaller pebs at £5 each. They cleaned up, because everyone would go to them for these cheaper deals. Andre's phone was still ringing a lot though. There wasn't any trouble, because I guess there were enough addicts to go round for everyone.

You're over there making your money, I'm over here making mine. Cool. Let's not bother each other. Let's just make money.

That was the vibe at that time. Mutual respect.

Those few days on the coast weren't all grinding, we had plenty of time for shining, too. We went to the town centre and on to the beach, messing around taking mad photos of each other. Andre took me out to eat and we lived it up a bit with cocktails on the little pier, it was fun. We went back to work in the evening for a while, then hit a club for a couple of hours, then back to work for the last rush before everyone crashed. We got in at about 5am, put a film on, went top-to-tail in the bed and fell asleep exhausted.

Then there was the tattoo.

We were out on the road and this nitty called the line.

"Oh mate, I ain't got no money. Can you tick us? You know I'm good for it."

"No tick, bro. Not for you."

"Come on man. What about your girl there, she want a tattoo?"

This guy had seen me on the road with Andre, who now turned to me and said, "You want a tattoo? He's saying he'll do you a tattoo if I give him two-on-two."

That's two wraps of crack, two heroin. Worth £30.

I shrugged. "OK. Why not?"

"OK," Andre said. "Let's go."

We drove to his address, a tall Victorian house, three floors up and a basement, where the guy lived in the top flat.

Walking in his place, it took a minute for my eyes to adjust to the light because it was very dingy. The tattoo guy was huge, scary looking, with designs etched into his shaven head. His mate was crashed out on a grubby, threadbare sofa in a drug haze. But the rest of the place was done out like a tattoo parlour, with the tattoo chair wrapped in clingfilm, a halogen lamp throwing a wide pool of cold, white light and a little table with rows of multicoloured inks lined up.

"What you got for me?" the guy said to Andre.

"Tattoo first."

"All right, all right," the guy said. "Get in the chair, love."

I climbed up on the chair and looked over his kit.

"You gotta give me a new needle," I said. "Let me see the new needle in the packet!"

He showed me the needle, then peeled open the packet.

"Put gloves on, man!" I tutted.

Laughing, he snapped on a pair of latex gloves and said to Andre, "Cor, this one's annoying ain't she?!"

I didn't want to miss a trick or have anything bookey go on. I knew the drill when it came to tattoos because I'd been getting them since I was 13, ever since I sneaked out of school sports day to get my first one.

Back in them days, if I wanted something I wanted it right there and then. The tattoo idea popped into my head as I woke up one morning. Pure spontancity. I don't know what came over me but I thought – *fuck it, I want a tattoo* – and nothing was gonna stop me getting one.

I shouted one girl I knew. "Hey, let me get your sister's ID." I knew she had an older sis who was like 27.

"What for?"

"Oh, I just want to get a tattoo."

No problem. She met me before school and handed it over.

In sports day, I dutifully ran in all my races – 100m, 200m and hurdles. You're meant to wait for all the other years to do all theirs, but I just cut.

"Where you going?" Haina asked as I gathered up my stuff.

"Don't worry, I'll be back!"

I didn't even go back. I found a tattoo parlour in Shepherd's Bush. The woman didn't bat an eyelid at my ID – the one for a 27-year-old woman who looked nothing like me, a schoolgirl of 13. I knew I wanted some flowers inked at the top of my leg. She showed me a design and I said, "Yeah, that one," without even paying much attention.

"This is a big one for your first tattoo," the lady said.

"Yeah, I want it!" I said. "I've really thought about it…"

These times, I never thought about things like that at all. I always decided on the spot.

I don't remember it hurting. As she started with the needle, I thought *oh wow, this is nothing*. That's been the case for nearly all my tattoos – and I've got over 30 now – except the ones on my feet and my belly. Those ones I felt. Ouch.

Of course, I hid my tat from Mum and Dave, but school was a different matter. I showed it off to all the girls, proud of it. They were shocked. I was the first one in the school to get inked.

Danielle, the wild one. Again.

A few months later, I had three stars tattooed on my hip, then got tats on my wrists. After that, I didn't really stop until I was 21. It became an addiction, a beast that needed feeding. I craved the sharp burn of the needle burrowing into my flesh, the itch on my skin as the tat scabbed over and then flaked off. Whenever something bad happened to me, I'd go get a tattoo. Maybe not in the immediate aftermath, but after a little time had passed and I'd got my shit together. Like after the incident with Jake and the rest of them boys – a few weeks later, I went and got a tattoo. To me, getting new ink symbolised turning the page on something awful. Years later, I was telling someone about this and they turned round and said, "You know what that is? It's like a form of self-harm."

I'd never thought of it this way before, but it made a lot of sense.

The one in country, though – that one was just for fun.

As usual, it was a spur-of-the-moment decision.

I pulled a lipstick out of my bag, and said, "Come here, Andre."

"What you doing with that?"

"Be quiet and put this on "

I smeared Andre's lips with lipstick, then snatched up a piece of paper. "Kiss it!" I said.

Using Andre's imprint, the guy worked out the design – a pair of red lips. His needle buzzed into life and he pressed its burning tip to my arm.

Afterwards, he was clearing up, leant over his set of inks, and I got a fine view of the tattoo that had long ago been needled into his head.

"That must have been hella painful," I said.

He looked up and flashed a grudging smile. "Nah, I was high, wasn't I?! Speaking of which…"

Andre handed him his little drugs, and we were out of there.

We drove back to London the next day. Landing back in the ends, Andre peeled two bills – couple hundred pound – off his roll.

"Here," he said, handing me the notes.

"You don't have to…"

"It's cool. You wanna come back some time?"

"Well, yeah. I better check with Dajuan though…"

Andre pulled a face. "He don't care, man. Make your money!"

Not for the first time, I realised, dealing drugs was work, this could be my job. If Dajuan wanted a good girl – a money, money, money girl – that's what he was gonna get.

12

VEGAS

That south coast trip was OT 101, just for fun. I kept Andre company on a few more seaside missions, but I had my sights set on bigger things. I'd heard Dajuan's lot talking about one middle-England city that had become their country HQ. I'm not going to name it, because for all I know it's still their drug-dealing home-from-home – even now.

"Who's got Vegas?" I'd hear Dajuan say. That was the code-name for his drug line. It can take months or even years to build up a line with a solid customer base, and he'd had his established in this one city since long. A select few got to work it, selling Dajuan's drugs, keeping a share of the profits for themselves. I pestered him to rota me in. As usual, he pushed right back. Nah, Dajuan was not keen.

"It's serious business," he said, trying again to talk me out of it. "Trapping's hard work, it's not a joke you know."

"I've seen the work. I've been there!"

"What? Seaside with Andre?"

"I can do it!"

"You don't need to, fam. Just stay in the ends. Get yourself a likkle job."

A job? Oh really? Like what?

Folding T-shirts in Primark or dying a slow death on a reception desk somewhere? For minimum wage? That just wasn't for me. I wanted something more open where the hours weren't set and I could work when it suited me. I'd seen the grind in Andre's spot. I was good at talking to the customers, and they responded to me. There were plenty girls running dogsbody errands, driving boys OT and dropping them off for a shift change or a re-up, but you didn't really see them shotting. It wasn't a very ladylike thing to do. Girls were usually happy falling back on the boys' cash – a little bill here, a few notes there, maybe treated to a shopping trip if they were lucky. Basically, treated like prostitutes. No thanks. If the boys could do it, so could I.

And I wanted the money.

My money.

"No," I said. "I want to come with you. I can do this."

"OK," Dajuan said finally. "You think you can handle it, you want to come – come. But you gotta bring food."

Food is drugs. Anyone going OT had to bring some up – that was the rule. You could chance it by sticking them in your pocket, but if you got a pull and the police were paying attention, you were getting nicked. That made you a liability to the people around you. So you needed a good hiding place, somewhere the police couldn't look when they blue-lighted you on the hard shoulder. Somewhere the sun didn't shine. For the boys, that meant sticking them up your bum – what we called 'banking'. If you're a girl, you basically made a drug tampon – an eye-wateringly big one – and… you get the picture.

Hold tight. There's some grim detail coming up.

A girl might bank a G-pack, or a G-wrap – £1000-worth of pebs in one wrap. It's about the length of an iPhone and half the width, but round like a tube. Yeah. It's as toe-curlingly uncomfortable as it sounds.

The boys would do a few smaller wraps, each worth £250 and holding 25 pebs. Reason being they go deeper inside the body and they're harder to get in and out. They always tried to make light of it, to lessen the grimness of the whole process. Whatever way you look at it, stuffing drugs inside you isn't nice, so they'd banter it off by cracking sly little gay jokes. "Nah, you man are gay about your plugging two G-packs!"

Dajuan had his own way of dealing with things, and as we got ready to hit the road I overheard him in the shower as he worked on banking his packs. "Gotta get through this! I gotta get through this!" he sang, to the David Bedingfield tune.

That first time, I did a 250. I wrapped it – super, super tight – in a triple layer of clingfilm, pulling and stretching until it was rock solid. To make it easier to get in and out I left a tail of cling hanging down like the string of a tampon, then smeared the pack with Vaseline. The lube helped, but nothing on this earth was going to make a fat stick of drugs feel comfortable stuffed somewhere it had no business being. I gritted my teeth as the sharp, angular rocks of crack scraped my insides. I'd packed it all wrong. It felt like a bag of spanners! Exasperated and feeling a little queasy, I pulled it out, started again.

Finally, I emerged from the bathroom. "I'm done. Let's go."

"Got your food?" Dajuan asked.

"I'm *ready*," I said pointedly.

Dajuan shouldered his weekend bag and snatched up a pillow and duvet. We headed out, picking up a boy called Mally en route. He was younger than Dajuan, more like my age, with dark skin and nice clothes. Real party boy. When he wasn't shotting, Mally was either in the club or in bed with one of his girls. He always had a huge grin splitting his face as he blasted his bashment music out of the car stereo, leaning on the windowsill and trying to chat up women passing in the street.

We had a rental. Not a banger that might give the police reason to pull us for a bald tyre or a dead headlight. And nothing too flashy that would draw attention. Something low-key basic like a black Ford Focus. Usually we'd get an automatic because there's loads of painful driving to do when you go country. Stop, start, pull over here.

Dajuan chucked a tub of Vaseline, tissues and hand sanitiser in the glovebox, and a spare roll of cling in the boot. Nowadays, this kind of stuff would ring alarm bells for any decent police officer, but back then, in 2011, the country feds hadn't cottoned on to what would come to be known as County Lines. And unless they turned up some drugs on us or in the car – or saw the shot going out and money changing hands – there wasn't much they could do about it.

"Can you explain why you have a roll of clingfilm in your boot?"

"Yes officer. I need it to keep my sandwiches fresh, officer."

"Why do you have Vaseline in your glove box?"

"It's because I sometimes get dry lips, officer."

Anything else? No? I'll be on my way.

The drive was about an hour and a half. I was excited, maybe a little nervous, but mostly just happy to be on the road with friends. Dajuan wrapped up a spliff and filled the car with sweet, pungent smoke. Mally killed time sweet-talking his girlfriends back in London, dripping liquid honey down the phone line.

Then Dajuan told him, "Hey, mans staying at Billy's. Give him a call."

Billy was one of the crackheads. Mally hollered him, "Billy. We're coming over." The boys were never short of somewhere to stay. Paying their rent in drugs, addicts were tripping over themselves to put them up.

15 minutes out of the city, Dajuan pulled a battle-scarred Nokia 8210 out of his pocket. Old school phone technology. No wifi, no GPS and no internet – which makes them untraceable. Essential kit for shotters. The battery powers through those long hours on the road, and they're just about small enough – if you're really brave and push real hard – to wrap in clingfilm and stick up your bum. No, I never had to. But plenty boys did. Plenty boys singing that David Beding-field tune while they did their thing.

Vegas started ringing within minutes and we lined up a few shoots for when we landed. Cruising through the city outskirts, green fields gave way to suburban estates, gave way to the quaintness and cobbles of the city centre. Clueless tourists on bicycles, wobbling all over the road, taking long. Cheery gift shops. Historic pubs spilling out ruddy-faced men with beer bellies. We drove on past all the nice stuff to the shitty end of town. Because however nice the city, there's always a shitty bit where for some reason the streetlamps don't glow quite as bright and rubbish collects in dusty hedgerows. It's where you find the prostitutes, the addicts, the forgotten.

"Pay attention now," Dajuan said, pointing the road names out as I drove. "Get to know your way around. You'll pick it up quick. You got the four main streets here, and all the shoots are off these streets."

I was no longer a passenger seat observer, gazing up at the pretty guesthouses and smoking fags out the window between cocktails on the pier. Serving up our first shoots confirmed: selling drugs is no joyride, and anyone who thinks differently needs some education. Dajuan was right. It *was* serious business. Mentally and physically exhausting. The laughs, the music and the banter masked the reality that every waking minute, I felt wired, nerves stretched to near breaking point. I was holding my own drugs now and risking police, undercovers and dodgy shoots looking to rob us. Later, even when I was done for the night, I couldn't properly relax – no one sleeps soundly with a lump of drugs stashed inside them.

"Look," said Dajuan as we pulled into one street. "See any cameras?"

I rubber-necked out the window.

"Looks all clear," I said.

"Yeah. This one's safe. But you gotta run it through when you're pulling up – always. Any cameras? Anyone looking? Can the shoot find you? Is the guy you see on the corner even the shoot?"

There was so much to think about. And while I was trying to stay on top of all this new information – heart pounding – Dajuan or Mally would be fiddling with the pack, trying to prise a few pebs out for the next shoot, and then get it wrapped up again without dropping everything.

Focused on selling drugs, I clean forgot to eat. Until, rolling round town, we passed the familiar sight of the golden arches and a little pang woke my tummy.

"I could go some nuggets," I said.

"You don't wanna do that, D," Mally said, shaking his head.

"Huh? What are you talking about?"

"Chicken in country ain't the same as London, fam."

"You're chatting shit!" Dajuan chipped in.

"I'm telling you – they use some weird country chicken out here, man. Country chicken is fucked up."

No doubt he was just messing with me, but I never did eat McDonalds in country.

We put hours into the grind, as day turned to dusk and darkness lengthened the shadows of the city's crack alleys. The night-owl addicts came down from crawling their walls, and their pale faces swam by our car window, one after the other. Neon-yellow teeth glowed under the streetlamps. Damp sores and runny wounds glistened black. By the end of the day, I was mentally and physically destroyed. My back and legs sang from being cramped up in the car for hours. All I wanted was the peace, quiet and solitude of my own bed. Fluffy duvet. Soft pillow. Maybe a scented candle. And… relax.

Instead, we went to the trap house. Billy's place.

Billy was a black crackhead, shacked up with this skinny white girl crackhead. I say crackhead, they smoked both white and brown, which is pretty standard. They lived on a terraced street, in a sparsely furnished, threadbare house with an airy sitting room. Billy gave us a bedroom between us on the top floor, with one, big double bed. To be fair, he'd tried. He'd done it out with bedding, but his sheets had that stiff and scratchy feel. We'd brought our own in any case, and I laid out a fresh, clean sheet on top of the bed, so we didn't have to sleep in Billy's bedclothes. That's only a little thing, but I think it's an example of how organised we were. I don't know about anyone else's operation, but ours was super calculated. We didn't really do chaotic. In country, or back in London, everything ran how it was meant to run. Like clockwork.

These rest hours we spent chilling in the trap in front of Billy's old box TV, weary from the road and sat bunched together on one of his grubby, cream leather sofas. Billy and the skinny girl got their little drugs for the day, and Dajuan wiped all the calls and texts from the day's sales off the Nokia. There'd be me and these two grown men, eyes drooping as we watched Disney movies, while the two nitties sucked on a filthy glass crack pipe or chased heroin smoke along a fold of tinfoil on the other couch.

The next morning, Billy was up bright and early to get to his job in the local factory. He was a functioning crackhead. An angry one – for no valid reason other than he had to go to work, while we were still lounging around his place in recovery mode, gearing up for another day being run ragged by Vegas. He railed at us over his morning cup of tea, "Get out my house! Get the fuck out!"

"Calm down bro," said Mally, wiping sleep from his eyes and handing Billy one rock. "Here's your fucking breakfast, now put the kettle on."

Billy snorted, his beef suddenly forgotten as he slunk away to do his thing.

"He's right though," I said, looking around the place. Billy's was a dump, which in my mind was good incentive to get out there and grind. Unless I was sleeping, or too tired to actually move, I wanted to spend as little time in Billy's as possible. "Let's get out of here, man."

We hit the road.

Regulating the shoots was half the battle. To make things easier, we bunched them up in groups. With 10 customers in one area wanting drugs, we told them to all go to the same road at the same time.

"Form a queue," Mally told them on the phone. "Don't make it a bait queue, but form a queue and then you come one at a time. Please – one at a time. Don't disappoint me."

They never listened.

Soon as they saw the car, they flocked on it. They mobbed the vehicle like Trafalgar Square pigeons pecking at a puddle of scattered birdseed. Desperate. "Me first, me first!"

The window was down just a crack and they shoved their mucky hands through the gap. My blood pressure cranked up a few points as they barked their orders at us.

"Three on five."

"Ten on ten."

"Two white, two-B."

It was like a scene from *The Walking Dead* – decrepit, shuffling zombies sticking their hands out.

"Move off the car," I said, trying to wave them away. "Move off the fucking car!"

They ignored me. Probably didn't even hear. All they heard were the voices inside their heads telling them they needed to get high.

If the police pull up, we're done for, I realised, as Dajuan tried to smooth out a fistful of crumpled notes. There was money everywhere. Mally had his pack out. The car was mobbed. It was chaos.

Dajuan spotted the danger, too. "Drive, D," he said, winding up his window. The zombies leant back as I started the engine and then slapped the roof and windows as we pulled away. Another lesson learned – better off losing sales than risk getting nicked.

The other thing that sent stress levels through the roof was if someone dropped a peb in the car and you couldn't find it. It was never us. I'd watched the boys and seen how they cupped their drugs in a closed fist, opening their fingers almost like a little sweet dispenser, counting the pebs as they dished them out.

The shoots though, they were a different story.

They'd get in the car, hands shaking all over the place and fumbling their money. Then it was, "Oh mate, I've dropped one."

Nightmare. A dropped peb is evidence if you get pulled over. It's grounds for arrest, in which case we're all going down the station and the boys are sitting in a cell with no toilet until they produce – shit out their packs. A dropped peb meant a trip to the car wash to hoover the car out, just in case.

Then there's the smell in the car, which – not gonna lie – was often disgusting. Even on the road, I had regular showers, used perfume and shampoo. If the trap didn't have somewhere to wash, I'd hit up a gym just so I could get clean. The boys though, some of the hygiene left a lot to be desired. Factor in nitties and rough sleepers in and out of the car, the packs going in and out the bum, covered in shit sometimes. Yeah, the aroma in that car was ripe.

All these little things I picked up on the road. And more. Like, never count your money at a traffic light. When you get to a thousand pound in cash, go put it down. Doing it and being there, that's the only way I was gonna learn.

It all sounds like a lot of hassle. But I think in those early days, I was still dealing with mental trauma and, despite everything, it was still a weird kind of fun. It was excitement, and risk and fun. Plus, I was drawn enough to Dajuan that I wanted to fulfil this persona of a little trapper. That's genuinely what I wanted to be. Not any old little trapper, but one who rolled with her hair in plaits tied with little bows, open-toed sandals and a cute dress. It wasn't an act, that's just who I was. All the stereotypes around drug dealing, I didn't fit any of them. I was probably the most girly, pink trapper ever.

And, therefore, an asset – flying low under the radar.

We'd been away about three days and, with all the drugs sold, it was time for home.

"You are literally perfect for this job," said Dajuan.

We hit the motorway and headed back to the ends.

13

COUNTRY GIRL

I didn't make money on that first trip with Dajuan – didn't expect to. I was still learning the ropes. I had a few more rounds of not doing a whole lot other than memorising streets and faces, before he said, "OK, the customers know your face now. You can do your ting."

That meant serving up the pebs from my own pack. Which meant I started to get paid. For the time being – until I began putting my own money into buying drugs – I was earning about £500 for anything up to a four-day trip. That doesn't sound like a whole lot of cash, given the risk, but at 18 years old it felt plenty. And remember, I wasn't paying for food, rent, petrol, electric. All those bills that usually chew through your disposable income and leave you with a couple pound were being covered by Dajuan. I had literally no outgoings, so there was always excess money. The only things I spent cash on were my hair, nails, trips to Westfield shopping centre and the odd bit of clubbing. I had money to save and from early on, Dajuan was telling me, "Look, you may as well buy into the box."

He might have been a drug dealer, but Dajuan had a money-motivated brain and plenty nuggets of sound financial advice. Although he always had stacks of money running through his hands, he was in many ways a frugal man. He had the crisp tracksuits and trainers, but apart from the odd splurge here and there he never really went crazy on designer gear. The big spends were on jewellery and – like the rest of the boys who wore their wealth on show – the line always was that gold is an investment. Diamonds are futureproof. They hold their value.

Instead of blowing all my earnings on acrylics and hair extensions, Dajuan was keen for me to squirrel some of the cash away.

"You wanna be putting half down," he told me.

I remember one time lusting after a Louis Vuitton bag.

"That bag is calling my name," I told Dajuan. "I'm having it."

"Stop a minute," he said. "Can you afford to buy three of them?"

"Well, no. But I don't want three of them! What am I gonna do with three L-V bags?"

He shook his head. "If you can't buy it three times, you can't afford it. Understand?"

That was his rule, the rule of three. Disposable income according to Dajuan. I still use that rule all the time, even today. Hundred percent. Many times it's stopped me buying stuff I just don't need.

I started saving, not thinking any further at first than buying a 'Z' or two of food. I can't recall exactly how much that cost, but I think it was around a grand. A Z is one ounce (or 28 grammes) and if you bought two Zs, the connect would chuck in a 'Q' – a quarter of an ounce – for free. 'Two-and-a-Q' was the deal.

I was a long way off having the cash for a box – a kilo of cocaine cost about £32k and heroin £28k. So there was work to do.

Not everyone was as keen to have me on board as Dajuan. Some of his circle were convinced that, sooner or later, I was gonna somehow land him in jail. That was the vibe from the get-go. They accepted I was involved, they knew I was never gonna snitch. But some of those boys couldn't move past the idea that girls either couldn't be trusted, or simply weren't up to the job.

"You hear what people are saying?" Dajuan told me. "Apparently you're gonna get me banged up."

"This is a mutual thing," I said. "If you don't want me here, then you don't want me here. Do what you gotta do."

But Dajuan kept me around, and he had my back too.

"She's cool," he told the boys. "I trust her."

We went OT. Back up the same stretch of motorway.

"We got five grand," Dajuan said to me and Mally. "Let's try and lick it out by the end of the day."

The shifts were long compared to my little introduction down on the coast. The phone rang all night and day, with no breaks at all. We never turned it off until we'd sold out, but at some point we had to snatch a few hours' sleep. We'd put the phone on silent and wake up to 15 or 20 missed calls. There was no point chasing sales by ringing them back. They weren't going anywhere. Couple hours, they would call back, hungrier than ever.

We fell into a routine. We'd go OT for however long it took to sell all the food, which varied from a couple days, to four or five. If someone in the ends was free to shuttle more drugs, we stayed OT. If not, we came back, grabbed a change of clothes and maybe spent a day or two chilling as we waited for the re-up. Sometimes I went country with a couple of the other boys, but Dajuan was there more often than not. He always had a big stake in the box, but I think also he low-key enjoyed the hustle.

In the car, the rule was that one person had a wrap out in a pocket, ready to bank if we caught a blue light. If you were behind the wheel and got a pull, you didn't stop until everyone in the car said "ready". In other words, all the drugs were concealed. Once everyone was cool, you could have your little chit chat with the officer. Otherwise, you did not stop for the police. Ever.

We were heading out on one of the early trips up to our usual tourist-town spot. We wrapped the drugs in London, and I offered to drive.

It was late by the time we arrived OT. Maybe 11pm. The city's darker corners were just getting lively, the night owls stirring. Hungry. The phone had been ringing so we had a couple shoots lined up waiting for drugs. There was no point switching seats, so I stayed driving. We hadn't even been to the trap to drop our stuff, and the boot was still stuffed with pillows and duvets.

We hit the first shot, somewhere deep in the city centre. All good. Dajuan had like 10 pebs cupped in his palm ready for the next couple of customers, plus the wrap in his pocket. I stopped the car at a junction. Mally's music was pounding out the stereo and – to be honest – giving me a headache. We had a long night working ahead of us.

"I'm just gonna turn this down, Mal," I said, nudging the volume. With that momentary distraction, I lost concentration – and pulled out of the junction, straight into the path of an oncoming police car.

Fuck!

I jumped on the brakes, emergency stopping just in time. But we'd caught the attention of these officers. I locked eyes with the WPC as she rolled by, and I forced a thin smile.

Yeah sorry. Please don't stop us.

"Shit!" I hissed, driving on, keeping one eye on the fed in the rear mirror.

"They're gonna spin," Mally said.

My heart was pounding. Dajuan was chill. "Nah bro. We're cool. Just drive, D. You ain't done nothing wrong."

I drove on. Steady.

Then, sure enough, the cop car span in the road behind us.

In seconds, Dajuan banked his pack. By the time the feds flooded the car with blue lights, he'd slapped his hand over his mouth and swallowed his pebs, too.

"Ready, D. Pull over."

"Mally?"

"I'm good," he said.

I parked up. A WPC sidled up to the window and did the usual checks. Insurance. Driver's licence.

"Can I have a look in the boot?" she said.

I popped it. She clocked the bedding and said, "The car's registered in London. What's all this for?"

"This is my girlfriend," Dajuan said, nodding to me "We're up for a few days visiting family."

She paused for a second, but Dajuan's story seemed to satisfy her and then she waved us on with a little caution: "Just try and pay more attention when you're driving, love? OK?"

We would use this 'visiting family' bullshit countless times over the next few years as the heat intensified and County Lines became a thing.

"Let's get to the shoot," said Dajuan. "Man's gotta get these pebs."

He was super calm, like he'd done this a million times before.

Often, if we had a regular shoot who we knew well, we'd go in the house. The problem with crap shoots – who get served up in the street – was it took long to get them in the car. Often they were grubby and came with a funky odour. Or they wanted shots out the window – and obviously that's so bait. It invited all sorts of unwanted attention.

We got to the shoot's house – she was cool, they'd known her ages, so Dajuan rocking up to vomit his pebs out was fine with her. We got in there, Dajuan done his thing, stuck his fingers down his throat and heaved up his pebs.

"Need any water, babe?" I said.

"Yeah. Let's go the shop."

The shoot got her drugs and we were out of there.

She paid cash. Always preferred, but we did take other forms of payment. The beggars always seemed to have the most disposable income to blow on crack and heroin, but sometimes nitties didn't have the cash to pay – in which case they'd go and rob for us. Sometimes they'd give us a little menu of stolen goods after tearing through a Boots or a Superdrug. It might be a load of shit like low-rent, £10 perfumes that no one wanted because they weren't even a brand, but then they might come with, say, 10 Gucci perfumes. We got perfumes practically every other day. There were hair straighteners, make-up for me, sometimes they robbed tracksuits from JD Sports. Some of them even stole on demand. For the ones who never came with money, payment might be something you told them to go steal for you.

One time we told this addict, "Go get us some baby clothes." One of our friends was due in a couple weeks, and we were planning to spoil her with a load of stuff for the new arrival. The shoot came back a couple hours later with two bulging bags of baby clothes from Mothercare, plus nappies, bath stuff, toys – the whole works for a newborn.

Shoots with a good credit history – a solid record of paying their drugs debts, on time and with minimum fuss – got ticked. We always knew what day these shoots got their benefit money on a fortnightly cycle, and we'd be there shortly after midnight to collect as soon as it dropped in their account. All these little debts, we kept in our heads. People who think you don't need any intellect to deal drugs are wrong. It's so fast-paced. You're thinking on your feet. Remembering names, faces, who owes what from last time. My brain would genuinely ache.

One night, we were so tired we pulled into a side road to catch some shut-eye. Just a few minutes' power nap was the plan.

It wasn't even late, but we'd been shotting all day and we were exhausted.

"Let's have a little sleep till the phone rings," said Dajuan.

Mally curled on the back seat, pulled his hood down over his eyes and lay his head against the window. I fell asleep with the streetlamp yellow seeping through my eyelids. I don't know how long we were out, but I was suddenly wrenched from sleep by Mally screaming his head off. The noise set me and Dajuan off, too, and when we looked around, a nitty was sat next to Mally in the back of the car! A Rasta man with huge, long dreads. We'd forgotten to lock the doors, and this guy had climbed in the back of the car while we were napping.

"What the fuck!" I screamed.

The guy just sat there, unfazed, totally calm.

"Get the fuck out the car!" I yelled.

But he was super chill. I mean, he'd sat there waiting patiently for us to wake up for maybe 20 minutes. "Relax. I ain't gonna do nothing," he said in a Jamaican accent, as he climbed out the car.

He got his drugs, and we got out of there.

It was another reminder that we had to be on point.

All. The. Fucking. Time.

"That could have been a fed!" said Dajuan. "We've got to sort out this tiredness, fam!"

Staying on point when we were tired meant rolling with the windows down, blasting our cheeks with cool, fresh air, chain-smoking cigarettes and listening to music. In any given day, we'd go through periods of being lively, up and bouncing, singing along to tunes, followed by slumping to seemingly bottomless lows. We'd feel tired and heavy until we got some food inside us. It was constant mood swings.

Inevitably there came a time when we couldn't take any more, and we had to retreat to a trap for a bit of downtime. We wanted to spend as little time as possible in these places because addicts are bait. They're known to the police. It was in these houses that I got to know some of the addicts and heard their stories. I couldn't help but feel sorry for them.

One woman, Ezra, had a strong, spiritual vibe about her. She wore her long, blonde hair cut in a fringe that she was forever pushing out of her eyes. Her house was always pungent with incense. Little clusters of crystals dotted the shelves.

Staying there was like stopping in a hotel. Ezra would do the room out with clean towels and scented candles. She had money – not big money, but she was comfortable, and she would buy drugs from us consistently throughout the day. Sometimes she'd even treat us to KFC out of her own cash.

"It's so nice to have a girl staying!" she'd say, poking around in my bag and checking out my clothes. One time, she pulled out a cute little tracksuit I'd bought.

"Oh my God, I love this!" she squealed, holding the top up against her. "Can I have it?"

"Yeah, take it. I've got loads of tracksuits. It's yours," I said. Whenever we returned to London, I got in the habit of leaving a few clothes behind for her. She attached herself to me, and if we were heading back on the road, she'd beg the boys, "Oh, can she stay here?"

"Yeah, cool, if she wants to. Make her chill!"

Ezra would chat for England while I listened. She could go all night. While she talked, she brushed my hair and tied it into plaits. The odd time, I made the mistake of letting her paint my nails just after she'd done her little shot of heroin, and my fingers would end up daubed in nail varnish because she couldn't use her hands properly. Her head would loll as she fought to stay awake. She was so high.

Another time, we came in from the road and found her slashing open the cushions on her sofa with a knife.

"Ezra! Stop! What are you doing?" I said.

"They're full of insects!" she said, high as a kite.

I noticed a lot of these addicts – not so much the men, but the women especially – had been in care, or had some kind of trauma in their past. With Ezra, she'd been run over by her own dad.

"He tried to kill me," she said. "And when it didn't work, he backed up and ran over me again."

I liked her. I don't know what happened to Ezra, but at some point in our back and forth, all of a sudden she was no longer around.

Which was a shame, because not all these nitty houses were as nice or as welcoming as Ezra's.

We often crashed with a girl called Jane, and her place was exactly like a movie crack den. In the hall, she had a thick beam of wood wedged between the front door and the stairs, to stop the police battering the door down. Every time we came in and out, she had to shift it out the way.

Her story was she'd been caught up in the Rotherham sex scandal. I know more about it now than I did back then, but

Jane told me how she'd been exploited, pimped out for cash and abused multiple times by multiple men.

"How did you get involved in that?" I asked her.

"It wasn't just me, it was a couple of girls from my care home," she said, explaining how a group of men had preyed on the young residents. She'd ended up pregnant, had her child taken into care and moved away to try and find some peace. In desperation, she'd turned to drugs to try and numb out the years of horrific memories – and the irony was she was paying for her habit by doing sex work.

The hallway in Jane's led to an upstairs flat where the set up was open-plan kitchen, living room, diner. There were a couple of mismatched chairs and not much else, save a few dishevelled bodies lying around the floor amongst the needles and patches of vomit.

Jane knew how messed up her situation was, and sometimes she'd sob, "I'm trying to get clean! I'm gonna do it!"

Nitties said this all the time. Said it – but never did it.

One time, I'd gone OT leaving Dajuan behind in London. The boys I was with had made plans to go meet some girls they knew.

"Yeah, it's cool," I said. "I'll stay in the trap – I don't care."

But, once they'd left, I did care.

This wasn't a regular crack house.

One of the addicts started pestering me for a couple of pebs. Weighing up the situation – four or five desperate nitties in various states of fucked-up – I didn't dare get my pack out. If they saw it, they were just gonna jump me. Game over.

"Yeah, I ain't even got it," I told the man. His eyes were rolling around his head and he was so close I could smell rancid vomit on his breath. "Let me just go downstairs and bring that two for you."

I went downstairs and called the boys: "Come pick me up, get me the fuck out of here!"

We came across girls like Jane all the time. I felt for her, and for a lot of the women we met on the road. Too many of them would come to the car with black eyes or fat lips.

"Rosie, what happened to you?" I'd say.

"Oh, Pete beat me up again last night."

Most of the women had stories like Rosie's. Did I feel guilty selling drugs to them?

Well, no.

They wanted the drugs, and we had the drugs. One way or another, they were gonna get their drugs. They might as well get them from us.

14

TOP GIRL

Dajuan and me were spending a lot of time together – on the road, in the trap or just chatting shit while we wrapped food and counted money. Office romances start with flirting over the water cooler. Ours was forged wrapping pebs, hitting the shots, making the money. We developed a bond.

Soon after I started going country properly, we became a couple and Dajuan made our relationship official. It was no longer a casual thing.

"So what, are you my girl now?" Dajuan asked.

"Yeah, I guess I am," I said.

"Well, OK. Don't move strange then."

In other words: *Don't see other boys.*

The news spread. In the micro-bubble of our ends, I was *the* girl. Connected. Known. I'd see other girls whisper between themselves and jut a chin in my direction.

Yeah. That's Dajuan's girl.

Boys stopped moving to me – instead of trying to flirt with me they steered clear and left me alone. Perfect. Still traumatised from the incident with Jake and them lot, I was low on trust with guys outside my circle.

Dajuan came up with a surprise to mark our relationship moving to the next level. At his place one day, I heard a car engine growl outside in the street. I looked out the window to see a friend of his parking up a smart-looking, black Audi A3. He popped his head around the door and tossed Dajuan the car keys. "Here you go, bro."

I was puzzled. "What are you getting a car for?" I asked. "You can't even drive."

Dajuan laughed, then took my hand and placed the keys in my palm.

"No, silly. It's for you."

"What? Are you serious?"

"Yeah, it's yours."

He'd had the car registered to me, and it came with what we called 'link insurance', where a connect at an insurance firm got a monthly payment to add my name and a few others to their database. If we got pulled, the car showed up as insured.

As word got around about me and Dajuan, people fell over themselves to buy me drinks and little stuff in the local shops. One time, I wasn't far from home when my car sputtered and lurched to a halt. The arrow on the fuel gauge was slumped in red. Within seconds, I had five boys pressed to the rear bumper, pushing me to the next garage so I could fill up. I wanted for nothing.

Most of all, I felt protected.

One afternoon, I was minding my own business, walking back from the local shop. A shambolic-looking guy approached from the other direction and – as we went to pass each other – he shoved me roughly into an alleyway. "Give me your money!" he hissed.

Up close, I realised I'd seen him around and even knew his name. He was one of those raggedy nutters that every neighbourhood has. Mad Man Wayne or something like that.

"What the fuck?" I said.

"I told you, give me your money," Mad Man insisted.

"Are you sure you want to do this?"

With that, he rummaged through his multiple layers of threadbare clothes and pulled out a knife.

"All right, all right!" I said. "It's not me you want to worry about, but here you go."

I peeled £50 from my purse and thrust the bottle of Hennessy I'd just bought from the shop into his hand. While he shuffled off, I called Dajuan.

"You'll never guess what's happened – my man pulled a knife and robbed me!"

"Serious!?" he replied. "You know who it was?"

I gave him a name and carried on home. A couple hours later, Dajuan phoned: "Come round mine."

And there was Mad Man Wayne, looking very sorry for himself. He handed me back the £50 and told me, "Sorry." He never bothered me again.

This protection, though, was a double-edged sword. Because in other respects, being with Dajuan made me a target. Everyone knew me now, and while in the ends Dajuan commanded respect, in other neighbouring parts of West London, he was considered an enemy. There was old beef with estates nearby, but this went deeper; it was more personal against Dajuan.

I remember driving down a North London road on one occasion when a group of boys spotted me. It was like an alarm going off in their heads. The mob descended on the car, shouting, "That's that girl! That's Dajuan's girl!" A red light and a queue of traffic blocked my escape. A couple boys stooped to pick up something in the road, and I winced as they dashed bricks against the car. They landed with dull thuds and all I could do was pray they didn't hit the glass. *Come on*, I willed, watching the lights turn to amber. Finally, we got a green. The cars in front rolled off and I hit the accelerator.

Certain areas were now out of bounds completely, including one neighbouring estate where the hate for my friends was strong. Previously – when I'd been invisible – I used to shop there. But now, locally, I was restricted to my small area. Being with Dajuan was limiting in that respect. Occasionally, rival boys would DM me, trying to move to me. Say I went to meet one, or, God forbid, ever slept with him, that would have been a massive one-up for them. A successful violation that would have incited a response.

Yeah, I slept with my man's girl!

I had to be careful.

Even the car came with a catch, because although it was a gift, it also meant we no longer needed rentals for going OT. Now, whenever we went country, we took the Audi. I drove, the number plate cameras on the motorway no doubt registering every trip. Plus, if Dajuan needed a lift somewhere, I couldn't really turn round and say no. I couldn't use the excuse of, "well, I don't have a car." Because he'd bought me one.

I don't think it was manipulation — it was just blatant, to be fair. Dajuan never came creeping round saying, "Hey babe, this is your present." He wasn't underhand about it. He'd given me a car, and as much as it was for me, it was also to serve the business. I was under no illusions. I was happy with the arrangement. I knew what it came with, but it was still a car — and a pretty nice one at that.

15

UNTOUCHABLE

O n the road, in the trap, I immersed myself in the grind – the line, the drugs, the money and the filth. It was a thrill ride. The adrenaline highs and the crash-and-burn lows masking what I'd lost. I couldn't get enough of this medicine. But whenever I was back in London, Lloyd was on my mind. The path I was on, I knew he wasn't safe at home with me, but I'd have leapt off it in a heartbeat at the sniff of a chance to have him back.

I remember shouting social services and feeling hollow, like my guts had been spooned out, as they told me, "Sorry, we don't seem to have him on our records."

How can a child – my child – just disappear?

In desperation, I called the police to report him missing. More incompetence. "The situation sounds like something for social services," they told me. "We'd suggest you contact them and take some advice from a family solicitor." I was going round in circles.

It made sense to me that Lloyd was probably with his dad, but no one had told me so and I had no way of checking. Aidan had changed his phone number after my flat got shot up. Clutching at straws, I went to his mum's place in the hope of catching a glimpse of my son, or just to see what was going down at the house. I'd knock on the door, only to be told, "We don't know where he is."

"If you hear anything, let me know, please. I'm still his mum…"

"Don't come here again. It's harassment. If you keep coming back, I'm calling the police."

Sometimes I'd take Haina with me. We'd park up, get a KFC and stake out the house for a couple hours. Nothing ever came of it. I burned with resentment. But I felt helpless – there was nothing I could do.

Around the same time, the feds were getting wise to the company I was keeping. They knew I was rolling with certain 'gang members', or whatever they wanted to call them. Like this one boy, Paul. Fair enough, he was known as a gunman. If you believed his reputation, he'd spray you up just for looking at him wrong. He was cool though. He had a sweet side, too, and I rolled with him a lot.

One night, he asked me to drive him over to one club to have, shall we say, a conversation with another boy over him sleeping with a girl Paul had been seeing. Paul was agitated, alcohol fumes steaming off him. I drove. He seethed, staring out the window, leg jackhammering in the footwell.

"Paul – you OK?" I said.

"Little pussy's taking the piss," he spat. "Taking me for a fool!"

Soon as we got to the club, Paul whipped his hood up, jumped out, pulled a pistol from his jeans and started waving it around, threatening this boy. The crowd scattered, girls screaming as their heels clattered on the paving stones. It was chaos.

The bouncers clocked me and they knew my face. "D, get him out of here!" they shouted. "Police is gonna come!"

"Paul, we gotta go. Feds are on the way. Let's go!"

It could have gone either way. Liquor, girls and guns make a potent cocktail. But Paul saw sense. He slotted his gun in the back of his pants and we cut.

I drove him home. He knew how close he'd come to fucking things up, but he wasn't sorry. Instead, he launched into a half-drunken tirade about how to handle the police if it came on top – his 10 commandments for arrest procedure, if you like. Top of the list was stuff I already knew – no comment, prepared statement, don't speak without a solicitor.

"Also, don't fight them, D. Just let yourself get arrested," Paul told me. "Don't resist. And when they put you in a cell, just say this prayer and everything will be fine."

He gave me one of his Muslim prayers. After that day, I never had a fight with a police officer again.

We'd been lucky that time, but because the police were now associating me with people like Paul, I was becoming bait. The city police had me in their sights and they made sure I knew it by stopping me more and more frequently.

OT, it was a different story.

The country feds had their own way of doing things, and I'm not sure they'd cottoned on yet that London 'gangs' were moving their business out of the city. Over the years, I'd seen a gradual increase in police presence across the more deprived inner-city estates, and people had inevitably found ways to do business away from that heat. Plus, in London, you ran the constant threat of violence. Country was calm. Plain sailing. Going OT was an inevitable response to the extra police scrutiny and everyday dangers of London hood life. Who wants to sell drugs on the doorstep when there's violence and feds every five seconds?

Instead, the problem just got moved an hour or two up the motorway. Sometimes, we'd pick a different town from our usual spot to go work. We'd rock up, dish out free samples along with a phone number, flood the place with drugs – selling non-stop until there was nothing left – then high-tail it back to the ends. It was too easy.

But it was our middle-England tourist town that saw most of our activity, and we felt pretty much untouchable there – despite some near misses.

One time, I was away with Paul. We didn't have a trap to crash at, so we'd booked into a proper bookey, dive hotel. The rooms cost £20 a night and the clientele was mostly prostitutes, crackheads and drug dealers like us. If you've seen the Netflix documentary about the Cecil Hotel in Los Angeles, where a bunch of people got murdered, this place was just like that.

It was freezing cold in this dump and we were both exhausted. I had my pack banked but it was hella uncomfortable.

"Same," said Paul. "Just wanna sleep, man."

"Fuck it, I'm taking mine out," I said. "It's safe in here."

Paul nodded and took his out, too.

We lay exhausted on the bed together, Paul spooning me against the cold. We both had our packs slotted between our legs – just in case – as we drifted into a light sleep. I don't know how long we were out, but suddenly someone was booming the door, smashing it over and over again. We jumped out of bed in a state of panic and banked those packs in five seconds flat.

"You cool?" I said to Paul.

He nodded.

The door boomed again. I tiptoed over and opened it a crack. A fed was stood outside. I was sure we were getting raided.

"Can I help you?" I said as Paul joined me in the doorway. "Is there something wrong?"

The officer poked his head in and glanced around the room, then said, "I'm really sorry to disturb you both. We're actually looking for someone else."

Relief flooded through me. "OK, good night," I said, smiling thinly as I closed the door on him. I felt like my chest was going to burst with anxiety. We didn't sleep a wink all night, and I was so shaken I barely ate for the rest of the day.

Another time, I was on the road with Dajuan and Mally again. We were stopping in a trap – a miserable apartment with a bedroom and a tiny, open-plan kitchen/living room. We put our blankets on the floor, lined up three pillows and slept in a row, cuddled up to each other because there was no heating. The bathroom was so disgusting we used to go to the gym to use the shower.

Tara, the woman who rented the place, let us stay with her whenever we wanted. Her boyfriend at the time had this insane shotgun wound in his shoulder. They both loved showing it off because they were super-proud that he'd lived to tell the tale. It was the weirdest thing I've ever seen. The flesh was hollowed out like a bowl, and the scar tissue had formed what looked like a glowing sun, with a white-hot burn at the centre and sunrays radiating outwards.

This pair only took crack, and they'd stay up all night smoking it. We'd be lying on the kitchen floor, while they had sex in the room next door. All night. Really loudly. We used to cuss them about it. "Mans' trying to sleep here! Shut the fuck up!"

But they were gone high, so they ignored us and kept at it.

I remember one time waking up in the morning to find our clothes and bedding wringing wet. The toilet had been leaking all night, and we were lying there in it. Soaked in toilet water. It was the most depressing thing ever. "Let's just go back to London," Dajuan said.

For some insane reason, we did return to Tara's a few times to crash, chancing another drenching from her loo.

We were chilling there one day, drugs out on the side, bits of spliff in the ashtray where the boys had been smoking weed. The flat stank of skunk. Suddenly a flash of blue strobed through the room. Dajuan popped his head over the windowsill to look outside, then ducked straight back down. "Shit!"

"What is it?" I said.

"Two bully vans. Bare feds."

"Coming here?"

The hammering on the door answered that one as a cop called Tara's name. Suddenly, she ran from the bedroom – and went to open the front door.

"No, no, no!" I hissed. "Just hold on!"

We dealt with our drugs. "OK, go on…" I said.

What else could we do? One way or another, those feds were coming through the door. But we knew how fucked up the whole situation looked – two black men and a little white girl sleeping on the floor, in a flat with two crackheads. It looked mad bait.

Tara opened the door a sliver. "Can I help you officer?"

"We've got a warrant out for your arrest."

What? The stupid woman was wanted!

"That's fine, officer," she said. "You can arrest me. Just let me put some clothes on and you can take me in. OK?"

Unbelievably, the feds let her close the door on them while she went and got dressed.

"See?" Tara winked. "I'd never rat you out!"

"You didn't think to maybe tell us you had a fucking warrant on you?" I hissed through gritted teeth.

She shrugged, put some clothes on, got arrested.

We breathed a sigh of relief. Another lucky escape for us. Tara was home a couple of weeks later, but we stopped fucking with her after that. Too close for comfort.

The more time I spent in stinking traps like that one, constantly surrounded by shotting's filth and smells, the more I became obsessed with cleanliness. Part of it was to do with that phobia I have about vomit, which was constantly tested by being around crackheads spewing up all over the place. It crept up on me, and then bled through into my relationship with food. *Actual* food, I mean, not drugs food. Cooking at home in London, if I touched raw chicken, I'd have to wash my hands over and over again, then scrub the kitchen with bleach. On the road, it was a nightmare. Often, we were too busy to stop and eat properly anyway, but there was usually time to grab a Nandos or a pizza. Even so, I pretty much stopped eating. It got to the point where all I'd have all day was a jumbo Twix bar or some Jacob's crackers. And lots of cigarettes. The weight fell off me. I looked physically ill.

Meanwhile, the drugs business was going well. After their initial reticence, the boys recognised I was an asset to have around – the women addicts were drawn to me, and the guys liked to flirt as they got their drugs. Shoots began asking after me if I wasn't on the road. "Oh, where's the white girl today, we miss her."

Plus, the more time I spent around the addicts, I started taking time to be nice to them. Just little things like, "All right, how's your day been?" So my customer service was a bit better than the boys'. Don't get me wrong, the shoots would still piss me off, but I did try to be kind, and I think I perhaps made them feel that bit more human.

The operation was making enough cash to rent a home-from-home in country. Dajuan tapped up one heroin shoot who worked as an estate agent, and got us a cool flat with Ikea furniture, Netflix, couple double bedrooms and an open-plan kitchen.

Most importantly, that place was *clean*. A pristine island in a sea of vomit and grime. We only used it for downtime, not trapping. The boys took girls back there. Dajuan would lend the keys to friends in London if they wanted to get out of the city for the weekend. Proper little holiday home.

We were smart about sales. Once, the guy who cooked crack for us made a special batch with a touch of orange food colouring. We called it cheesecake, just for the banter, and hyped it up in country. "Yeah, cheesecake! This one's mad strong."

The shoots heard the word on the street and came flocking. "Hey Vegas, you got the orange cheesecake one?"

Another time, our chef stuck a bit of molly (ecstasy) in the cook. Crackheads were still begging for it long after it sold out.

In truth, we didn't really need to do this stuff because we had 80 percent of the shoots regardless. If someone new rocked up and rolled around town trying to get nitties' numbers for their line, they were likely to be told, "Nah mate, I see Vegas." Nitties needed us, badly. Our shoots were loyal to the soil. Even if they did manage to scrape a few customers together, no matter. There were enough addicts to go around. Some South London boys showed up at one point. We saw them on the road and knew straight off what they were on. We'd pass each other in the cars, give a little nod. Mutual respect. "We're cool," said Dajuan. "Phone's still ringing. They ain't dippin' in our pockets."

That was the vibe. Maybe a little tension, but nothing serious. Nothing that was gonna spill into violence. My lot weren't like that. It was never a case of "Oh, they're stepping on our toes," because being a gangster and doing crime to make cash are two very different things.

Any heat was more likely to be over the same old, postcode-based bad vibes than protecting business and territory. Some boys from a neighbouring estate back in the ends did show up in our spot OT – and it was taken as the deliberate provocation they'd almost certainly intended. This was ancient, historical beef that had been simmering for years. I wasn't party to how it was dealt with, but I heard mutterings about going to the garages – where boys in the ends kept their guns – before a little convoy headed up the motorway. This other lot never showed their faces there again.

The main thing was to avoid selling to an undercover. I had a UC checklist in my head and we all thought they were easy enough to spot. Anyone who looked too clean, had good teeth, or wore Superdry clothes, got marked down as UC. Superdry was the one, bait undercover police uniform. They always seemed to be driving Vauxhall Vectras or the Focus saloon. Three white men in a Vectra was guaranteed UC as far as we were concerned. Also, we knew the number plate prefix for the local police force, so if we spotted a plate starting with those two letters, we cut. Bare times, we'd be on the way to meet a shoot and spot an unmarked car just as we went to pull up. We'd have to bell the shoot and divert them.

There were rules. Random-number callers didn't get served. "Two white, two what, mate? I dunno what you're talking about. Goodbye."

New shoots were preferred as face-to-face referrals. If a random person got through on the phone claiming to know an existing customer, we'd bell them to check. Even then you couldn't be certain. We were always edgy about the undercover threat and there were all kinds of mad little conspiracies that only served to ramp up our paranoia. One was that the under-cover officers weren't allowed air fresheners in their cars, so if we couldn't see one hanging from the rear view, alarm bells rang. Another was that the undercovers were taking blockers, so they could use drugs without getting high. I don't know if it was true, but this was supposedly a response to shotters making customers prove they were crackheads by doing drugs in front of them.

We had this one potential new shoot, and he looked hella clean to me. Smooth, well-cared-for lips over pearly white teeth. Styled hair. Tidy clothes. Nothing about him fit the usual, run-down nitty profile. The first red flag was that he got the Vegas number from someone else.

"Yeah? Who d'you get it from then?"

He told us. And it actually checked out. But still the boy just wasn't sitting right with any of us.

"Get in the car, bruv," said Dajuan.

He looked freaked out and took a big step back. "Nah, I ain't getting in the car mate."

"Relax. We're not gonna do nothing to you, fam. But if you want your ting, you're gonna have to get in the car."

Reluctantly he got in the car. We had no drugs, no money out. Even if he was UC, there was nothing to nick us for. Going all round the houses to avoid incriminating himself, Dajuan broke it down for him, making it clear he was gonna have to do a tester in front of us. Even then the boy was still acting weird, because any normal nitty who smelt a free sample would be straight on it.

"This guy is proper bookey," I said. I'd have told him to fuck off, but the call wasn't mine to make.

"OK, OK. I'll do it," the boy said.

"Take us to your place," said Dajuan.

He directed us to the house he shared with his mum and Dajuan followed him inside. He came back out 10 minutes later. "He did it," Dajuan shrugged. The boy got his drugs.

There really wasn't much getting past us. But what is it they say? *Pride comes before a fall.* That fall – a big one – was just around the corner.

16

JUMP OUT GANG

Back in the ends, the police were on a mission. I got stopped practically every day, sometimes multiple times a day. I had my own personal team of stalkers – and they wore police uniforms. They never turned up anything suss in my car or in my pockets, but they did find certain 'gang' members sat in my passenger seat. They pulled me one time with that gunman, Paul. They seen me walking out the chicken shop with Dajuan. They clocked me chilling with various other boys whose names had no doubt been plugged into their gang matrix of organised criminals. Jail cats. Boys with reputations, police records and time served.

So they knew. *OK, she's chilling with this lot now.*

Probably my name appeared at the top of that matrix alongside Dajuan. Maybe they thought that with the right kind of pressure, I could be turned. Because now I was a target, too. To be fair, their intelligence was accurate – somehow they seemed to know exactly what I was up to. They just weren't very good at catching me at it.

I had the odd lucky break – always with the regular feds who generally went about their policing duties with a lighter touch. Take this time when one of the YGs – the youngers – asked me for a favour. He was desperate to get his driving licence and he tapped me up for some lessons. "Yo, D – teach me how to drive."

"Yeah, no problem. Come."

I had this kid in my car, first time behind the wheel. Rather than draw attention to ourselves kangarooing up and down the street, I made a suggestion. "Let's go to the car park down the road. Get you used to the controls."

We ran through using the clutch, lurched across the car park a few times, crunching up and down the gears, me wincing at the damage he was doing to my gearbox. Finally, he started to get the hang of it. The creases in his forehead smoothed out and his mouth cracked into a grin.

"You're doing great," I said.

"Can we go on the road now?" he asked.

"OK, sure – do your thing."

One important detail: although this YG lacked experience behind the wheel, in other matters – Class B drugs for example – he was an old hand. For some reason, he'd brought barc weed along to his first driving lesson – maybe to sell later, or go stash in his house. This pile of bud was in a Tupperware slotted into the passenger door.

We got on the road, YG driving, taking it slow and cautious. Maybe too cautious, because we caught the eye of a police van that pulled out of a side road behind us. We hadn't gone far when we got blue-lighted. There were no L-plates on the car, YG wasn't insured. I don't think he even had his provisional.

"Keep driving – swap seats with me," I said.

"Do what?!"

"Swap seats, come on."

I don't know how we managed it, but – yeah – we did. I slid across so I was sat on his lap. As I took the controls, he wriggled out from underneath me, slipping into the passenger seat. Blue lights were still flashing so I pulled over to the kerb.

YG had forgotten about his weed in the chaos, and the police wasted no time in finding it.

Shit!

As the car was mine, they had me in the back of the van, and I was stealing myself for an afternoon in the nick wearing a bored expression as I said "no comment" over and over again. But the sergeant had a heart, and he wasn't scared to show it.

"I've got a daughter your age, and on this occasion I'm not going to do anything with you," he told me.

"I can go?" I asked, barely able to believe my luck. Clearly, he hadn't bothered searching my name, because that would have been a huge red flag, and I'd have been cooling my boots in a cell in no time.

He nodded. "Just this once. Treat it as a warning."

"Well – thank you."

This was a rare positive experience of policing. Other times, I wasn't so lucky. During a random stop one day, a police officer ran the usual checks and said, "You're not insured to drive this vehicle." I told Dajuan later, who got onto our insurance connect. Turned out the system had glitched and my name had dropped off the database. I ended up on a ban and because there was no way I was letting something little like that get in the way of business, I began racking up the driving convictions. Every time I went country, I was now breaking one of our cardinal rules: never commit two crimes at once.

Our activities were also getting attention from another type of fed, a supposedly specialist group of officers who worked in notorious 'gang' hotspots like Peckham, Brixton and West London, rolling around mob-handed in a little minibus.

They called themselves Gangs Unit.

We called them Jump Out Gang – because that's literally what they did. They jumped out on you, at every opportunity.

When I was younger, boys on the corner just scattered when feds showed up. The police never bothered running people down, you just got moved along.

Jump Out Gang, though, would literally leap from the van, rough you to the floor, slap you in cuffs without even telling you why. You could be on your way to get a can of drink from the shop and they'd have you splayed against the wall. All they needed was 'reasonable grounds' to suspect you were carrying, say, a weapon or some drugs. They 'suspected' me all the time – but never found a thing on me. If I saw Gangs Unit in the ends or on the road, guaranteed I got stopped. Sometimes, I'd be in the car and they'd roll up next to me, wind down the window. "Hi D! Come on, pull over."

"I'm not doing nothing! I'm just going Westfield!"

"You know we gotta do what we gotta do. Pull over."

Then I'd get sly little comments like, "Oh, where's your boyfriend Dajuan today? Saw him with another girl today – nicked him in this other girl's car."

Or they'd tease me with some intel showing my car getting picked up on the number plate recognition cameras: "We've got your car on the motorway like 30 times in the last month. Where are you going, D? Going country?"

They were looking for a way in. Leverage. Like I'm gonna snitch because they tell me my man is fucking around.

Other times they'd box me in at the petrol station while I filled up and detain me for a search under the Misuse of Drugs Act. Every time I was searched, they gave me a receipt. In the space of a couple of years, I collected over 300 of these stop-and-search sheets.

"Give me a break, guys. I'm literally going to the corner shop and you're stopping me, holding up my day."

"Come on, D…" In that patronising tone.

"You're not finding nothing though! It's not like you've stopped me before and you've found something. You're wasting your time."

They always put me in cuffs because they thought I was gonna run or do something crazy, then I'd stand by my car as they searched under the seats, emptied out my glove compartment. Sometimes they dashed everything in my boot out on the floor. Depending how they were feeling, they might bring a dog down. Often, an officer would wrinkle his or her nose and say, "It smells of weed in your car, so we're taking you for a strip search."

Ah the joys.

I got strip searched so many times, I grew immune to any embarrassment. It was as normal a part of the day as brushing my teeth. The rules are, it has to be done in a police station, so usually they took me to Belgravia. But occasionally, they'd invent some reason why it had to be done in the van.

"Station's busy. Custody suite's full, D. Van it is."

If there was no female officer on scene, they had to radio for one to come and conduct the search. I'd wait on the side of the road for her to turn up, then I'd get in the van while the men stood outside. I'd incrementally take off my clothes, so I was never fully undressed at any one time. My top half off first, put it back on, then remove my bottom half. A tiny bit of a concession to dignity, there. Countless times. Nothing ever found.

Worst of the worst of the Jump Out Gang was this one officer who I'll call Gary.

Gary was a brute. Gary was bent. Gary was a conniving sleazebag.

In some ways, I felt like Gary was torn between enforcing the law and being part of the hood lives – our lives – that he was trying to police. He'd sit in his police van and listen to the same rap artists that we listened to on the block. He loved it. When he was off duty, he'd sometimes roll up on me outside the club in his own personal car.

"Hey D, get in, I'll give you a lift home."

Strange creature.

I was sat in my car on the estate one time, and Gary pulled up with another fed in an undercover car. Gary wound down his window.

"Oh, all right Gary? What – are you stopping me now, are you? Are you gonna search me Gary?"

"No, we don't want to search you," he said. "I've just got a question for you."

"OK. Go on then."

"Have you ever thought about writing a book?"

"Shut up Gary."

"No, I'm serious. If you ever want to, you know, talk to us, we can get that arranged."

What he wanted was for me to come down the station and snitch. For the record, Gary had nothing to do with this book.

"Gary – fuck off."

Another occasion, I watched with my own eyes as he pocketed a bribe. I was getting the tyres done on the car. A bunch of boys were chilling on the road nearby. Jump Out Gang rocked up and had them all up against the wall for a search. They strung them out along the pavement, splitting them up, and I watched as Gary walked off down the road with one boy. He was straight in my line of vision. The boy pulled out some weed and gave it up. "Here, I've got weed on me," and then, as well as the weed, he handed Gary some cash.

Gary pocketed both and patted him on the shoulder as if to say, "Good boy, off you go," and then walked away.

Bare times I heard people chatting about him taking bribes that you could pay to get out of him nicking you.

I think he took other forms of payment, too.

One afternoon, Gary pulled up on me on the estate. It was mad timing because I was sat waiting for someone to come out of this house to go country – and that boy had all the drugs on him. I fired off a quick text to him: *Gangs Unit. Stay in the house.*

Gary walked round to my window. "Come on D. Step out the car." He started with some excuse about having intelligence on me. "We know what you're doing tonight."

"Whatever Gary, do your thing. Let's get it over with."

Gary made a grand show of searching my car, found nothing, then actually *walked* me to the local police station.

I hadn't been charged or even accused of anything, but Gary had me in a room in the station and, out of nowhere, he said, "Look, give me a blowjob and I won't nick you."

Pardon me?!

"Suck your mum," I said. "Fucking nick me for what anyway? You haven't got anything."

Gary was trying his luck. Did he really think I was that easy? I've no doubt in my mind that if I'd said yes, he'd have gone through with it. But really, he'd picked the wrong girl to bribe – it's not like I'd done something and was desperate to get out of it.

Gary laughed and tried to brush it aside, like it was just a bit of hilarious police banter. "I'm only joking. Come on, I'll take you home."

Telling lone female suspects they can duck a charge in return for sexual favours?

Great gag, Gary. I'm laughing.

He took me out the back of the police station and my car was sat there waiting – he must have had a colleague drive it over. Gary had the keys and he drove me back to my flat. On the way, he was coming on all flirty, asking sleazy questions like, "What you doing tonight, D? Have you got a boyfriend coming round tonight?" Fucking weirdo.

Gary dropped me off and I said my goodbyes – until the next time. I chilled until the coast was clear, but I had to go get my money. I went to pick up that boy and we carried on doing what we were doing. We went country.

Sometimes, this heat touched people close to me, people who were totally innocent. The police knew Haina was like a sister to me. One night, we were out together and she got talking to a boy I knew. He was trying to move to her so I said, "Yeah, cool, you go with him. Have fun!"

This boy had a Porsche, and not long after leaving the club, bare police cars descended on his vehicle – only instead of stopping, the boy put his foot down and gave them a chase. They careered through the streets of London pursued by blue lights and wailing sirens, Haina terrified in the passenger seat. He was only ever gonna get so far and eventually lover boy pulled over, but rather than dealing with the situation, he opened his door and ran. Haina was left there on the side of the road, in her little dress, to get nicked by the feds. They had fuck all on her and, this one time only, it was me picking *her* up at five in the morning. "I got you babe."

Dajuan always said, the feds only had to get lucky once, while we had to be lucky every single day. And there did come a time when our luck ran out.

It happened in the ends.

Dajuan was round mine wrapping drugs. We'd spend hours and hours doing this. Stuck in a room together, listening to music, talking shit or just spending long moments in silence alone with our thoughts. I think that's why we were so comfortable being around each other. It didn't have to be bells and whistles all the time, we were content just being quiet in each other's company.

During a lull in the conversation, we caught the sound of Muslim prayers drifting up from the flat below.

"This is so peaceful," Dajuan said. "Let's just be quiet for a minute and listen to it."

We listened, carried on wrapping, and by the time prayers had finished, we were ready to roll.

I banked my pack, and said, "We going then?"

But Dajuan was hesitant. "I don't know... I've got a weird feeling," he said.

"Don't worry," I told him. "It's cool."

Listening to those prayers had really got to Dajuan. "It don't feel right banking this food, fam," he said, explaining that it was 'haram', or sinful. "I'm just gonna roll with mine out."

It was risky – but the choice was his.

We got in the car and drove as far as the shop on the corner at the end of the road.

"Just stop here," Dajuan said. "I'm gonna get some Ribenas and snacks for the trip."

I pulled up and he went in the shop. I'd been sat outside less than a minute when, out of nowhere, three police cars T-packed mine: one in front, one beside and one behind. I was boxed in. Trapped. We were being busted.

I knew these officers from around the ends. And they knew me.

I heard a familiar voice yell, "Open your door, Danielle!" Fucking Gary. "Open your door!"

"No, fuck off!" I told him. "I ain't opening nothing!"

I wasn't so worried for me – but Dajuan was in the shop with his G-pack in his pocket.

I was screaming at the feds, they were screaming back at me when suddenly – bam! The car window shattered as one officer battered it with his riot stick.

The glass caved in then disintegrated, and the feds reached in to try and drag me out the smashed window. Meanwhile, the road was blocked by all the commotion and the traffic was building up around us.

Somewhere, a car horn beeped.

"What the fuck!? Get off me!" I screamed at the top of my lungs. I was trying to alert Dajuan – still in the shop – to what was going on outside so he could do something with his drugs, or duck out back. I was trying to say *we're being busted,* without actually saying *we're being busted.*

Gary must have clocked me eyeing up the shop because the penny dropped and he shouted, "She's with someone! Check the shop!"

From there, it was game over.

The feds ran towards the shop – just as Dajuan was coming out. In desperation, he threw his pack – but managed to hit Gary in the head with it. It sounds comical. But we were both getting nicked. It was a whole shambles.

Down at the station, I felt safe the police weren't finding my drugs. I got strip searched, but there was nothing to see. I had confidence in my technique. My pack was well hidden.

Instead, they tried to pin Dajuan's pack on the both of us.

I was distraught. Not through fear of getting done, but because I felt like the whole thing had been my fault. I sat in my cell sobbing, inconsolable, trying to summon up Paul's Muslim prayer that would make everything OK. Eventually, the police took pity on me and let Dajuan in to sit with me to try and calm me down.

He sat on the floor, shuffled up next to me, and I lay my head on him.

"I am so sorry," I told him. "Looks like everyone was right! I got you nicked, didn't I?"

"It's not your fault, D," he said. "We're cool. And don't worry, I'm saying it was all mine. They're letting you go tomorrow."

Half of me was unsure. Was he really gonna take the fall for this?

But true to his word, he did.

I went home the next day, feeling like shit.

And Dajuan – he went jail.

17

JAIL MAN

The public gallery was packed. Maybe 20 local boys and girls, family and people from the block who'd come to show their support for Dajuan. Court appearances were always a big occasion in the ends, and this one was no exception. Fuck knows what the judge must have made of it. There was no jury for this hearing, but still, with hindsight, it wasn't the best look. Mad bait.

Security brought Dajuan into the dock and a ripple went through the gallery. He flashed me a cold smile and gave a little wave to his mum, sat beside me. I swallowed hard on the lump in my throat as she pulled out a tissue, but I couldn't hold back the tears any longer. I glanced around at my friends, seeking a bit of sympathy and togetherness – but the vibe I got was fury.

Apparently, it was all my fault. I'd put Dajuan in jail. Not the feds. Not his decision to keep his G-pack in his pocket instead of up his arse where it should have been.

Me.

By the time this bail hearing had come round, Dajuan had had plenty cell time to stew on the circumstances of our bust. Specifically, he'd remembered hearing a car horn beep in the road outside the shop while he was still inside loading up on snacks. He'd got it into his head that it was *this* noise which had alerted the feds. He'd gone and put the same idea in a few other heads, and from there it had been passed round the ends like a foot-long spliff at a block party. This stupid rumour was inhaled deep, taken as gospel. It sent all my friends crazy.

Mascara ran down my cheeks like black tar tracks. I was crying because I ached for Dajuan, but also because I'd taken on the burden of guilt everyone was now flinging like sticky shit in my direction. Through the blur of my tears, I watched the to and fro playing out in front of us on the courtroom floor. Guys in gowns and wigs deciding my man's fate. I had a firm grip on Dajuan's mum's hand and together we tried to follow the legal argument. His barrister wanted him out on bail until the actual court date, which would either convict him or set him free. Meanwhile the prosecution barrister was saying if they let him out, he might run, so justice would be best served by keeping him locked up.

"The defendant is to be remanded into custody," the judge concluded. I swallowed hard once more as fresh tears welled in my eyes. Dajuan shook his head and stood to let the security guards lead him away.

As I shuffled out of court, broken, Mally turned on me: "It's your fucking fault! You sent him jail!"

Really? I thought. *Please don't make my life any more difficult!*

Part of me wondered whether I'd ever regain their trust, whether they'd ever get over this, whether they'd ever believe it wasn't my fault.

First, I had to convince Dajuan.

I had his name and prison number, so it was no hassle booking a visit. I got one in as soon as I could. Did not go well. I was in the bad books.

"Why d'you beep the horn? Are you dumb?"

"I didn't beep any horn. I swear!" I said. "They smashed the window and had me out the car! I didn't even have time to beep the horn!"

"I'm in the shop paying for the snacks. Fucking car horn goes off and next ting I know it's bare feds."

"Yeah. There was a horn," I explained, laying it all out. "Because the road was blocked with like five police cars. I shouted and screamed and made a scene. But I did not beep."

Dajuan glared at me, kissed his teeth and looked away.

By the second visit, it seemed like he'd straightened out his head. I was just making sure he was cool. Dajuan had been jail before. He was a jail cat. He could handle it. He got the same respect on the wing as he got on the block. He was getting treated well. So yeah, he was cool.

Between trips to country, I did some running around for him. Sorting out a solicitor, getting paperwork together. But the main thing was to keep things ticking over OT. Where Dajuan had been fronting the money for buying a whole box at a time, we started buying smaller amounts between us, running back and forth between London and country on three-day cycles for re-ups. Everyone banded together to keep the business running smoothly. In country, we'd sell drugs for Dajuan, then do ours, putting cash down for him, just in case it went pear-shaped in court. He was convinced he was going to do time.

"Man needs some clothes," he told me on one visit. "Can you send some?"

"You're gonna be coming out soon!" I said, not wanting to believe he might be going away.

He got quite agitated. Far as he was concerned, his fate had already been sealed.

"Look, I'm fucking going jail. Send me my clothes. I'm asking you for clothes, send me the fucking clothes."

It was a tense time, and I spent these weeks on tenterhooks still feeling like I'd done something wrong, wondering if maybe I should have taken the fall for him. Dajuan still wasn't convinced at first, and the rest of our circle followed his lead by pointing accusatory fingers in my direction. They couldn't blank me completely, because we still had to work together, but it was hella uncomfortable. I felt on edge and lonely as I caught sly, disapproving looks.

"D, I've got to ask. Did you really bait him up?" Mally said as we drove OT one day.

"No! What the hell? Why would I do that?" I said. "I don't like it any more than you, but I did not hit that horn."

Mally shook his head and looked away, went back to messaging his little girlfriends. Everyone was looking to the boss – Dajuan – to pass judgment. If he said it was cool, everyone had to be cool. Until then, I was kept at arm's length.

We were on the road when he called. Dajuan had access to a phone smuggled into jail by another prisoner and he phoned three or four times a week to chat business, organising the teams and discussing re-ups. We'd pass the phone between us. My conversations with him were often awkward one-word-answer affairs. He was chatting to Paul, who flashed a look in my direction before handing me the phone.

"He wants to talk to you."

I took the handset. "Yo, you OK?"

"Yeah, I'm cool. Listen D, about that ting. I still reckon you baited it up, but I've been thinking about it and it's not that deep."

"If I could change places with you…"

"Nah, you made a mistake, I'm gonna get over it."

"We're cool?"

"Yeah, we're cool. Put Mally on."

If Dajuan was over it, everyone else had to be over it too.

Dajuan agreed to take a guilty plea on his drug offence, but asked me not to go to his sentencing hearing, so when the day came I stayed away. After the last time in court, I guess he wanted to spare me the emotion. Plus, he probably didn't want the embarrassment of one crying girl in the public gallery.

I was steeling myself for him getting two years, doing one. On the day, I went gym to take my mind off what was coming, but lasted like 10 minutes in the place before I headed home. Jordan, Mally and Paul showed up at the flat to chill – then word came back from the court. Someone must have been smiling on Dajuan, because somehow he got away with a two-year suspended sentence, with six months of that time to be spent under electronic curfew – tag, in other words. Smiles all round. I was so relieved.

Jordan picked him up and I met him at his mum's house later that evening.

"Hello Mummy!" I said, as she opened the door to let me in. I always called her that – she loved it. His mum was cool. Tall and slim like a model, with pale skin and her hair done in an afro puff. She seemed to float around the place almost like a ghost, silent and smiling. She was probably gone high half the time from all the weed that got smoked in there.

Me and Dajuan had our awkward little reunion. He gave me a hug and I felt then we could start to put it behind us. I hadn't been there long when the guys from G4S showed up to fit his ankle bracelet and install the box that would monitor his movements, making sure he stayed housebound for the 12 hours between 7pm at night to 7am the next morning. Later, the rest of the boys came round for a catch up, few drinks and a big smoke, bodies perched on the arms of sofas, while Dajuan's mum passed around dishes of mutton, ackee and salt fish.

While Dajuan was happy and relieved he hadn't gone jail, part of him was also pissed off because the curfew meant he was still in a kind of prison, albeit at home. His wings had been clipped. During night-time hours, he couldn't leave the house. Instead, the party came to him. There was never an evening when Dajuan was alone in the house – it was a team effort. He'd call me when his curfew time started. "Yo, D. Can you bring me dinner?" Them lot would go around, smoke weed, talk business and listen to music. He was basically the CEO of the area – if he needed something, he only had to snap his fingers and someone came running.

Which gave us plenty of time to get operations back up to speed. Then we'd spend hours and hours bagging up drugs. I remember one time covering the floor in a maze of black bin liners, and we got down on our hands and knees to process a fresh brick of heroin. Dajuan carefully slit open the plastic wrapping with a pair of scissors, weighed the block then began cutting it down. In half, then half again – and half again. Bigger quantities were held back and wrapped for wholesale, and we pebbed up the rest for country.

Mally had come round to lend a hand and we'd been wrapping for a few hours. I felt so lethargic. I couldn't get my head round it because it wasn't heavy work. It was just monotonous.

"Why do I feel so tired?" I said, letting go a yawn. I felt like I could nod off – and a bit sick and wobbly with it.

Mally laughed. "You're high!"

"I'm what?!"

"You're high! It's the fumes!"

"Fuck, I need to get some fresh air!" I said, rising unsteadily to my feet and heading for the front door.

The insane thing about Dajuan's tag was he could still come country. Sometimes he'd just come up for the day with us lot to roll around and chill in the car, before someone ran him home in time for curfew. Other times he'd hang out at the OT flat. Or he'd get someone to drive him, and shuttle drugs OT to the rest of us, meaning we didn't have to go back to London for the reloads. It got so that I was barely leaving country while he was on tag. Dajuan dropped off drugs and collected his money. We stayed OT making ours. Lots of it.

For a long time, it was solid flow. Whereas I'd been making about a grand every time we went OT – maybe over the space of between four and eight days – I was now making two or three a week. I had money to burn.

18

BIG SPENDER

It was a blazing hot summer's morning, stripes of light angling into the alleyways, the estate's concrete towers gleaming in the bright sunshine. It always took me a couple days to wind down from the stress and tension of being OT. Often there was barely a moment to catch my breath before I was heading back up the motorway with a reload, but now I was having some downtime. I'd caught a good night's sleep between clean sheets, showered the trap-house funk from my skin and hair, and I was loving the feel and smell of brand-new clothes against my clean skin – a pair of tiny tracksuit shorts with a matching hoodie bought off a girl who robbed stuff from Westfield.

Nothing made the memory of country fade faster than a shopping trip up Knightsbridge. I was planning some retail therapy to hurry things along when Dajuan shouted me. His tag days were behind him and the ankle bracelet had gone back to G4S. "What you doing today?" he said.

"I'm gonna go Harrods. Seen a bag I want."

"You know the rules – can you afford three?"

"I can afford five! You wanna come?"

I already knew the answer would be a no. Knightsbridge for Dajuan meant sending a YG on ahead to check there was no rival roadmen in the area. Even if the coast was clear, it meant rolling with a stab or bullet-proof vest, maybe carrying a blade just in case. Bare hassle just for some shopping trip.

Dajuan laughed. "Nah, you're good. Got some business to do innit. But if you're going, I want something too."

"Tell me."

As it happened, Mally also wanted stuff from Harrods. Paul wanted stuff. This boy who I'm gonna call Warren who was doing well in the music business wanted stuff. Basically, all the local big hitters had a Harrods shopping list and money to spend.

"Come round mine," said Dajuan. "Get the P, then you go shopping and do what you want to do."

"Okay, cool."

By now, shopping in places like Harrods was standard for me. The first few bits of designer stuff I'd bought, it was a mad thrill. I got such a buzz out of buying the stuff, I didn't dare wear it. Just knowing I owned and could afford it was enough. I used to keep my purchases in the box because they felt too special to even take outside the flat. Now and then I'd get them out to look at them, turning them over in my hands. I even hoarded all the carrier bags they came in.

I guess when you haven't had much and you get something nice, you just don't want to use it, because you're scared you might never have it again. But there comes a point, after however many bags or pairs of shoes, that it gets a bit samey, and eventually I used to just shop out of boredom.

I jumped in the A3 and shot round to Dajuan's, where everyone unloaded like three grand on me. Dajuan wanted a Louis side bag, few other bits. The rest all wanted trainers. Three of them wanted the exact same Balenciaga shoe, for fuck's sake.

"Here," said Warren, handing me a Harrods reward card. "Put all the points on this." It was a 'Black Tier' card, for the store's biggest spenders – you had to put £10k a year through their tills to even qualify for one. So I ended up with about £20k – in cash – plus the black VIP card. Whatever. No biggie.

I drove over to Harrods and parked up in the car park by Harvey Nics, then walked around to the store. I'd spent money in Harrods plenty of times before – on Gucci belts and hats and sunglasses, couple handbags – but I'd never walked in there with 30 grand on me. Not even *my* 30 grand. Besides the money in my open-top Louis bag – folds banded together in bundles worth a grand each – I was carrying huge responsibility. Feeling that weight on my shoulders, I tucked the cash tight under my arm. Hella pickpockets up Knightsbridge.

I was browsing – pulling dresses off the racks to check them out, picking up trainers, trying on sunglasses – when a security guard came over, chest all puffed up like a proper jobsworth. He eyed me up and down, taking in the shorts and hoodie, and said, "I'm sorry, you can't be in here wearing that."

"Excuse me?" I replied. "Wearing what?"

"I'll have to ask you to leave. It's inappropriate."

"Inappropriate how?"

"It's sportswear. I'm sorry, if I could just show you the way out…"

I looked around the store. It was a hot sunny day. In London. Literally everyone else was in shorts and little skirts, dressed for the weather. I thought, *what the fuck? If only you knew how much cash I've got in my bag, you might treat me a bit better!*

"Look," I said, "I've got money to spend."

"It's not really about the money," he began.

"OK, well, I've got *big* money to spend. Does that make a difference?"

I could see the cogs whirring in his head: How much cash was the store missing out on versus how much embarrassment would it suffer by letting this mouthy little estate kid shop there in her tiny shorts and matching hoodie combo? I wasn't prepared to open my bag and literally show him how much cash I was carrying, but I was willing to help him out a little bit.

"Let me speak to a manager," I said.

He slumped, looking deflated, then set off, returning a couple of minutes later with some supervisor type.

"How can I help you madam?"

"I've been asked to leave the store, but I'm shopping for someone," I said, handing over Warren's Black Tier card. "Check this."

"Very well," he said, and scanned the card.

I don't know what exactly came up on the screen, but the vibe changed pretty damn quick. Presumably, it showed Warren spent hella money in Harrods. Must have been some big numbers because the supervisor wiped his condescending frown and shitty look off his face, and replaced them with a welcoming smile. Nothing was too much trouble.

"Oh, I'm so sorry madam," he said, my 'inappropriate' clothes suddenly no longer an issue. "No problem at all. Let me get someone to assist you."

He clicked his fingers and two young women came bouncing over.

"How can we help you today? Are you looking for anything in particular?"

"As a matter of fact, I am," I said, parking myself on a sofa. I handed the women my list and they ran and got everything for me. It was a sweet moment.

When it came to paying, I handed over the cash, all in billfolds wrapped in elastic bands. Classic drug-dealer look. They never questioned the cash, but let's not pretend – it was bait as fuck where the money came from. I remember them looking at me and I got the sense there was maybe a touch of jealousy – here was this hood girl, dressed just like a hood girl, dropping £20k on bags and trainers like she's buying a can of Coke from the Esso.

There's been times, in other stores, when I felt people were maybe looking down on me. Like, you can never get away from the street because no matter how much money you've got, people are always going to look at you like you don't belong, that you're not worthy. I'm buying Louis Vuitton or Loubs while having a conversation on my phone about some ratchet business, and the man's looking me up and down. I'd get it a lot if I went shopping with the boys. I don't know what people thought – that maybe I was some kind of escort? But I didn't get that in Harrods on this occasion. If anything, these two young girls were looking on the encounter with envy.

They bagged up the boxes of trainers, mine and Dajuan's Louis gear, and I walked out with a spring in my step, making light work of the clutch of Harrods bags hanging from my wrists. As I reached the door, I caught the eye of that security guard and gave him a little wave. That was a good day. I drove home on a retail high and distributed the gifts.

The jewellery shops of Hatton Garden also scored big off our ill-gotten gains. I shopped there for chains and rings. A lot of the boys wore chains with low-slung, custom pendants. Rather than going up Hatton to shop, the biggest spenders had Hatton come running to them. Jewellers were dispatched to the ends to discuss designs, or took orders by phone and delivered them in person. In our area, wearing grills was a strong look. Dajuan was a big fan and some of the boys gassed me up about getting a set made. "You'd look so cute in them!" they said. "Get them pink diamond ones!"

Slave to the peer pressure, I went up Hatton for a fitting, pressing my teeth into a mould shaped like a gum shield. I dropped four and a half grand on them, had them iced out with top-end, VVS1-clarity pink diamonds. Truth – they were a total waste of money. I wore them maybe once. Should never have done it.

As well as somewhere to burn money, Hatton was the place to get paid. Get paid *big*.

In the ends, there was a separate group of boys to the shotters I rolled with, and their thing was robbery. I'm not talking Oyster cards and iPhones. They robbed millionaire

Hampstead Heath townhouses, smashed up West End jewellers with hammers, stole Rolex watches and precious gems worth tens of thousands of pounds at a time. They took their trade so seriously that one of the boys had done a diamond course, so he'd know exactly what he was robbing. On smash and grabs, they gave themselves 40 seconds to nail the job – that was the rule – and one of the team would count out loud "One... two... three..." while everyone filled their bags with shit grabbed from the shattered glass cases. Once they hit 40, it was time to go. These were big, big guys in our area of London, and a totally different kettle of fish to my drug-dealer circle.

"Robbery is big risk, big reward," one boy used to tell me. "I would never sell drugs – money's too slow! You go jail for like 10 years just for selling a one little drugs and you don't even make no money!"

These robbery boys thought the drug game was a joke, some pussyhole thing. I was making my way in it and doing OK, but what they were into was another level, hundred percent a man's world. They were very 'live fast' guys, because one job might bag 70 grand, and they'd just go and spend it. They'd burn through their money, party hard, drinking lean and taking molly.

I don't care. I'm spending it right now, because next week I'm gonna make another 70 bags.

By comparison, the drug boys were way more calculated. They'd save up for a splurge or make plans to invest. There was a point when it seemed like everyone wanted to buy a shop, a barber's, or an off licence – to wash out the money but also to do something for the community and maybe create some jobs, on some kind of Pablo Escobar trip. The boys who did robberies, they didn't think for the future at all. Didn't need to. They had money on tap.

Sometimes, I'd roll with them as they unloaded the spoils from their latest jobs on their link in Hatton – often as many as 10 Rolexes at a time – and I picked up some little knowledge along the way. Like the best watches to grab, besides Rolex, were brands like Audemars, Patek Philippe and Richard Mille. Also, some of the shotters liked getting their Rolexes iced out by having diamonds slotted in the face or bezel. For the robbery boys, this was a massive no-no – because instead of making the watch *more* valuable, it devalued it instantly. Fucking with it meant it was no longer authentic. The watch was now defiled and basically worth shit.

Personally, I didn't have a clear plan on what I was going to do with my cash. I was saving some – I'd put maybe couple grand in the bank from time to time – and I kept about £15k in shoeboxes stashed under my bed. But mostly I spent it. £100 on nails and lashes every couple of weeks. £400 on hair extensions. High-end make-up at £200 a time. Tom Ford and Louis perfumes. If I wanted it, and if I could afford three of it, I bought it. I was generous, too. If someone wanted something, cool – I was the girl. I'd get it for them.

With money in my pocket I could afford to kick my social-ising up a gear. Whenever I was back in the ends, I filled my nights with clubbing and dinners. I still went to the ratchet, dive clubs with bulletholes in the woodwork, bashment music on the sound system and bottles of Magnum tonic wine imported from Jamaica behind the bar. But I was also living it up in Mayfair clubs like DSTRKT and Tape, booking VIP tables with a minimum spend of a couple grand a time, bottles of vodka and cognac £500 a go.

The Tape vibe – according to Tape – was all about the "elegant party experience for an elite, global crowd". When I started going there, my hood girl face didn't really fit among the preened Essex dolls and top-flight footballers, so I caught a lot of stinging, catty looks and side-eye.

Tape could gas their clientele up all they wanted, but that "elite and global crowd" soon had to get used to sharing the dancefloor with fraud boys and drug-dealer types from the estates of inner-city London – hoodlums from the ends who had hustled their way into big money. The champagne corks flew. We'd earned our spot on the velvet banquettes alongside the rich kids of Chelsea.

I remember one night at a club called Sugar Hut in Essex. I hadn't booked a VIP because it had been one of those spontaneous outings, and now there were none free. Me and Haina stood by a table and the girls sat there were cackling and pointing at us over their cocktails. I overheard one say, "Look at them! They don't even have enough money to buy a table."

Yeah, I definitely do, I thought, turning away and taking a sip of my Courvoisier and Coke. *There just aren't any unavailable. If only you knew!*

If I was home in London, out on the town, Haina was often by my side. Usually my treat. She had her own money and was happy to spend it, but I always offered. She wasn't around me for the cash, though, and didn't know the difference between

Gucci and Balenciaga. That stuff held zero interest for her. Haina had her own thing going. She'd got a new car and was doing a degree. She still had boy trouble, though and, like me, she found an escape by dipping her toe in my hedonism.

A few times she brought another friend, Cheryl, along for the ride. Cheryl was a normal girl, with a normal job, but once she clocked on to what I was doing, she was in total awe of the shotter life and tried to stick to me like glue. She wanted to come country, she wanted to chill with the boys; any time I bought something new, she'd ogle it with envy. She never had money for drinks and cigarettes, so by putting herself close to me, she always got a free night out. If I was going shopping, Cheryl wanted to come – because she knew I was good for a freebie. We'd be in JD and she'd pick up a pair of trainers, turning them over in her hands and cooing over them. "Oh, these are so cool." Then she'd go to put them down, looking a little dejected because she couldn't afford them, or didn't want to spend the cash.

"I'll buy them for you," I'd say. My money was ill-gotten, so I didn't care about spending it.

One time, I was due to go country and Cheryl piped up, "I'll come. I'll carry the drugs if you want."

She was desperate to be a part of it – I don't know what was wrong with her. "OK," I said. I never wanted to intentionally put anyone in harm's way, so if someone was coming OT with me, they got told, "This is serious. You know what this is about, you're responsible for yourself. If anything happens, it's on you."

Cheryl nodded, bouncing like an eager puppy. She thought it was the coolest thing ever. *Fine*, I thought. *If she wants to carry the drugs, she can carry the drugs.* Cheryl stuck the pack in her bra. Like *that* was going to work if we got pulled.

Haina, too, knew exactly where my money was coming from. I was upfront about it, told her everything that was going on in my life. Plenty times she was happy to roll along in the car to country with me if I was dropping a reload or collecting cash – but she never ever touched any drugs. Haina was always very clear about that. She didn't mind being in the room, so long as she was strictly hands off.

One time, she was there when me and Dajuan were up to our elbows in rocks of crack, setting up some reloads and getting ready to head OT.

"Hey, Haina, grab some clingfilm and wrap some of this with us," Dajuan said.

Top boy or no, she didn't take shit off Dajuan.

"Are you stupid?" she said. "I don't know who the fuck you think I am! I would never in a million years."

Dajuan just laughed.

"OK! OK!"

He respected Haina all the more for that. He liked the fact that she was just rude.

Although Haina kept her distance from the drugs, she never lectured me about what I was doing, or looked down on me for the choices I'd made.

"So, what's going to happen?" she asked me over dinner one night in Zizzi's. "Are you doing this forever?"

"For now, this is what I'm doing," I shrugged. "I can't see anything else at the moment."

"I dunno, university maybe?"

"Not gonna lie, I'm jealous you're going uni. It's such a good look!"

"OK – so there's something."

I shook my head. It was weird. Haina and me were at such different stages in our lives. She was in uni studying accounting, and I was going country selling crack. It was so opposite, yet we managed to stay best friends. But me and university? My school years had been a disaster.

"I don't think so," I said. "Education's not for me."

If I'm honest, I felt like I was above all that in some way. The people I was spending time with didn't have an education and they were doing fine. Better than fine. I guess; for the time being, they were my role models – and not Haina, who was in uni.

"Think about it though."

"Nah – I'm good at this. I know what I'm doing. I enjoy it. This is what I'm on."

Dajuan and me never really discussed the future like I have done with boys since – those chats about marriage, houses and babies you have when you're still feeling your way, trying to suss out what your future looks like.

Dajuan was the kind of boy who, if he wasn't making money, he wasn't happy. He was all about getting P. And if he wasn't dealing with country stuff, he was dealing with politics – either in our group, in the ends or with outsiders with scores to settle. He was the one who had to calm things down, one way or another.

That's where I was. Shotting was so fast-paced, I wasn't making plans beyond the next re-up. That life didn't leave room for anything else. I realised later that it was all just a distraction.

10,000 nightclub tables, a shop full of Balenciaga shoes, a walk-in wardrobe dripping with Louis Vuitton bags – none of it was ever gonna make up for losing my son.

19

HIGHEST STAKES

"What d'you fancy tonight then?" I asked Haina. I was kicking back in London; she was on a lunch break. We were sat outside her work in my car, plotting out our weekend.

"I'm easy," she said, as my phone lit up with a number I didn't recognise.

"Hang on, let me get this," I said. I answered, "Hello?"

"Good afternoon, is that Lloyd's mum?" It was a woman's voice. Friendly. Professional. Upbeat.

For a second, I froze.

Not even a second. It was the blink of an eye – and then I regained my composure. "That's right," I said. "Can I help you? Is something wrong?"

"It's the health visitor," the woman said. "Nothing to worry about. Can I just confirm Lloyd's address, please? According to our records you're at…"

And then she read out an address.

An address I'd never heard of before – but presumably Lloyd's address, I realised.

I snatched a pen off the car console and motioned to Haina for something to write on. She flipped the glove box and dragged out a garage receipt. Scribbling the address down, I said, "Yes, that's correct."

"That's great, thanks for your time. Bye."

"Bye, bye. Thanks for calling."

I hung up and sat there speechless for a moment, barely able to breathe. Haina was looking at me wide-eyed: *Well? What the fuck?*

"You would not believe what just happened," I said.

"Who was it?"

"Some health-visitor woman. She's only gone and given me Lloyd's address!"

Haina gasped. "No. Fucking. Way. For real?"

"Hundred percent."

"Oh my God! Let's go! Let's drive there now!"

I stared out the windscreen.

Haina slapped the dashboard. "Come on! What you waiting for? Let's go!"

I'd wanted this for so long, replayed over and over in my head how it might pan out.

The big reunion.

You imagine it'll be like some Hollywood movie moment – you call your kid's name and they come running into your arms across a sunlit park. But does that ever really happen in real life? Confronted with the reality of it, I wasn't so sure. I should have been buzzing, ecstatic, but part of me really didn't want to check out this address at all. Part of me wished I'd never answered that phone, and that the nice health visitor lady hadn't been so bloody stupid!

She'd fucked up, and I was now heading into some unnecessary drama. In official terms, I still had joint parental responsibility over Lloyd. All this time, I'd just had no idea where he was. Knowing what I knew now, I couldn't just ignore it.

I started the ignition. "OK. Cool. You got me, Haina?"

"I'm right here babe."

We drove round there.

As we pulled into the street, Haina pointed. "That's my girl's car! That one right there!"

She had some little knowledge of the girl Aidan had started seeing after we split, and recognised her vehicle straight off. There was nowhere to park in view of the house, so I drove past a couple times, looking for any signs of life. Someone at a window, maybe, or a light flicking on.

"Looks dead," I said.

"Park up at the end of the road."

I reversed into a parking space and we sat there for a couple of minutes. My thoughts were racing. The address was right, the car was right – but what the fuck was I gonna do if Lloyd was home?

Hi baby! Have you missed your mummy?!

Would he be frightened? Would he even recognise me? Where did we go from there?

I couldn't stand it any longer. "Come on," I said. "Let's go knock it."

We walked down the street to the house, and then up a short tarmac driveway. I glanced in the front window to see if anyone was home, then knocked on the door. We listened out for footsteps, but I felt like I couldn't hear a thing over my pounding heartbeat. We waited, I knocked again, waited some more.

Haina shrugged: *What now?*

I flicked open the letterbox and had a peek through. Again, it looked like no one was home.

"I dunno about this…" I said. "Don't you need to be back at work anyway?"

"I'm cool. It's up to you though. You wanna go, we'll go. You wanna stay, I'm with you."

We tried knocking a couple neighbours to see if they knew who lived there, but it all sounded pretty vague. Drawing blanks, we headed back to the car. I slumped into the driver's seat and slapped the steering wheel, then rested my head against it for a moment. This was torture. I'd had some anxious moments in country, but nothing compared to this. It was off the scale.

Haina turned the radio on. "We just wait," she said. "As long as it takes."

We'd been sat there maybe two or three hours, when a car turned into the street and rolled right by us. Haina grabbed my arm and said breathlessly, "That's her!"

"What the fuck!"

"She must have slipped out the other end of the street!" Haina said.

As the car threaded its way between the rows of parked vehicles, I could just about make out the top of a little boy's head through the rear windscreen.

"That's Lloyd!" I gasped as tears welled in my eyes. "Oh my God, Haina. It's him!"

The car pulled into a parking space outside the house and I blindly scrabbled to open my door. Me and Haina jumped out and ran over. By now, tears were streaming down my face. As I got to the car, I could see Lloyd in the back, sat in his car seat. I grabbed for the car door handle and gave it a tug, but the door was locked. Then Lloyd saw me and his face crumpled. "Mummy! Mummy!" he yelled.

It was more than I could bear. The next few moments are a blur as I fell to the tarmac, a mess of sobs, while Haina tried to placate Aidan's girlfriend. She couldn't understand why we were there, or how we'd got their address. All I remember is the rough tarmac under my knees and Lloyd's voice, seemingly coming from way off, as he wailed inside the car.

I was still on the floor when another car pulled into the street. This time, it was Aidan behind the wheel. And as he got out, his girlfriend drove away – with my son on board.

Once again, my son was gone.

Aidan was as calm and collected as ever. "What are you doing here, Danielle?" he asked. "How did you get this address?"

"I just want to see my son!" I said. "Where is he?"

"You can't be here," Aidan said.

As we argued, more of the family showed up. I was in the middle of it, a crying heap, getting nowhere. In the end, Haina put her hands up and said, "OK, enough. Let's just go. Come on babe."

Haina helped me to the car and we drove back to mine. I felt like absolute shit, heartbroken. She stayed a while, then Dajuan came over. Situations like that, he always knew what to say.

"This isn't gonna last forever," he told me. "You carried that boy for nine months – he knows you're his mum."

"I can't see an end to it."

"I'm telling you though – that bond can never be broken. You'll always have that."

Next steps, my plan was to just monitor the house.

"What you thinking?" Haina asked me next time I saw her.

"Let's go back in a couple months' time, sit outside and see what's going on over there."

We did exactly that.

But by now, the place was deserted. Lloyd was gone.

I was at a loss. Some people around me said I should find Aidan's car and stick a tracking device on it. Stupid idea. I wasn't gonna do that.

And there was no way I could go court.

Fact check: I was a drug dealer.

I think that was the moment the seed was sown for me turning my back on the life. There was no conscious decision at that stage, but the idea had burrowed deep and, in my heart, I knew I couldn't sustain it forever. I had to be in the best position possible if I wanted to get my son back.

In the meantime, though, a voice in my head was telling me, *go get your money.*

I wrapped some drugs, got back on my grind.

OT.

I was in country with Dajuan when his mobile lit up. He took the call.

"Wagwan my guy?" I saw his face drop and then he clamped a hand over his temples. "What fucking shooting?" he said. "Who's been shot?"

My heart plunged into my stomach.

"All right, keep me updated, yeah?" He hung up.

"The fuck?" I said. "What's going on?"

"That was Mally. Someone from the ends been shot OT. Dead. Couple of our lot gone jail."

"They done the shooting?"

"Don't know. This is a mess."

"What d'you wanna do?"

"Let's get back to London."

On the drive home, I turned this news over in my head. My nerves tightened and that familiar knot of anxiety bloomed in my chest. Someone taking a bullet demanded a response. At that stage, we had no idea what was what, but I was worried there would be repercussions. Bloody repercussions. What was going to happen to my man? Was he gonna go do something crazy and get nicked himself?

These things rarely stopped at one shooting. There was always some back and forth. Shit always got messy.

Between taking calls, Dajuan pondered on next steps. I didn't envy the responsibility that came with his position. He was always happiest just making his money, or planning making his money. Problem was there was always some stupid little hood politics getting in the way, some argument to resolve, or some external beef threatening the safety of the group – or needing an answer.

"Do we know who it is yet?" I asked him.

Dajuan told me a name. I knew him from around the area, back when we were 10-year-old kids scraping our palms sore swinging on the climbing frame and buying ice pops from the corner shop. He wasn't part of our circle, so whatever he'd been doing OT, he had his own thing going, but it didn't make sense that a couple of our lot would take him out.

"We're gonna make sure his mum and girl are looked after innit," said Dajuan.

The mood in the ends was low. There'd been murders in our bit of London before, but this was the first time I'd actually known the boy. The threat of violence hung round the hood like some sewer stink on a hot summer's day. You pushed it to the back of your mind with the good times, the nice clothes, jewellery and cash – but it was always there.

One time, I'd been on the high road when shots rang out from a drive-by. A scream went up as a young girl caught a stray bullet. Luckily, she survived, but I remember it happening so quick, all I did was jump at the noise. There was barely time to react, let alone take cover. And I'd been in the club before when the night got shut down because boys started shooting. Gun play in them ratchet clubs was a normal occurrence.

The feds made progress on the boy's murder, and news got back that our guys had been picked up just because they'd been in the house where it went down. They would spend some time on remand while loose ends were tied up, but they were in the clear. Arrests followed, and the police got the actual shooters cooling off in jail awaiting their day in court.

I breathed a sigh of relief.

OK, cool. No one's gonna go off doing crazy revenge shit now.

Saying goodbye in the ends was a big deal and once the police had done what they had to do with forensics, the boy's body was released for the funeral. Our lot put money in the kitty. On the day, everyone wore white. Some people had T-shirts with the boy's face printed on. I remember standing outside the church – I couldn't get inside because there were that many people – and hearing this animal-like scream. I never heard anything like it in my life. It was the boy's girlfriend, just howling in pain, cut to the absolute corc. It broke me, that sound, and then I burst into tears, too.

Weirdly, knowing someone who got shot didn't make me feel unsafe in the life I was living. In our bit of the ends, with Dajuan, I always felt safe and protected. And it turned out this boy's death was nothing to do with territory or dealing drugs. It all came down to a boy he knew sleeping with the wrong girl. Just being friends with some other kid had cost him his life. Insane.

After a funeral, it was traditional to have what we called a Nine Night, a celebration in honour of the person's life.

Any event we went to, there was guns coming with us. No disrespect, but this was no different, regardless of how this poor boy died. For us, there was no going to a big occasion without guns. It just wasn't safe.

The way it worked, there would be two or three gunmen who carried the guns for everyone, maybe two straps each, in a man bag, ready to distribute among the group if things went left. They would be what we called shop boys. *Hey, run down the shop and get me a Mars bar.* That's a shop boy.

Part of their job was to absorb the risk of getting banged up for firearms, and they would get some little money for their trouble – not a salary as such but they were looked after and their shit would be paid for. Weed. Bills. Phone. That way, if police come, it's only a couple little shop boys going jail instead of six olders.

Nine Nights were for celebration as well as remembrance. Big venue, plenty food and all comers welcome. They usually bumped along until the early hours of the morning. Emotions and tensions were always running hot, you pour some booze on the flames and – boom!

I didn't see the argument, but there was some beef among the group, among our lot. I was minding my own business, drinking a Coke, when one of the boys came running over. "D! D! Go get your car and bring it round the front."

"What's going on?"

"No time to chat. The police are coming. Go."

I didn't need telling twice. I grabbed the car and swung round to the front of the venue as the wail of police sirens closed rapidly in. The boy come running out the place: "Open your window! Open your window!"

I did as he said – and he tossed in a gun, to land on the passenger seat right beside me. It had been wrapped in a bandana, but the cloth slipped off as it came through the window, so it wasn't even covered up.

Gun.

In my car.

Police on the way.

"Go and put it down!" he said. "Go!"

I'd seen guns before, held one before. I'd been in the room when them lot were wrapping guns up to put them away. One sawn-off shotgun and a couple handguns. I'm not into guns, but, not gonna lie, I had been intrigued and so I'd picked up the handgun and waved it around, pretending I was shooting people. Just to see what a gun felt like in the hand.

It had felt heavy. And dangerous.

Only now I had one on my passenger seat with bare feds pouring into the area. I picked it up and stuck it under the seat. Lame, I know, but there was nowhere else to put it.

I set off driving, mind racing. If I got stopped, I was looking at five years' jail. Five-year sentence, do three.

I thought, *Do I drive slowly and avoid drawing attention, or just floor it all the way home and get the fuck out of here?*

I floored it. It was one scary drive, fuelled by fear and anger – I'd had a gun dumped on me and I wasn't generally known as someone who deals with hiding guns. But at that time, I was so compliant. I wasn't going to make a fuss about it.

I drove to the garages – one of the places where our lot kept guns – and phoned one boy who told me exactly where and how to hide it. They had multiple locations across the ends, and a select few people knew where they were. Boys always wanted to buy a gun with their first savings from drug money. If they didn't have one and needed a strap for whatever shooting or robbery they were scheming, they had to go through a certain person who might give them permission to go grab one or two from the stash.

Anyway, the boy directed me to this hiding spot. I was eager to get rid of this gun. I cleaned it down to remove my fingerprints, dug in the dirt in a specific spot as instructed and put my hand down the hole, then up inside to push the gun into a gap behind the wall. I could feel there were at least a couple other guns already there in the hiding spot.

Back at home, I headed out on the block to catch up with the boys – but I couldn't get this gun thing out of my head.

"What if my prints are still on it?!" I said to Paul.

"Did you wipe it down?"

"Well, yeah, but what do I know about guns? What if I didn't do it right?"

"If you wiped it down, you're good. Don't worry!" Paul said.

All those straps were dirty: they'd been bought from all over the place and used in God knows what shootings even before they came to my people. So my worry was this one particular gun getting found and somehow linking back to me. Suddenly police want to speak to you about something that happened five years ago in a city you've never been to.

"I'm not sure though," I said to Paul. "Will you go get it for me? Clean it down?"

"No need. You're good!"

"Please!" I said, begging him.

"Now you're just being annoying," said Paul. "But OK, if it's gonna keep you quiet, I'll go."

I'm under no illusions. He probably never did.

20

THE SHOW GOES ON

Neat rows of cash covered my living-room floor – stacks of notes worth £100 each, arranged 10 stacks to a row, so each one was worth a grand. I counted the cash in my hand and put another £100 down on the rug. We'd totted up about £70k. It had been a good few weeks OT and we were putting together the funds to reload on a couple fresh bricks of heroin.

I went through to the bathroom to wash my hands, working the soap between my fingers. A big count like that one always left a layer of foul-smelling grime on my hands. The water in my sink turned black – our money was, quite literally, dirty.

"Where's the counter, D?" I heard Dajuan call from the living room.

"In the drawer under the TV."

Between the group, we were turning over so much cash that electronic counters had become a necessity, and we kept one in a few of our key money-drop houses. Dajuan turned ours on and ran cash through it, double-checking the manual count. The machine stacked up the notes with a satisfying whir and we snapped elastic bands around each £1k billfold, putting them down until the re-up was due.

Dajuan's drugs were on the street through various shotters in cities around the UK, and he was banking something like £8k a week profit. Long term, his plan was to move to a more hands-off operation, stepping off the country grind and simply acting as the drug connect to people like me who wanted to work OT.

Money flooded back from country in various ways, and there was no set routine – it depended on how business was going, who was around, who was doing what. Sometimes a runner or one of the girlfriends would drive up from London to grab a carrier bag full of money folds and go put it down in whoever's house. If I was in the city and bored, couple times I'd go country myself and bring cash back, just for the drive. If it was a busy time OT we might throw the money down in a pile, stuff it in a bag and split it up when we got back to London. The better option – which we always aimed for – was to be efficient and organised, keeping the money counted and shuttling it back to the ends in values of no more than £5k a time. But if we were busy on the grind, and a couple weeks slipped by, we could easily find ourselves on the motorway with £15k cash in the car.

Which was not cool.

I hated rolling with that much money. It's not illegal to carry cash, but that's how it felt. Driving around with a pile of money gave me a feeling of dread, like something was gonna go wrong – even if I wasn't carrying drugs. Plus, having that much cash in your car looks bait. I didn't need the heat or the attention. I'd been stopped before with maybe a few grand on me – enough to arouse suspicion – but always managed to find a friend with a legit job who'd vouch for having given me a cash loan.

The other tool we'd use for getting our cash back to London – and 'use' is exactly the right word for this situation – was the country girlfriends.

A lot of the boys had girlfriends and baby mums back in the ends. They had kids, homes, responsibilities. And plenty of them also had secret, second lives OT. When their girlfriends in the ends kissed them goodbye before another country excursion, they were sending them off to another woman in country.

Our London boys held a special attraction OT, and the country girls found their charms irresistible. Half the time they were so gassed to hear a London accent, a boy only had to lean out the window, ask for their number, and they were putty in his hands. Our guys said they were looser than the girls back home quick to chat with them, and more 'free' – if you catch my drift. They didn't really care what these girls looked like either. They served a purpose: clean house, comfy bed, sex, somewhere to stash drugs. And mule cash back to the ends. On demand.

Say if we'd had a good run and were loaded down with money, we'd send a girl to London with half, and bring the rest ourselves a day later.

"Go take this 10 grand and put it here."

I never saw a single girl say no, because she would be just in awe of this man.

At first, these girls really took to me. "Oh wow! You're from London! Lemme see your Louis bag!" But after a while, jealousy crept in – because I was on the road all hours of the night with the boy who they thought was theirs. Now they saw me as a threat. "Oh yeah? You're with D again are you?" And then there'd be some fall out.

They didn't appreciate that we were only there to do business, and they were part of that machine, dutifully taking bags of money to whatever drop-house address we gave them back in London. In a way, I felt sorry for them. They were the real victims of country – not me. I was there by choice. But they were sold a dream. "Oh yeah, I want you to be my girl." All bullshit. They were tricked into doing what we wanted them to do, all under false pretences. They didn't even get paid. It was all done for the illusion of love.

Buying in new batches of drugs was now a streamlined process, designed to minimise the risk and exposure to us. There seemed to be a never-ending supply of cocaine via Jordan which was cooked up into crack in the microwave on demand. The flow was constant. Vac-packed bricks of heroin, often covered in gift wrap like some bizarre birthday present, arrived from the connect via courier, usually one of his little young bucks in a taxi carrying a JD bag.

Before we put it on the street, we had a local heroin connoisseur come test a new batch and tell us if it was the real deal. Our supplier was solid: we'd spent hundreds of thousands of pounds with the guy and built up a rapport over years. If the batch was low quality, or the texture was a bit off – what we called 'dusty' – it went back for a refund, no questions asked.

One batch came in and we could tell it was a weird one as soon as Dajuan slit open the brick.

"Colour don't look right," he said. "And the smell is off too."

"Let me see," said our tester dude. He was an old hand, with years of experience using heroin. He was never wrong.

He spooned a little onto a strip of foil and sparked up a disposable lighter. The heroin melted reddish-brown over its dancing yellow flame.

"It's burning red – you see?" he said, before sucking up a curl of smoke. He gasped, his breath taken away for a moment by the intensity of the rush.

"Power," he nodded. "My guess is it's cut with fentanyl."

Fentanyl.

That's the killer one.

It's like a synthetic heroin, but it's mad, mad potent.

"If you're putting it out, tell your customers it's only for smoking," our guy counselled.

The sale went through, we hit the clingfilm, wrapped up some G-packs and took the new gear OT to our usual spot. Serving up our regular shoots, we knew who usually injected. "This one is mad powerful," I told Jane, Ezra and the rest. "You can't inject, OK? You gotta be careful."

Some took the warning on board.

Others thought they knew better.

Between phone orders, we started getting calls about near misses. "What the fuck, mate? Nearly died last night off that gear!"

Then there was this one guy and his girlfriend, both in their 30s. They both injected. The guy bought off us and came back for more a few days later.

"Yeah, it's fire that one!" he said. "I only smoked it." He took another couple pebs.

The next morning the line rang and this time it was his girlfriend. We thought she was just sticking another order in for more drugs, but instead she was in floods of tears. "He's died," she stammered between sobs. "He's overdosed."

He'd injected it.

She wasn't angry, it was like she was just informing us. Thinking about that now – about the role we played in the guy dying – is painful. At the time, part of me felt sad and part of me felt like, *but we told you – don't inject it.* Dajuan though, he had a big heart and he was broken. We rolled around town working out what to do next, as Dajuan chewed it over on the phone with someone back in the ends.

"We can't be killing people, bro. We got to stop selling it," he said.

The call was on speakerphone. "Nah, keep going innit. Just finish it off," the boy replied.

Dajuan decided though, whatever was left we'd just take the hit on it. We were in the drugs business, but we weren't on killing people.

After that rogue batch, Dajuan must have been keeping an ear to the ground for a new heroin connect. He called me one morning: "Fancy a road trip?"

"Yeah cool, whatever." I knew it wasn't country business. "Where we going?"

"South. Wear something cute, yeah?"

"OK."

Cute as in, *I want you to make an impression*. Whatever was going down, it was quite a big to-do. I can't remember what I was wearing that day, but 'cute' at that time would have been jeans, a little top and designer belt and shoes.

I drove round Dajuan's. A couple boys were already waiting there in another car – one of them I recognised as a big-time heroin connect. He rarely got his hands dirty, was never short of money and spent most of the year overseas. I never clocked him doing business with Dajuan, but they were good friends and they'd get together to scheme from time to time. Whatever conversations they had – they were way above my pay grade.

Mr Big Time was coming along for the ride. I remember there was confusion over the meet because none of us had ever really ventured south of the river before. I swapped out my car and slid behind the wheel of a plush BMW 3 series that Dajuan had on a long-term rental for whoever fancied a little prestige motoring. He had a few of these smart rentals parked in the area and if the boys wanted to use one – to impress some girl, for example – they only had to ask nicely. I think it was a more-money-than-sense kind of vibe; I never blew my own cash renting fancy cars.

We pulled up in a street in South London, and not long after, a Range Rover swung in behind us.

"Wait here," Dajuan said.

He climbed out and together with Mr Big he got in the Range with this potential new connect, an Arabian-looking man. What they discussed over the following half an hour, I don't know. Most likely volumes and prices. We never came away with food that day and I never saw the guy again. Possibly he gave Dajuan a sample to test with our local guinea pig and it turned out to be rubbish, because the regular connect came through the very next week with new drugs. I'd got all dressed up for nothing. I didn't even see the point of me being there.

There'd always been a music community around our lot, making up raps and putting them with a beat – it was a hobby, a nice stress reliever. The boys would go studio, turning the place into a hotbox as they chilled on the sofas, smoking spliff after spliff and making the air thick with smoke. They rapped about their lives. Same shit – money, drugs, girls. Literally what was on the doorstep. I never heard anyone get deep with a love song.

Some of the boys were shit, but a few really shone. A couple in particular.

They had something. Talent.

Even though no one was really taking this stuff seriously, around the time I started going country, a few names started getting known. Boys like the rapper I'm calling Warren became hood famous. We were telling him, "This is cold! You're actually really good."

Warren was intelligent and relaxing to be around, but his mean streak was never far below the surface. It came out if he wasn't getting his way, because he was so used to being surrounded by people who said "yes" to everything.

To us, it was no revelation that he had musical talent. Warren was already *the guy*. His family name meant he had a reputation to live up to, and he filled those big shoes from young. Alongside a certain business acumen, he had the star quality, the charisma. He was destined to become the face of the area. But even though he probably wouldn't admit it, Warren's confidence was low. He wouldn't have it. "Nah, you lot are chatting shit."

Who was right? Him, or us?

The buzz grew. The word spread.

As big artists sat up and took notice, the music got traction beyond the confines of the block, beyond London even. Radio plays, record deals and an army of fans followed – bringing everything that comes with music business success.

Early Warren music-video shoots had been amateur efforts, funded out of his own pocket – a handful of boys, couple bottles of alcohol and a guy with a camera. But as his fame grew, a Warren video shoot became a hood-wide, major event, with a record label budget behind it. We had Porsches, Lamborghinis on the ends for filming. It brought a good energy to the block – street party. Jerks going on

The buzz built over a couple of weeks. *Video shoot. Saturday 15th. Get ready!* Ready meant get some designer clothes; if your watch is in Hatton getting cleaned – go grab it, get your chains and ready-up your jewellery. Boys go get your hair done. Girls go get your hair done.

As a drug dealer, I didn't want to be in a music video that millions of people might see. Way too hot. I had Insta at the time and I was already getting DMs from randoms in places like Bolton – just off the back of the hood being famous. "Oh, do you know Warren? Do you know so and so…" I didn't need the exposure. But even though I wasn't going in front of the camera, I always put on a nice dress and did my hair, just because I knew it was going to be a party.

Shoot day, unless they were really on their grind, everyone came back from country. That aspect of it was nice. *Everyone's here, everyone's safe, we're all together.* Filming took long – like 12 hours long. I'd drop in and out because there was lots of standing around between the action while they did changes and set up scenes – and I didn't have time to stand in that all day. More times, Haina came with me too because she was into the vibe. Warren never left anyone out – he had a barbecue or a jerk pan going and anyone who wanted to come fill their belly or have a drink was welcome.

For the youngers, having those dreams of big money, gleaming supercars and music-biz glamour pop into life right on their doorstep – while the streets echoed with lyrics about selling drugs – was without a doubt alluring. And dangerous.

This is attainable. Get on your grind, get that P, and all this could be yours.

I was in a different position: I'd been shotting since long before the Ferraris started growling up and down the block. I wasn't allured or dazzled, but for people like me who were already on the grind – in a 'gang' – being part of these shoots and the party vibe around them was necessary to let off steam. To have fun and relax for maybe just one day of the year. Even then, anyone local with a big name and hood reputation wore a bullet-proof vest at these shoots. Some of us didn't know it – plenty still don't – but we were all suffering PTSD. If it makes people happy to come together to shoot a video, then that's a good thing. I see why boys in this life do this stuff, I get why they spend money frivolously. They're all going through trauma.

Warren was generous with his success and he got a buzz out of sharing it with his friends. As his music spread, he was in hot demand for performances. For us, that meant a free night out. It was a privilege.

I called Haina: "Wanna come? Free show."

"I'm there!"

30 cars lined up in the estate. It was ridiculous. We were shipping out in convoy to see Warren do his thing in one university town. Anyone who wasn't driving got allocated a lift, and one little gunman thought I was his ride for the night.

"No, no, no," I said, because I knew he was one of two boys carrying a gun. Multiple people wanted to bring their guns. Someone had to do the honours.

But not me.

"You're gonna have to find another car," I told him.

By now, I was driving a Mercedes A-class. I'd bumped the Audi so many times – and I was so bougie – that I couldn't be bothered fixing it. Plus, I'd got ban after ban in that car. It was too bait.

"I was told to get a lift with you!" the boy said. He was sat in the back of my Merc. He peeled his pack off his back and settled its considerable weight in the footwell. Bare guns.

"I don't give a fuck. No way I'm driving with guns – come out my car."

One of the boys came over and tried sweet-talking me around. "Come on, D. No one wants him in their car, fam."

Not this time. I was standing my ground. "I'll stay in the ends, man. I don't care! He ain't coming with me."

There was some kerfuffle, lots of side-eye in my direction accompanied by kissing of teeth. End result: little gunman came out my car and got into someone else's. I took a couple of YGs who couldn't yet drive.

We rolled out. In convoy.

In theory, this was a good idea because it meant everyone knew where they were going and everyone arrived en masse at the same time.

In practice: major hassle.

Soon as we set off, everyone's gotta go petrol station. Everyone's gotta queue. I drummed my manicured nails on the steering wheel as we waited in line.

"What time's he on?" Haina said, glancing at her watch.

"Don't!" I said, then laughed. "These boys can't organise shit!"

Finally, we hit the motorway and managed to get to the venue in one piece. Walked to the club. Round the back to the artists' entrance. By this time, the guns had been distributed to their owners. There was security on the door but no one was checking the entourage for weapons. We breezed through with enough hardware to equip a small army.

We hit the green room, but we were already so late there was barely time for drinks before Warren got called on stage. Maybe 25 of us joined him. Me and Haina stayed near the back, sat on a ledge at the side, looking out over a sea of sweaty, student heads.

The beat dropped in. Warren prowled around the stage, spitting his rhymes. Some of the boys postured and strutted in the background, beefing up the whole stage-presence vibe. Already they had plucked some little groupie-type girls out the crowd and had them on the stage, sweet-talking and dancing with them.

Stood just in front of us was the little gunman who'd tried to get in my car, and I knew he had a strap. Young buck, remember. Still finding his way.

The crowd was bouncing, usual mad crush at the front. Then, all of a sudden, a boy jumped out of the audience and vaulted up on stage. Next thing, he took a swipe at Warren's chain, trying to snatch it off his neck.

This was a cardinal sin. Sacrilege.

Warren took a step back and dodged the grab, but the young buck by me and Haina didn't hesitate. He had that strap out and aimed at the stage raider in a split second.

Time shifted, slipped into queasy slow motion.

I looked across the stage where one of the older boys was motioning to the young buck, shouting, trying to make himself heard above the pounding bass: "No! Don't fucking buss it! Put the gun away!"

Then everyone on stage started panicking – they'd seen the gun. It was surreal. Beat was still throbbing. Lights flashing. And we're all on show doing a headless chicken act thinking someone's getting shot.

By now, the stage-raider dude had got some of his little boys up there with him and they'd started punching it out with our lot.

Warren clocked the gun, dropped his mic and gathered people up. "Come on, get your stuff. We're leaving. Go!"

I grabbed Haina. "Let's go babe," and we just cut, heading for the door at the back, where one groupie girl was dithering in the doorway, blocking the exit.

"What's going on?" she said, rubbernecking around. A sniff of drama had put a dumb grin on her face.

I gave her a nudge. "Can you move please? We're going?"

"Why's everyone going? What's going on?"

I stopped short of telling her, *because someone's about to get shot* and gave her a shove instead. "Just come out my way!"

And then we were through the green room and out into the night.

Thank God, no shots were fired. The young buck with the gun was a compliant dude, he looked for instruction before doing anything. One of the elders had ordered him not to shoot, and he'd done as he was told. Could easily have gone the other way: if they'd told him to pull the trigger, he'd have unloaded that burner, crowd or no crowd.

The chaos spilled into the street outside. Couple people got bottles wrapped around their heads. Anyone who didn't want to join in the madness made their way to their cars – me, Warren and Haina included.

"Fuck music," Warren said. "No money is worth this shit for someone to get killed. This is ridiculous! It don't make sense!"

I had to agree.

And anyway, the music business was a fickle industry. I was cool doing what I was doing. Selling drugs was a damn sight easier.

21

POSTCODE

London's a small town in the hood world, a patchwork of beefs and petty rivalries where connections are everything. Who you know, who you're around and where you're from – it's all life and death. Little things – like what boy your second cousin is sleeping with – take on an insane and potentially deadly importance. The streets be talking, they say. But, their message shifts all the time. You have to keep your ear to the ground if you want to understand their intricate dangers.

In West London in 2015, if you were part of this culture, the safest bet was to stay in your own area. Just walking down the wrong street could get you slapped, stabbed or shot. A five or ten-mile radius round our blocks was basically a no-go zone, and it didn't stop there.

Some of the people who didn't get on with us had affiliations in the East End, so certain areas there were off limits, too. Same story south of the river. Even then, even if you managed to get a handle on the Google map of London 'gang' wars, all it took was some rival's uncle or brother to move to a new postcode, and then you had problems there, too. This shit ran so deep that if, say, Haina had her eye on some prospective new boyfriend, we'd have to have a conversation.

Where's he from? Who does he know? Who's his family?

Because she'd been in rooms that she maybe shouldn't have been. She'd heard secrets that could make her a target.

Even now, my original block is a dirty secret. Boys I've been with don't want to talk about where I'm from, because they know their friends will warn them off.

Don't be around her. She'll bring you trouble.

The origins of these problems went back years, to long before my generation was even born. No one knew what anyone was fighting about anymore. The grudges were inherited. I only knew this stuff because I'd listened to the streets.

One thing I'm sure of, this violence rarely had anything to do with trapping. Yeah – I'd been at the sharp end of it when my flat got shot up, but my lot were on making money. Selling drugs was a business, a career. If violence needed to happen, there was always a discussion, always someone trying to be rational about it, trying to limit it. I wasn't party to these conversations. I sold drugs – I wasn't a getaway driver or a shooter. Guns and knives were to my mind – and theirs – a man's world. I knew what food was coming in and when, where it was going, who was due back from OT and who was wrapping up to go. But those occasions when boys went to the garages, leaving their phones behind at home, were never spoken of. The fewer people who know what you're up to, the better, because the streets be talking. Sooner or later they give up your secrets.

In all my time, I can't remember an occasion when someone was chatting, "Let's go get this guy," just for the sake of it. Violence brings heat. It just gets in the way of making money.

Violence also left its mark on us all. Physically, of course, but mentally, too. Living life constantly on edge because of hate from another 'gang' and being exposed to violent situations, or being victims of violence ourselves, left me and so many of my people with deep, ingrained trauma. The vibe was, *we're in a war.*

Boys rolled with bullet and stab-proof vests. I knew guys too afraid to sleep on the ground floor in case someone bust in through the window and unloaded a gun on them. Jail men who still woke religiously at 6am, even when they weren't locked up. They wanted to be treated, helped, like soldiers coming back from an actual war. I gave my shoulder to many of them to cry on. Beyond that, they didn't know where to go for help, or where to ask.

So the violence continued.

It could come out of anywhere, when you were least expecting it.

I was home chilling with Haina one night. We had nothing planned so we were slobbed in our PJs watching *Love Island* on catch up. It was already late. I had one eye on the beach bodies parading on my TV screen and another on my Snapchat.

"Do you think he loves me," I said to Haina. I was having doubts about Dajuan.

"Does he say he does?"

"Yeah, but…"

"But what? I've told that boy he better not mess you around. He better treat you right!" That girl always had my corner. "Has something happened?" she asked.

I thought about the time a few weeks back, when I'd walked in Dajuan's house and spotted a pair of false eye lashes on his bedroom windowsill, sat there like a pair of dead spiders. It had felt like a punch in the belly. There – staring me in the face – was a conversation I was unwilling to have, an ugly truth I wasn't ready to confront. I'd opened the window and tossed them out.

What eyelashes?

Never happened.

Same as the message on his Facebook. *Thanks for last night. I'm covered in love bites though – my mum's gonna kill me.*

Never saw it.

I thought of all the rumours reaching my ears – those talking streets again – about Dajuan and other girls.

"Nah, it's cool," I said, pushing those thoughts away.

"D?" Haina probed. "Come on."

"Forget about it," I said, and swiped on through Snapchat. I seen a few boys we knew were out and messaged one: *Where you all at? What's poppin'?*

He fired back, *In the club. Come.*

I told Haina. "What you saying? I could go out. You wanna go out?"

"You know me. Let's go."

We got ready, jumped in my car. It was already 1am by the time we got there and the doormen had secured the venue. "Sorry girls, you can't come in."

Yeah, we can, I thought.

I messaged the boys. *We're outside. They won't let us in.*

Few minutes later, security had a change of heart. A couple of palms got greased and all of a sudden it was open sesame.

We had a good night. Haina had her little drinks, I caught up with some of the group. Everyone was cool. Boys wearing their chains, flashing new sets of grills. There was no edge, no threat, nothing bookey going down. Just a good vibe.

Until we left.

The club spilled out onto the street and everyone began making their way back to their cars. I was a way down the road with Haina when we heard shouting behind us.

"Hang on," I said to Haina. "Let me just go back. All my people are there."

"Sure."

We walked up the street, following the noise, to find a loose mob of people. In the centre was one of my friends, Jermaine, grappling with a random guy who was stabbing him over and over again in the back. It was surreal – here was one of our people getting stabbed up, while everyone stood around with their mouths open catching flies.

"Hey!" I yelled, elbowing my way through the growing crowd.

"D! Where you going?" Haina said, trying to snatch up my hand.

"Can't just leave him, man. The boy's gonna fucking kill him!"

I pushed through into the middle and grabbed hold of the knifeman. He was a tall guy and really strong. One fist gripped a four-inch kitchen knife.

"Get the fuck off him!" I screamed, seeing red. "What the fuck are you doing?!" Fury pulsed through me from my toes to my fingertips. I didn't give a moment's thought for my own safety.

And *now*, as if some spell had been broken, everyone else began shouting, "Get off him! Leave him alone."

Knifeman took a step back, weighing things up. Meanwhile, Jermaine collapsed to his knees, one tattooed arm supporting his weight, gold chain swinging out from his black T-shirt.

I took a stance between him and the knifeman, who now stared me down. I was like a mama bear shielding her cub. My desire to protect this boy came from deep inside. It was innate. But I was just a little girl with a rage on, and he was a six-foot-something thug armed with a knife!

"Do what you're doing then!" I yelled. "Come stab me!"

Looking back, I don't know what compelled me to taunt him. Dumb move. But, actually, it worked. The knifeman wasn't on it no more. He turned and ran – and the crowd surged after him, snatching up bricks from the floor and launching them in his direction.

Jermaine struggled to his feet. "I'm OK," he said, then groaned and clutched his side. "I don't even know why he was punching me, fam. What's the boy's problem?"

"I dunno. Come here, let me look at you," I said.

Haina joined me, and together we helped Jermaine limp to a side alley. He slumped heavily against the wall and let go a moan as his body succumbed to a shivering fit.

"Nah, I feel mad dizzy."

"You know you been stabbed, right?" I said.

Panic flashed on Jermaine's face. "I thought he just punched me!"

Where he'd been knifed in the back, he couldn't actually see his injuries.

"Can I look?"

"Yeah, tell me how bad it is."

I lifted his shirt, already slick and heavy. Jermaine was riddled with stab wounds, pouring blood. One – on his flank towards the back of his ribs – hung open, revealing bone and glistening, yellow fat. A clear liquid oozed.

"Yeah, it's fine," I lied. "It's just a scratch." The last thing I wanted to do was send him into shock. In truth, I thought he'd probably got a punctured lung. "I'm just gonna put some pressure on it and then we're going to the hospital, OK?"

Jermaine nodded. I think he even believed me.

Haina was looking at me: *what the fuck?*

Poor girl. More fun and games on a night out with Danielle.

I flashed her a look back, shook my head imperceptibly. *Just follow my lead. OK?*

She was stood in front of Jermaine, holding his hand. "Just breathe," she said. "You're going to be fine."

By now, he was struggling to get his breath. The one big wound was gushing blood and shit. I had to put some real pressure on it. We weren't rolling with a first-aid kit so I had to improvise. It seemed the most natural thing to do: I took my dress off and wrapped it around Jermaine's body.

What else was I gonna do? I was in a tight little dress: the stretchy material was perfect for a makeshift bandage. I tied it firm around his torso and managed to cover most of his wounds – but the worst ones still bled through in moments. I couldn't have cared less that I was stood there in my bra and knickers. *This is my friend,* I thought. *He's not gonna die today.*

We helped him to my car and laid him down across the back seat. Luckily, I had a few spare clothes in the boot from trips OT – pair of joggers and a hoodie. I put them on and drove to A&E.

I pulled up outside, before Haina and me struggled in with Jermaine draped between us. "I need help! My friend's been stabbed!" I yelled.

"If you could take a seat in the waiting room and someone will be with you shortly," said the receptionist.

"Waiting room? My friend's been stabbed!"

"It's a Saturday night. We're very busy," she shrugged.

We waited with Jermaine until a triage nurse came over five minutes later. She decided his injuries were serious enough to be seen to immediately.

"Do you want me to stay?" I asked him. "Or can I ring someone?"

"Can you stay?"

"Yeah sure."

Jermaine gave a false name and they took him in to get stitched up. Later, we were allowed backstage to see him. Besides the stitches criss-crossing his back like crazy train tracks, he had a tube draining fluid from the nasty gash on his side.

"He needs to stay in for the night, until the drain's ready to come out," the nurse told us. We all nodded. "And the police are on their way to take a statement."

"Sure, thank you," I nodded again,

The nurse left.

"I'm not talking to the police. Get me out of here," Jermaine said.

"Yup. Let's go," I replied.

Jermaine says to this day that he'd be dead if it hadn't been for me and my little dress. I don't know if that's true, but I did feel proud. We never found out why he'd been stabbed. Maybe just random jealousy. Perhaps the guy liked the look of that nice chain looped over Jermaine's neck, perhaps Jermaine liked the look of the wrong girl and the guy took it to heart. But note how Jermaine didn't want police. That was standard. No one wanted feds, even if they were a victim. Street justice rolled around eventually – or not. Regardless, police involvement was to be avoided at all costs.

One guy from our ends, Reon, got shot five times and wouldn't even go hospital. He was like the man with a hundred lives. Reon had been shot and stabbed so many times over the years, no one knew how he was even still standing. He was a guy with many talents who was as good at hacking computers as he was stripping and cleaning guns. Like Paul, he was a total gunman. He *loved* guns – they were his favourite thing. And he was one of the rare ones that loved violence. He lived for it. He was the madman who people went to to do their mad business. If someone needed a shooting doing, they better go to Reon because he would get it done. "Oh, shooting? Yeah, cool. Where am I going?"

He was short, stocky, with hand tattoos and a good-looking face. It hid some pain though, that face, because he was a tortured little soul and would openly admit to me that he was suffering from PTSD thanks to the things he'd seen and done.

He vanished from the ends for a while and when I saw him back on the block, I asked, "Where you been? Haven't seen you around in long."

"Got shot, fam. Not once, not twice – five times."

"The fuck!?"

"Still here though. Reckon I used up another one of my nine."

Reon had been south, in Wandsworth, seeing a girl. Some boys spotted him and chased him across a park, shooting at him. He took five bullets but didn't go down, circled back to his vehicle and somehow set off driving back to the ends.

"Started passing out," he told me. "Had to stop and call a cab."

"Did you go hospital?"

He shook his head.

Reon made it home and, from there, to one NHS nurse we knew who lived in the ends.

"Two of the bullets went in and out," Reon said. "She got the other three and sewed me up with a needle and thread."

He pulled up his shirt and showed the wounds. The stitching looked legit but the wounds were red and inflamed.

"Shit – you need to go hospital, man. It's the infection that's gonna get you!"

But Reon wouldn't have it. "I'm cool."

He'd told me before about a messed-up childhood, how he felt like it had shaped him to be on violence. He wanted to stop, but he couldn't. Knowing Reon, when those wounds healed, he'd have gone stalking back to Wandsworth to take his revenge. But he never told me about it. The fewer people who knew, the better, because sooner or later, those streets be talking.

22

ROBBED

London. Early hours. While most of the city slept, the hidden workers who kept its wheels turning went about their business. I loved this time of night. The Mercedes carving tarmac. Alone with my thoughts as I drove home from Dajuan's.

Swinging hard through a corner, my phone intruded on them. I didn't recognise the number, or the voice on the other end of the line. A woman's voice.

"Oh, is that Dajuan's girl?"

The hairs on the back of my neck prickled. "Yeah, it is. Why?"

"I just wanted you to know, woman to woman, that I've been seeing him."

My stomach lurched. "OK," I said, and instantly hung up. I was in such denial, I couldn't speak, certainly didn't want to know the details. It was finally happening. My relationship with Dajuan was slipping through my fingers.

I drove on under the streetlamps.

These things done in the darkness always come to light eventually, and I'd had my suspicions for a while. Maybe even from the start, if I was being honest with myself. Who knew what Dajuan got up to while I was in country? Or while he was OT and I was home in the ends? Well, someone did.

In the last six months or so, the block had been bristling with rumours about girls coming and going from his place at all hours. I'd clocked how, when his phone rang, he'd sometimes flip it over instead of answering. I'd pored over his Instagram checking what girls had liked his posts, trying to work out who he was sleeping with. It was impossible. With Dajuan's links to Warren and all the hype around our ends, he was getting more hood famous by the day. He'd racked up thousands of followers on Instagram. Everything he posted was showered with likes.

Problem was, our relationship and work lives were so entwined. I was basically sleeping with the boss, I'd run through the scenario in my head – *What if we split up? What if I stop doing this? Where would I live?*

Dajuan was paying for my car, bills, food. I was earning money off his drugs. I was totally reliant on him. If we went our separate ways, the most I'd be able to afford was a room in a shared house somewhere. He was literally funding my lifestyle and – shallow as it might sound – now I'd got to that level, I wasn't sure I could just let it all go. I felt like I couldn't really say anything about my suspicions. If I accused him of cheating, I ran the risk of him leaving me. I still loved him, but by now I was just as worried about losing my business as I was my boyfriend.

I couldn't let it go completely, though.

I was at his the next day – and dropped that bookey phone call into the conversation.

"Yeah, this weird girl rang me up and she was saying that you're seeing her or something? What's that all about?"

"Girl's chatting shit. That isn't true! You're my girl! It's only you!"

We carried on dancing around it. I knew he was lying. He knew that I knew he was lying. And he also knew I wasn't going to do anything about it.

There were two or three girls in particular that I had my suspicions about, but it wasn't the done thing to go and confront them. I was never allowed to be ratchet. The rule was: *stay classy*. Confronting another girl, causing a scene, is not classy. I had to take the high road, even if – while I was taking the high road – Dajuan was taking other girls to his bed.

The few times I tried to talk to him about what the streets were saying, he'd gaslight me. "Why are you looking for these things?" he'd say.

As though the only reason they were coming out was that I was searching for them.

The work, too, was becoming monotonous. It was nine to five vibes, but still silly hours. I was starting to feel trapped in the grind, and the shine had lost its sparkle. We'd fallen into a routine, with three little teams rotating constantly between London and country. The adrenaline jolt I used to get from the daily peril of class A drug dealing had wound down to a dull static hum, studded with the almost daily exasperation of hassle from Jump Out Gang whenever I was back in the city.

Maybe I'd even got a little bit complacent about it. Maybe I needed reminding the grind could still deliver thrills and spills, that country still had a trick or two up its sleeve.

It was a balmy evening. Dusk. I was OT with Dajuan in our usual spot; Mally was chilling in the B&B. I'd made my money and was looking forward to heading home. In my head, I was already cruising south on the motorway.

We had a couple of deliveries down what we called crack alley, where almost every house on the street bought drugs from us. Out of the blue, crackhead Tara came tottering up the street. At first I thought she'd put on weight, which was unusual for an addict, but as she drew closer I realised she was actually pregnant.

"All right, Tara?" I said as she hinged into the open car window. "Haven't seen you for a while."

She attempted a weak smile, briefly flashing her filthy, yellowing teeth. Tara may have been carrying a baby, but she had been short-changed on the pregnancy glow. Poor girl looked like a charcoal drawing.

"Yeah, I'm all right thanks," she said, and absentmindedly stroked her tummy.

"When are you due then?"

"Another three months," she said.

I nodded as we danced around the elephant in the room – we both knew the chances of her keeping this baby were hella slim.

"Look, can I get one white?" she said. She must have caught the look of horror on my face because she quickly added, "Oh, it's not for me!"

I didn't even have to think about it. True – I was a drug dealer. I sold heroin and crack cocaine, but I had my limits.

"Nah, I can't do it Tara."

She reached through the window, gripped my arm. Normally I would have recoiled, but we had history and she looked so broken.

"I looked after you, remember? When the police come? I could've grassed you up!"

Beside me, Dajuan kissed his teeth. I put a hand on his thigh to quiet him.

"I'm not gonna help you kill your baby, Tara. I'm sorry."

"Please! Please!" she cried. "Just one!"

I gently prised her fingers from my arm. "We're gonna go now, OK?" I said. "See you around, yeah? Hope it all goes OK."

She stepped back from the car, tears streaming. I started the engine, drove away, and Tara disappeared from my rear-view mirror as I turned the corner. That was the last time I saw her.

We still weren't quite done, so I pulled into a side road to meet the next shoot. Music on the stereo. Windows wound half down to let some air in the car.

"You think she'll be OK?" I said to Dajuan.

"Probably not, but there's fuck all you or me can do about it."

"She's just gonna go somewhere else."

"At least it's not on you though."

Thinking about Tara, we'd both let our concentration slip.

Neither of us saw them coming. The first I knew we were getting robbed was the gun stuck in my face. Almost like a replay of five years earlier. Only this time it was an older, white guy concealed under the black hoodie. And this time, I wasn't going quietly.

"Give me your fucking bag!" he snapped.

I had an LV bag perched on my lap. No way was he having it. I hugged it to my chest. "No! What the fuck? You can't have my bag!" Stupid, maybe, but I wasn't letting it go.

The guy reached in, gloved hands trying to wrench it from my grip.

"Get the fuck off me!" I said. This bag was new, cost the best part of a grand. "I said no!"

While this was going on on my side, two more boys were tugging at the passenger door on Dajuan's side.

The guy fighting me for my LV then spotted my holdall on the back seat – where there was *another* Louis handbag – and reached around, groping for the rear door lock. Meanwhile Dajuan had now spilled out of the car and was trading punches with his two in the street. My man gave up trying to take my stuff and went to help his two little friends fighting in the road with Dajuan.

I got out and dashed to the other side of the car to try and secure the drugs and the phone. The pack had been out. *Let me at least get them,* I thought.

"Get back in the car!" Dajuan shouted. "Just go! Drive!"

"I'm not doing that!"

Then, suddenly, this trio just cut, set off running down the street.

Dajuan pounded after them, shouting back to me, "They've got the food, fam. And the phone!"

I saw him snatch a loose brick off a wall and then disappear around the corner. All I could do was sit in the car and wait. Five minutes crawled by. Then 10. Dajuan finally reappeared.

"You OK?"

He nodded, gasping for breath.

I saw the knife in his hand. "Where d'you get that?"

"Shoot's house round the corner. Spin the block. Man's gotta find them pussyholes!"

We drove around and around, necks craning, trying to catch sight of them. Then Dajuan spotted one, trying to make a break for it, heading for an alleyway.

"There!" Dajuan yelled. "Run him over!"

I drove straight at the boy. He dodged the car and I reversed up – into a wall. I tried again and the car's front bumper crumpled agonisingly against brick. I was just too slow. As I fumbled slotting the car back into reverse, gearbox howling like a wounded animal, the boy ran. He was gone.

Dajuan slapped the dashboard, then sat back in silence, seething. It was the angriest I'd ever seen him. Phone was gone. Food was gone – maybe a grand's worth. The money wasn't the end of the world, but the phone was a disaster. We'd lost all the shoots' numbers.

"Are you cool?" I said.

Silence.

"Talk to me, please."

He looked out the passenger side window. The vibe I got was that this was somehow my fault, even though it wasn't, just like the car horn when we got nicked and Dajuan went jail. *He's gonna turn this on me,* I thought.

He had a little cut on his face that was oozing a trickle of blood. It was already turning crusty. I got a tissue from my bag and went to dab it, but he slapped my hand away like he was swatting a fly.

OK. He's really angry.

We sat in silence for a few minutes before Dajuan finally said, "Drive to the B&B."

Mally slumped as we filled him in on the drama.

"I've still got a pack to sell," he complained.

"No point taking it out with no phone," said Dajuan. "Store's closed for today."

There was nothing else for it. We drove back to London.

Home in the ends, I didn't see Dajuan for five days. In all those years, it was the longest period of time we'd gone without talking to each other. My calls went ignored. Unheard of. The only times he wouldn't take a call from me is when he was in shower or toilet. I didn't deserve it, none of this was my doing.

I felt completely isolated. As far as I knew, our line – our business – was gone. Where did we go from there?

The night we got back, my own phone lit up – and when I clocked the number, I nearly fainted. Vegas was calling *me*. I answered with my heart in my throat.

"You want your phone back, it's going to cost you," said a man's voice. He was trying hard to disguise his voice but just came across like a dickhead.

"Sorry, who is this?" I said innocently.

"You know who it is. We took your phone off you."

"I don't know what you're talking about. I'm sorry…"

"Don't fuck with us! You think you're bad? *We're* bad!"

"*We're bad?*" *The fuck was this guy on?*

It was scary in a way but also a little bit comical, hearing this man trying to act all gangster. But I wasn't admitting to anything; for all I knew the guy was undercover.

"You'll do as you're told if you ever want to see your phone again!"

Ridiculous. This man was acting like he had my child or something! "I don't know who you are or why you're calling me," I said, and hung up.

I needed guidance on how to play this. On the surface it looked like I now had a connection with the robber. Maybe I could get him to meet me and them lot could do what they gotta do? I called Dajuan. Phone just rang and rang. No answer.

The next day, the plastic gangster dude called me loads of times.

Let him sweat, I thought, leaving my phone to ring. When his calls went unanswered, he texted.

Pick up the phone you little bitch.

I know where you live.

And so on.

Without any guidance, I tried to long the conversation out, thinking I'd keep communication open and when Dajuan came back on line he could take over. We went to and fro for three days, but – by then – the guy had had his fill.

"We know what your phone is worth to you," he told me. "The price is 75 grand." He gave me a time and a place – some car park out east in Bermondsey – and told me he wanted the cash in a Tesco bag. This went on for the best part of a week, but while Dajuan was blanking me, I had no idea how to play it. Honestly, I was getting tired of talking to the guy.

Then, out of the blue, Dajuan called.

"You ready to go?" he said, almost like nothing had even happened.

"OK," I said cautiously. "Are we cool?"

"We're cool. Food's ready, come get your piece."

I drove round to Dajuan's, filled him on the phone development. "He says 75 bags if we want it."

Dajuan snorted. "We've got the Vegas number and all the shoots are backed up." Turned out he'd had a sim card stashed with all the shoots' contact info. Vegas had been offline for the past week, but it was now active again.

OK. Phone was cool. But never mind that. "I was worried. Are you sure you're OK," I probed gently.

"Honestly baby, I'm fine."

"Did you find out who done it?"

Dajuan gave a dark little chuckle. "Yeah, don't worry about that. He ain't gonna be phoning you again."

"What happened?"

"We don't need to talk about that."

I left it, for the time being.

Over the next few days, piecing things together, I learned a few people had gone up to our spot OT during that week when Dajuan went dark. They'd figured someone on the road would know something about what went down, and our reach in that city spread far and wide. We knew nitties, regular civilians and other drug dealers who weren't part of our operation. We had links with nightclub door staff and pub landlords. We were so established that we'd get invites to barbecues at the homes of country girlfriends and their parents. My lot listened to the street – and it gave up its secrets.

On the road, we had new rules to prevent a repeat of the hijack. We had to be super on-point. We couldn't afford another loss like that – not so much in terms of money – but reputation.

"We been slipping," Dajuan told us. "Sooner or later it was gonna happen. I want everyone back on their A-game. Does everyone understand?"

That meant, windows up unless you were driving. Engine running while you served the nitties. Three people in the car at all times.

"And don't be lacking by the side of the road unless you can see the shoot," Dajuan added. "If they don't show in a couple of minutes, move on. Spin the block."

The gun incident should have rattled me, but bravado had taken over in the heat of the moment, and I felt safe OT with the boys around me. There'd been a time when I'd thought I should maybe develop my own line, but while I had some business smarts, decent customer service and a certain entrepreneurial flair, I'd always be an easy target for guns in faces without the boys around me for protection.

I was back to the grind, back to the money.

For now.

Dajuan was on it when it came to business, but when it came to *us* I was no longer so certain. I tried to reach out to him, but there was now a gulf between us.

How long did I have before he pulled the plug?

23

SINGLE

Top boy doesn't get his line taken off him. Top boy doesn't have his drugs robbed, or get slapped in front of his girlfriend.

It didn't matter that revenge had been swift and absolute. I wasn't there to witness the return show of force. And even though Dajuan had held his own in a scrap with three other boys, I think he felt belittled in front of me. Something in his head had shifted. The robbery had driven a wedge between us. Now it was prising us apart.

"His ego is bruised," Haina offered. "He's meant to be the big man, he's probably embarrassed."

It made sense.

In the hood, Dajuan was untouchable. No one had him down as a fighter, but reputation and standing meant he never got troubled. Only now he had been – and I'd seen it happen. We both felt it. We both knew. We'd been through a lot, but whatever we'd had had now run its course. There was no great break up, no floods of tears and slamming doors. After the robbery, our relationship seemed to just fizzle out.

"Look, even though we're not together, you're still my ride or die," said Dajuan. "You're one of my best friends. We're always gonna be cool. We're always gonna be there for each other and we can still do what we're doing."

It was sad, but I also felt a weird sense of relief. Freedom even. I didn't have to worry anymore about what he was up to while I was OT, I didn't have to tune out the rumours, or fret over those snide, woman-to-woman phone calls from rival girls. We were both free agents. They could have him.

The split gave me a renewed sense of work ethic, too. *I'm going hard now*, I thought. *I've not got him around, I'm a single girl. Let me really, really make this money.* A weight lifted off me. My head was more in the game. Going country was fun again. Rolling around the streets in my car, music on, good vibes. More times, I'd bring Haina or Cheryl with me for weekends away and we'd go clubbing.

The *idea* of being newly single was exciting – for a while.

But after little time the reality of my situation and how limiting it was began to hit home. I had money pouring through my hands, it should have been the key to boundless possibility, but actually I was still very dependent on Dajuan. As well as being the closest person to me, he still provided for me, covering all my bills and paying for my car. The only thing that had changed was that he was now talking to other girls and not sleeping with me. Otherwise, things were still the same.

On top of that, meeting new guys was fraught with dangers and awkwardness. Some boys wouldn't even give me a chance. Maybe they were frightened. Maybe with good reason.

I remember chatting to one boy in a club.

"Where you from?" he asked me.

Usually I kept things vague, but for some reason this time I told the boy my ends.

His face dropped. Looked like he'd seen a ghost. "Nah, sorry. Can't do this," he said.

"What do you mean? Why you moving like that? Are you scared?"

"No, it's cool. It's just, you're not for me, OK?"

Even boys I chatted to online around that time would say, "I can't really come and see you." They'd clocked my Insta photos and seen the people in my circle. What they were saying was kind of true. Coming to the block would have been hella intimidating for an outsider. I wouldn't even have felt comfortable putting a guy in that situation; my lot didn't want some random boy getting in the way of their business. I was a big part of the operation, and anything distracting me from that potentially stood in the way of someone else's money.

So… boys couldn't come in.

But there was nothing to stop me going out, right?

Wrong.

I couldn't face the predicament of having some boy say, "Hey, shall we go south today, I know this place…" and then have to explain why I couldn't really go in that area.
Too weird.

And where would I even start with the "What do you do for a living?" conversation?

Oh, I trap. I'm a trapper.

There'd been a time in the early years when I thought it was cool, but I was 25 now and still on the road. It wasn't exactly an alluring look. No one could say I was a prize catch. Other girls – normal girls – had proper jobs and actual careers. Now I was trying to mix with new people outside my small circle of drug-dealer friends, being a drug dealer myself was a bit embarrassing. It was beginning to dawn on me that my situation was, frankly, abnormal. Yet I was still so entrenched in it, so petrified of change, I couldn't begin to contemplate an alternative life.

This was all I knew. Accepting change was going to take something drastic.

Things have a way of working themselves out. Maybe it was fate. Maybe I even wanted it to happen. But that something was in the post. It had been watching us. It was lying in wait.

* * *

Dajuan texted: *Dinner's ready. Coming over?*

That was code for: "Food's here. Let's go country."

We took my Mercedes up the motorway to the usual spot. Me, Dajuan and Mally. Paul was coming too for a change – there was a birthday coming up and he needed some money, so he'd swapped a shift with a boy on one of the other teams.

We were taking a more relaxed approach to this trip OT, so we were staying at the flat in our downtime, instead of some shithole trap. We hit a club one night after work and went back to the apartment, where I slumped on the sofa.

"Man, I'm never gonna meet a boy with you lot around me all the time!" I moaned.

"What you talking about D? Loads of boys in that club – you just need to up your game innit. You're not trying hard enough!"

"I'm trying all right. You lot are cock-blocking me! I never go on no dates or nothing!"

Dajuan caught my eye and I felt the familiar butterflies. No denying it, the chemistry was still there. We would always have a bond. "We're back in London in a couple days," he said, twisting the end of a freshly rolled spliff. "Go on some dates. Have some fun. No one's stopping you."

He was always chill like that. I don't know if he was fucking with me, trying to make me believe he wasn't bothered. I think if I ever let slip I had someone coming over, it would have been a different story.

"Yeah, we'll see," I said. "Anyway, what you got going on?"

I knew Dajuan had been seeing multiple girls. He'd tell me everything about them. All the detail. It was weird having these conversations with a guy. Too much, sometimes. He was a total gossip.

This one smells. That one's shit at sex. That one's ratchet as fuck.

"Ah, you know, got some bad bitches," he said, grinning, pulling hard on his joint. Thick smoke jetted from his nostrils in twin plumes. By "bad" he meant promiscuous, loud and a party animal. A big bum was a requirement. It was hurtful hearing him talk this way, because what he was on was the total opposite to me, and even though we weren't together, I still cared for him.

"But I can't open up to these girls like I can with you," Dajuan said. "Don't trust them. Don't want them in my house, don't want them around my shit."

"You'll find someone," I said, not really believing it. In our world, I was learning that finding someone you could trust with your secrets was some tall order.

I pulled a blanket over me. The heavy cloud of weed fog draped across the room was making me sleepy.

Next day, we did the rounds in our usual spot. Them lot were in high spirits, relaxed, hotboxing my car with endless spliffs. The line rang incessantly. We hit the shots.

It was around mid-morning when I noticed this one car, a gunmetal-grey Toyota four-by-four. There was nothing remarkable or stand-out about it. Yet for some reason – pure instinct maybe – it caught my eye.

We rolled around town. Couple hours later, I saw it again.

"That's weird," I said. "I swear that's the same car I saw a while back."

Dajuan squinted. Boy was so stoned I was surprised he could see anything at all. "Nah, it isn't. You're being para," he said.

But a while later, that same car slowly crossed the street in front of us.

"There it is again!" I said.

The boys kissed their teeth. Mally leant over and turned the music up, dismissing my concerns.

OK. Maybe I am being paranoid, I thought. It didn't *look* like a regular undercover car. It was too old and crusty, and often with an undercover car you could see a glint of the blue light casing stashed behind the front grill, or there'd be an extra aerial sticking up in the back.

But then I spotted it a fourth time and felt my nerves tighten.

There were three guys in the car. Every time I'd seen it — same three guys. One million percent, it was police.

I turned the music down. "Listen, something bookey's going on here. That four-by's following us. I swear — that's feds."

Dajuan looked again. "Nah man! That's not police. We're cool."

"I'm telling you!" I said.

"Turn the music up," Paul said. "I can't hear a thing in the back."

Conversation over.

"All right then," I muttered under my breath, cranking the sounds back up. "Don't say I didn't warn you."

We went KFC. Everyone was chilling. Staying at the flat had put the boys in a relaxed mood. But as much as they liked to say they were on point, bringing their A-game, the only one who was *really* paying attention was me. They were all high from smoking weed. I was on edge, frayed, from fretting about this car all morning.

We drove up to one estate to see a shoot. We did the deal and were about to head back to the city centre when a regular police car pulled out of a side road behind us. *All right,* I thought. *We're definitely being watched.*

Dajuan caught the look on my face and checked out the fed in his wing mirror. "It's just a regular patrol car," he said. "Take him for a spin round the block, see if he stays with us."

I did as I was told. Back into the estate. Pulled a few odd turns, and sure enough after a couple the patrol car peeled off in a different direction. My grip on the steering wheel relaxed as I settled back into my seat.

"See?" said Dajuan. "We're cool."

We drove back into town, lined up the next couple of shoots. I was feeling calmer by now, thinking maybe the boys had been right after all. Perhaps I was just being paranoid.

But then, we were parked on a side road when I caught the gunmetal Toyota in the rear-view mirror.

"It's that car again!" I said. "Behind."

The boys swivelled to get a look.

The Toyota rolled up on us, then passed slowly by on our right, the three men inside swivelled to meet our stares. My eyes locked with the guy in the passenger seat. He held my gaze. Understanding flashed between us.

It was police. Dajuan saw it too. Plain as day.

They'd made us. We'd made them.

No more games. It was on.

24

BUSTED

"Yeah, I think we go home now," said Dajuan, calm as ever.

"I told you!" I said.

"Head for the motorway."

I drove to the dual carriageway, taking it easy. There was no panic in the car. Didn't matter that we'd left everything back in the flat, including our phones: it would all still be there when we next went back. We got on the motorway and I headed for London, keeping a cautious eye on my wing and rear-view mirrors.

We'd been driving maybe 20 minutes and it looked like we'd given them the slip. Home free. The music was booming. Everyone was on a little adrenaline high from the thrill of evading the chase, when...

Suddenly the car in the outside lane next to us strobed blue lights.

The BMW in front lit up like a UFO, the driver touching his brakes and forcing me to kill my speed as I came up hard towards his bumper. From nowhere, another BMW sped up behind me, almost tailgating me, blue lights pulsing.

We were being T-packed.

Hard stop.

My heart pounded. The usual rule of not stopping until everyone's ready went out the window. I had no choice as I was forced over to the hard shoulder by the three police cars boxing me in. We were surrounded.

"Is everyone done?" Dajuan said, as I snatched up his weed from the centre console and stuffed it down my knickers. He was still my guy. I didn't want anything bad happening to him. Taking the rap for a bit of weed was cool with me.

By some miracle, the boys got their food banked. Even the Vegas phone had been broken down and the sim card had gone up someone's bumhole – just as a marked police car swept in behind us and four armed officers piled out, boots crunching on the gravel.

One drew his pistol and pointed it at our car.

"Hands where I can see them! Throw your keys out the window!" he barked.

I wound down the window, tossed the keys.

We sat there with our hands up as more police cars – marked and undercover, maybe 10 in total – flooded the hard shoulder around us.

"OK. Slowly get out the vehicle," the armed officer said, keeping his gun trained on us.

We did as we were told, and a posse of plain clothes officers swooped on us, dragging us apart and lining us up on the hard shoulder. We were cuffed, hands behind our backs, as police patted us down and more searched the car.

"Clear for weapons," I heard one say, with maybe a hint of disappointment in his voice.

The armed officer slid his pistol back in its holster and the takedown was handed over to CID.

"Look, I've got weed," I said to the one officer holding me.

"Yeah, we'll sort that out," he said, indifferent to my confession. The way police officers were crawling over my car, inside and out, they seemed convinced they'd scored massive. Thing was, we didn't even have big cash – we'd sent five grand back to London with a runner just the day before. I caught some exasperated looks as the car search drew a blank.

"We're going to take you down the station and bring your car in for a thorough search," my officer told me.

They read us our rights. We were being arrested on suspicion of possession with intent to supply Class A drugs – no problem there, I knew I didn't have any Class A on me.

But they were laying out another potential charge: conspiracy to supply.

Conspiracy.

That was the killer.

Getting caught live and direct is one thing. Conspiracy was way worse.

As they led me to a waiting police car and folded me into the back seat, my mind began racing. *What did they have on us?*

While they drove me to a local station, I turned this conspiracy thing over in my head. Not gonna lie, I was panicking. How many times had I been through the same ANPR camera on the motorway? Had they tailed us and taken photos? Tapped our phones? We always tried to keep conversations semi-coded, and some of the big hitters had special EncroChat phones – on a secure, encrypted network – for dealing with the drug connect. But I'd got lax in sending texts to Dajuan: *Is the box in yet? We going country tomorrow?* Stuff that screamed 'drug dealer'.

But wait, I thought, as we got to the police station. *My phone's in the flat! This is a lifesaver!*

We got to the station and they put me in an interview room. As I was on a driving ban, my car was registered in Haina's name. Likewise, the car insurance, all with her permission. The police asked my name, and I gave them Haina's, along with her address and date of birth. It all checked out. The police actually seemed satisfied. It looked like they not only had zero physical drugs evidence, but nothing to make a conspiracy stick either.

"OK," the officer processing me began, "you've told us about the cannabis, that's fine, we can deal with that with a caution."

I could sense their frustration. They knew exactly what we'd been doing. They'd probably seen us doing it earlier that day. But they didn't have anything. They were stuck.

We rattled through the caution paperwork and I was literally being walked to the door to freedom when another officer walked in – fresh from searching my car – carrying my purse.

My heart dropped. I knew what was inside.

"Who's Jess Beeney?" the officer asked me.

I laughed innocently. "Oh yeah, she's a friend of mine, she forgot her ID on a night out, I'm just keeping it safe until I see her at the weekend."

Besides a bank card of Haina's, in my purse I had an ID belonging to one other girl. The officer narrowed her eyes – and I knew then I was fucked. "I'm not convinced you are who you say you are," she said. "Can we get her fingerprints?"

They ran my prints – and of course my real name came up. And the previous arrests, and the driving bans, and the gang marker. The mood changed very quickly. They were pissed off I'd lied to them and from thereon the charges racked up.

They got the easy stuff out the way first – driving on a ban (again) and with no insurance (again). No one was gonna do me any favours now, so the weed caution was off the table and I was formally arrested for possession of cannabis with intent to supply. I surrendered my clothes for evidence, changed into the little grey tracksuit number and got shown to a cell. The door clanged shut, the noise echoing off the bare walls. There was a low, narrow bench against one wall, with a thin, plastic-covered mattress and a stainless-steel toilet in one corner. That was it. Things were going from bad to worse. I lay down and closed my eyes.

I hadn't been in there long when the officer returned and nicked me for lying about my identity. Then she came back again and said, "We've found white powder in your car."

"There's no drugs in that car," I said bluntly, knowing full well nothing we sold was in white powder form.

"It'll have to go for testing. It'll be at least 24 hours before we know for sure, so just sit tight in the meantime. Do you want something to eat?"

"Nah, I'm good. I do need a tampon though."

Not eating was one of the little tricks I'd picked up for killing time in a cell; it made you tired, so you slept. I was fine going without food, but I was on my period and had nothing with me.

"I'll send someone along in a minute," the officer said.

That someone never came. The tampon never arrived. I buzzed. They promised – and did nothing. It was degrading.

The second day, the hatch in my cell door rattled open.

"You've got a phone call," the officer said.

"Who is it?"

"It's your mum."

I almost blurted, "My mum?", but I managed to keep my cool and took the phone.

"Hi Mum," I said.

"What the fuck is going on?" Haina said. It felt amazing to hear her voice.

"Yeah, I can't really talk."

"I know, but – basics?"

"I'm in a police station."

"When they letting you go?"

"I dunno. I'll have court first. Can you come?"

"When is it?"

"Not sure yet. Keep ringing back and I'll tell you as soon as I know."

A fed came and took me for a sit down with a solicitor, and then into the interview. I did the standard *no comment* and offered up a prepared statement. *I was just doing a favour for a friend and didn't really know who these boys were. To my knowledge, there was no wrongdoing occurring in the car. The reason I lied about my identity was because of previous bad experiences with the police.*

That's all I was giving them. They answered by hitting me with the possession with intent to supply charge. Back to the cell.

Won't lie, sitting in that box was scary, man. I tried to distract myself by reading anything they'd give me. But with that conspiracy charge dangling over my head, my mind played tricks on me. My solicitor was up and down like a yoyo every time the feds came up with a new charge, and I expected him to rock up any minute with a sheaf of surveillance photos showing me hitting the shots out the car window. The bit of weed I couldn't care less about. I knew the sentencing guidelines – the most I'd get was probation. But the conspiracy was jail time, and there was no way I could go jail.

The police longed the to and fro out over four nights and three days. Sunday they charged me with obstructing arrest and attempting to pervert the course of justice, but there was some relief when they told me the conspiracy accusation was being dropped.

"You'll be appearing before court in the morning," an officer told me. "Would you like a shower before court?"

"Well, yeah," I said. I'd been wearing the same filthy tracksuit for three days. I looked a whole mess.

"We'll wake you at six."

I felt isolated and a bit forgotten about. There'd been no more calls from Haina. As far as I knew none of the boys had tried to get in touch. I was on my lonesome in a country police station. That night I barely slept, and although the shower next morning felt amazing, I was told to put the rank tracksuit back on.

"Can I have a clean one please?"

"No, sorry. We haven't got any."

Hands cuffed together, I climbed into the sweatbox van that would take me to court and was locked in a little cabin. I stared out of the tiny pane of blackened glass, certain I was going to be made an example of. Before this, I'd done a few overnights in police cells, but after three nights in one I was certain I couldn't do prison.

Arriving at court, I was taken in through the back and put in a holding cell. I stared at the walls, willing the minutes away. But I couldn't do it. I pressed the buzzer over and over again. Every time the court staff came to the door, I begged them, "Please! I've been in the cell for three days. I'm not doing this! Open the door for me!"

I kicked up such a fuss that in the end, my solicitor told them, "Look, she can sit in the interview room with me."

I was itching to get this over with. It was just a case of sticking guilty pleas in the boxes, and I was out of there. But my solicitor had news.

"I'm afraid we've got a problem," she said, as I dragged out a plastic chair and sat down.

"OK," I said cautiously. "What kind of problem?"

"They want to remand you in custody."

"What?! What for?" I said, trying to swallow the lump in my throat.

"There's an unpaid fine of £1500 – from your last court appearance? Unless you can pay it right now, they're remanding you."

The room lurched as I racked my brain.

She was right. There *had* been a fine, for a driving thing. Had I really forgotten to pay it?

"Look, that's not a problem," I said. "Let me make a phone call and I'll sort it."

"The court won't facilitate that, is there any way…"

The clock was ticking. The magistrate would be calling me any minute. I gestured as if to say, *Look at me!* I had nothing. I was wearing grey prison sweats. Yeah, I was big and bad for the police – until they said I was getting remanded! Then I was crying! I'd always thought I'd be able to do it, that it held no fear for me. I'd known so many people go jail and say it wasn't scary. When it came down to it, though – I just didn't want to lose my freedom.

"I can't go prison," I said, wiping away tears.

My solicitor slid her phone into my hand and said quietly, "I'm not really supposed to do this, but one call. OK?"

"Thank you!" I breathed. I dialled – you guessed it – Haina. "Babe, I don't know where you are, but I need you to pay this court fine for me," I said.

As always, Haina came through. By the time I appeared before the magistrate, the fine had been squared away.

I pleaded guilty to everything and stood there trying to look remorseful as the magistrate did his little speech.

"You've come very close to going to prison," he began. He was insinuating that he knew exactly what I'd been doing. "If I were you, I'd stop while you're ahead. Please take this as your last chance."

He gave me 250 hours of community service and a year's probation. I breathed a sigh of relief. I was free to go.

I walked out of the court clutching my bag of clothes with "EVIDENCE" written across it in bold capitals – and nothing else. No phone. No money. A tiny part of me had thought maybe Dajuan or a couple of the boys would be waiting outside to pick me up, but I was one hundred percent alone. I found my way to the local railway station, dodged the barriers and bumped a train to London Paddington. At the station, all the hoardings for the *Metro* newspaper were headlining the Brexit vote. It was the crunch day. I was pissed off because I'd wanted to stick my cross in the box to stay in Europe – but I couldn't face going home to get my polling card. I needed some Haina-style TLC. I made it to near the ends then stopped one young boy. "Hey, they just let me out the police station, can I borrow your phone?" I must have looked a state. Intimidating even.

He loaned me his mobile. I called my rock. "Haina, can you come pick me up?"

She had a hot bath, clean clothes and a roast dinner waiting.

25

LYDIA

I woke at Haina's the next morning under a plush duvet. After four nights in a police cell, a fresh pillow and a comfy bed felt like a solid dose of luxury. My back and shoulders were still stiff and crunchy, but I could already feel my muscles softening.

Haina made coffee. I called Dajuan

"Thank God you're alright," he said. "Feds were talking about a conspiracy thing…"

"It's cool," I told him. "Just some little PWITS bullshit and driving."

"What d'you get? Probation?"

"Yeah, a year. Plus some community. And another ban."

"Don't worry about it. It's nothing."

Them lot were all back in country. Maybe that sounds bold considering just five days earlier we'd been hard-stopped by armed response and arrested at gunpoint – but selling drugs was our job. We had to roll with the punches. Getting busted was just an occupational hazard.

"All your stuff's here," Dajuan said. "It's up to you, I'll get someone to bring you up if you wanna come?"

Was I about to let a little bit of probation stand between me and my money?

"I'll come," I said.

I chilled until early afternoon and one girl from the ends took me back OT. It felt like the most normal thing in the world. Only difference being it wasn't my number plate getting pinged on the motorway – my Merc was being held prisoner in a secure car park around the back of the police station.

I met the boys on the road and jumped straight into their rental. Smiles all around. The arrest, nights in the bare police cell and court drama soon felt like little more than a hiccup along the way.

Almost.

There was something twisting in my belly. I had to get it out.

"So, what happened with you lot?" I asked. I was pissed off that no one had hung around to see if I was OK. I'd felt stranded.

The boys told me they'd been strip searched, informally interviewed and were free to go. Mally and Paul had drugs plugged, but without any other incriminating evidence there wasn't enough to hold them to see if they 'produced the goods', as it were.

"We waited for hours," Dajuan told me. "We saw them bring your car in for a search. They told us you weren't coming out and said we might as well go."

"How come no one even came to court to bring me back?" I complained.

"Feds said you were gonna be up on Friday. We stayed OT, went court when they said – but you weren't on the list."

"Right," I nodded. Whether that was all true or not I'll never know. What more could I say? I'd made my point.

It was going to take probation a couple weeks to line up some appointments. In the meantime, I went back to work.

"What about my car though?" I asked Dajuan.

"Just leave it there. It's hot now innit."

"What do I do with no car?"

"We'll set you up with a rental."

One of the boys was dispatched back to London to fetch up a fresh car for me, and we all swapped into the new vehicle.

By now, I was on a three-year super ban. I didn't even have a licence anymore. No biggie. I was still going to drive. I had drugs to sell. In my head, I had it all figured out: probation maybe one morning a week, a nice early appointment over breakfast coffee, all wrapped up by mid-morning, and the rest of my time OT.

My probation officer, though, had other ideas.

Lydia called me before our first appointment to introduce herself and set things up. I must have had a gang marker on my file because right from the get-go the vibe was – *OK, you're from this gang, so you can only come in at these times, when the other gang's not going to be here.*

Fair. There's only so much probation to go around in West London. My gang and the other gang had to share. Lydia's remit was to prevent bloodshed, not facilitate it. She didn't want gangs stabbing each other up in her office.

What struck me from that first call with Lydia was how young and chill she sounded. *Perfect*, I thought. *This girl sounds practically normal.*

"Also, I don't want you sitting in the waiting room," she told me. "For your own safety. You'll come straight into the appointment room."

"OK, cool."

"And I'd like to see you three times a week. Monday, Wednesday, Friday. OK?"

Beg your pardon? Three?

"No, really, I'm fine," I told her "There's absolutely nothing wrong. That's not necessary."

"All the same, I'd like to see you three times a week."

"Seems a bit extreme to be honest."

"Nonetheless, that's what we'll be doing."

I knew what she was on.

Her plan was to break the cycle of my offending, disrupt my drug dealing by eating into my week. My heart sank. Lydia was smart – and I really thought she'd already won.

"This ain't gonna work," I told Dajuan later. "She wants me in the probation office every 10 minutes! How can I go country if I'm stuck in there!?"

But Dajuan was cool. "Look, don't worry about it. We're still gonna flip your pack for you. Just make sure you're up here when you're not in probation."

This was a massive deal.

Usually, if you didn't go country, you didn't get paid. End of. I never asked for any special favours, but Dajuan had my back. No one argued. Plan was, while I had this probation shit, I'd just be a driver. I'd take people up, ferry reloads and bring back the cash. Dajuan and the rest of them were sure they could make it work. They were cool with looking after my end.

I got my first appointment. Lydia dropped me right in a 2pm slot – another spanner in the works. This was no accident. She was intentionally cutting my day in half.

I recalled some advice from Paul on dealing with probation: take everything, give them nothing.

"They're there to help you, fam," he'd told me. "Use them for stuff like help with housing or sorting out benefits if that's your thing. But don't ever forget – they might be called probation, but they're police. Deal with them how you deal with the feds. Be polite and don't tell them nothing."

The office was just down the road from me. The place looked like a doctor's surgery – reception, waiting room, rows of plastic chairs. Most people would sit and wait for their probation officer to call them. I buzzed in and was ushered straight into a meeting room.

Lydia introduced herself. She was dressed casually in jeans and sliders. Tall, mixed race, with dark, curly hair and tattoos.

Fantastic, I thought. *She really is a normal person.*

She'd sounded young on the phone, and in the flesh, she looked the same age as me. Because, in fact, she was, I learned later. It made me think, *Wow, I'm really sitting here, and she's a whole probation officer.* She had a responsible job; meanwhile I was driving around with Class A drugs hidden inside my body, selling £10 deals of crack from a car window. Looking back, I think that was the moment the first domino toppled and began falling in slow and uncertain motion into the next.

Our first meeting was just an initial assessment. A get-to-know-you. We sized each other up. Lydia was cool, but she was no pushover. And to my mind, she was still the enemy, part of law enforcement. She asked me how I was doing for money, whether I had a partner, what my family situation was. All this, I realised later, she already knew.

"I don't have anyone," I told her.

For now, I kept the rest of my cards clutched tight to my chest, giving away the bare minimum. Yes and no answers all the way. Far as I was concerned, Lydia was basically police, and there was a strong chance that anything I said to her would get back to them. She could return me to court with a click of her fingers. I had to watch what I said. Plus, I didn't want to long this one out.

"So, what are you doing after this?" Lydia asked.

"Nothing," I shrugged, knowing full well I was going country. The boys needed a re-up.

For the next month I kept selling drugs, earning my money. Lydia hassled me for a home visit, but I found excuse after excuse to keep her at bay. Not that I had anything to hide in the flat – we weren't keeping drugs there at the time – I just didn't want her in my home. Yet in other ways, despite all my front, she was getting through to me. The wall I'd thrown up between us was beginning to crack.

I started my community service. I was on painting duty, redecorating the communal hallways in one block on a nearby estate. I was the only girl and it was actually super fun, hardly punishment at all. First day I turned up and they tried to give me a set of overalls and some clunky, paint-splattered shoes. The laces had stiffened with dirt over time.

"Nah, no way. I'm not wearing them," I said. "They've had someone else's feet inside."

The guy running the show told me they were special safety shoes. "If you don't wear them, I'm going to have to send you home."

"They ain't going on my feet. They don't even fit! They're two sizes too big!"

So he gave in, and after that we were cool. I wore my own trainers. We put dust sheets down in the block hallways and took our time over treating the walls to a fresh coat of paint. I tutted as flecks of white emulsion messed up my manicure. As the weeks went by the boss dude started low-key flirting with me and everyone on the painting detail did less and less actual painting. It was summer. The sun was high. Most of the time we'd chill on the grass outside the block, chatting with people off the estate.

Lydia must have felt like she was making progress in our meetings. We'd have long conversations. She'd tell me about her life and what she was up to. I at least listened, and showed an interest, even if I wasn't giving anything away about mine.

I didn't really need to. She knew exactly what I was on.

"I see you around," she told me. "I know who your man is…"

"I ain't even got a man."

"OK. Then I know the boys you're rolling with. I've seen you in the music videos with them. We analyse social media. I know exactly what's going on."

I didn't agree or disagree. "Cool. Well, you know then," I shrugged.

Lydia looked at me for a long beat. "Don't you want to stop? You're better than this."

"Stop what? I already told you I'm not doing anything."

She let a silence settle between us, then said, "OK. Let's leave it there for today."

The next time I went in, besides Lydia, there were two smartly dressed women in her office. I looked at Lydia as if to say, *who are they?*

They introduced themselves. "We're from the sexual violence team, and we were concerned that you might have experienced some sexual violence."

No shit, I thought. *You're about seven years too late.*

I was furious. "Why the fuck are you bringing police officers in here to ask me about sexual assault?" I yelled at Lydia, giving it both barrels.

The two officers left and Lydia apologised. "I'm sorry, I can see your frustration," she said.

I didn't get why she'd brought them in. We'd discussed the rape that had happened all those years earlier, because it had been part of my mitigating circumstances in court, but I'd never talked about being sexually assaulted since. I think she was on the same bad trip as everyone else, that I was coerced into this life – and that just wasn't the case.

I closed down on her.

Lydia started again. Every week with the same mantra.

You can do so much better.

It doesn't look good on you.

You can do other things.

As I ferried drugs up the motorway, I'd turn it over in my head. I couldn't deny Lydia had a point. I was 25 now. It was getting long. Where was this heading? Was there really something else I could do?

On the other hand, what did my life look like without trapping?

In my chats with Lydia, I'd seethe with frustration. Thinking about getting out was one thing, but how would I make it work? I was in turmoil. In the end I snapped.

"OK, what do you see me doing instead?"

"You could go to university," Lydia suggested.

I snorted. "Uni ain't for me."

"Trust me, you'd like it. You're clever."

"You don't understand the upheaval it would bring to my life," I said. "How am I supposed to live? How do I pay for my flat, bills, everything else?"

"To start with, there are benefits…"

"I've never done benefits – I wouldn't know where to begin!"

"We can help you."

With each meeting, this idea that Lydia had planted in my head wormed deeper and deeper. It began to feel like it might actually be possible. And I started to warm to her.

One day, a couple of months after we'd first met, I walked into her office to be introduced to a caseworker from London Gang Exit.

"I'm going to leave you two to it," Lydia said. She gave my shoulder a reassuring squeeze and left the room.

At first, I prickled with discomfort. It was moving too fast. But Marcia talked through her background. She'd been in a gang herself. She'd got out, she'd stayed out – and now she was helping people like me do the same.

"We can rehouse you," she told me. "You can start again somewhere new. Do you want me to help you?"

I don't know what, in that moment, made me say it – and I'm not certain I even meant it at the time – but I heard myself saying, "Yes."

"That's great, Danielle," she said, pulling a bunch of forms out of her bag. "I'm going to go through the paperwork with you and get your autograph on a few forms, and we'll get the ball rolling. OK?"

"OK," I nodded, still not sure. Still feeling like I was being swept along and hoping that at some point I'd come up for breath. Marcia was damn quick getting me to sign on that line, bless her!

Later that night, lying in bed, I wondered if I had the strength to go through with what she had planned. *What did I just agree to?* I thought, my heart pounding, doubt gnawing my insides. *This is not good. This is my whole life. I don't know how to do anything else.* I was already regretting it.

Other than probation, the only person I could talk it through with was Haina. "Do it! Why not?" she said. "Aren't you bored by now?"

In theory, it sounded simple. In reality, not so much. If turning your back on this stuff was so easy, everyone would do it the second they'd had their fill. But leaving made me look like an informant, and the truth was – I knew too much. My friends wanted me in their sights. If they found out what I was planning, they'd be asking themselves, *Where the fuck is she going? What ends is she gonna go to and tell people our business?*

Behind the scenes, by saying "yes", I'd already set the wheels in motion, and Lydia and Marcia moved so quickly that I was swept up in it. I barely had time to give it proper thought. I knew – if I didn't do it now, I was never going to do it.

"OK, start packing up your stuff," Lydia said, next time I saw her.

"Wait – I can't just get a removal van to my flat!" I said. "The whole ends is going to see. That's madness."

Lydia agreed. "OK, every time you come for a meeting, bring a bag and I'll get permission for you to store your belongings here."

"So, a few bags of clothes? Is that it?"

"You'll be going into emergency accommodation. It'll be a single room…"

This is what I meant by upheaval. I had a banging flat – and I was going to have to leave it all behind. My sofa. My 60-inch TV. All my kitchen gadgets. Boxes and boxes of trainers that had barely even been worn. I'd have to walk away from it all.

"How do I get the stuff here?" I said. "I'm on a driving ban, remember?"

"Just drive," Lydia said.

It hit home. They were so concerned about my safety, they were willing to condone me breaking the law. And they were probably right. These people that I'd been so close to, when it came down to it, probably would have harmed me – not directly, but via someone else acting on orders. Or I just wouldn't be allowed to leave, full stop. It would have turned into some kind of hostage situation where now I *would* be forced to go sell drugs. I'd probably be shuttled off to go live in some country trap and no one would hear from me again.

Over the space of a couple of weeks, the pile of stuff stashed in the corner of Lydia's office grew. It looked like a stack of donations heading to the charity shop – couple suitcases and one of those big Ikea bags – but they contained my life. What was left of it. All those years in country, hundreds of thousands of pounds earned in the grind and it all came down to a few bags of clothes and 12 grand in billfolds. Even my designer stash had been depleted. Bits lost or loaned out and never returned. A couple Louis bags were all I had left.

Every time I deposited the remains of my life at Lydia's office, I felt an overwhelming sense of betrayal, not just of the people close to me, but the whole ends. I was constantly on edge. Without even realising it, I was pulling away from the team – and it hadn't gone unnoticed. Out of the blue, Mally hit me up on Snapchat: *I can't hear from you – where you been? Wag1?*

I'm here bro! What you talking about?

A'right sis – cool.

And then he left it.

My predicament was agony. I felt like I was letting everyone down, but the walls were closing in on me. I wanted out, but the idea left me cold. Then, suddenly, I *needed* out. I wasn't the only one who thought I was betraying my people.

Dajuan knew.

I was chilling, scrolling through my phone, when his Snap popped up: *Anyone see D on the roads, grab her, hold her and don't let her go until I get there.*

He was OT, but somehow he'd found out I was doing a runner. Top of my list was a leak in the probation service, dripping secrets in his ear.

"We've seen it," Lydia told me. "We're working on it."

They had eyes on the internet and had picked up on a flurry of chatter across social media. This was exactly the kind of nightmare scenario I'd been desperate to avoid – everyone thinking I was a snitch. But there was nothing I could do about it; there was no hiding in the ends, not for someone like me. Everyone knew where I lived. If anyone wanted me, they could come get me. Anytime. Day or night.

"What the fuck am I gonna do now?" I said to Haina.

"It's too late. You just gotta pretend everything's cool and hold it down till you get out, man. You ain't done nothing wrong. No one's gonna get nicked from this. Ride it out."

In my favour, Dajuan and the other big hitters were either gone country or out of the area living the showbiz life thanks to their music-industry success. There was only the YGs left in the ends to do the dirty work. As it stood, Dajuan's command hadn't yet filtered down to these eager little foot soldiers. Just as well. They were quick to violence

Even though there was now a new and pressing sense of urgency, I still wasn't expecting the call when it came a few days later.

I was stretched out on the sofa one afternoon on the phone to Haina. Boy troubles. Again.

Another call broke into our conversation.

"Hang on," I said, and put Haina on hold.

It was Lydia.

"We're moving you," she told me.

"Today?" I replied, my pulse quickening.

"Right now. Get yourself to the probation office. It's time to go."

26

GONE GIRL

ydia hung up and Haina came back on the line.

"It's happening!" I told her, fighting a rising trepidation. "I'm leaving. Now."

Haina caught the wobble in my voice. "It's cool. Just organise yourself. It's gonna be fine. You got this."

Deep breath. "OK. I better go."

"Call me. Good luck."

My focus in that panic-driven moment was on pure practicalities. I didn't have time to process how huge or pivotal this moment was. Instead, I moved methodically from room to room, grabbing the last of my belongings – clothes, toiletries, passport – and putting them in a cabin luggage case. *You can't come back here*, I told myself as I scanned each room in turn. *What have you got in here that you hundred percent cannot do without?*

Kneeling beside my bed, my cheek brushed the cotton fabric of my own duvet for the final time as I reached for the shoebox underneath. I scooped the twelve billfolds inside

– each worth a grand – into my case. Back in the living room, I paused for a moment, looking over the framed photos studding my walls.

Dajuan. Warren. Paul. Happy times with my people. But behind our smiles, I realised now, lay unfathomable trauma. I feel like I should have cried, but disbelief had smothered my emotions. Grabbing two photos of Lloyd, I traced a manicured fingernail around the outline of his cheek, then added them to the suitcase.

One day, I told myself. *This is the first step. One at a time.*

For some bizarre reason, I even gave the place a little clean – not that my flat was ever dirty, but I wiped down the surfaces and straightened the furniture. Maybe I was trying to long it out because I still wasn't sure I was doing the right thing. Then I grabbed my keys, unlocked the front door, stepped out and closed it behind me. I scanned the street outside, half expecting to get steamed by a squad of balaclavas, dragged kicking and screaming into the back of a car. But all was quiet. A normal day, people going about their businesses. No one even gave me a second look.

Heart thudding, I posted the keys to my flat through the letterbox and left the keys for the rental car on the wall outside. Then I pulled out my phone and Snapchatted a panorama of the ends.

Summer days in the hood, I posted.

Never gonna have that again, I realised.

But there was no more time for sentimentality. I strolled down to the probation office, where Lydia and her manager met me.

"The police are waiting for you. They're going to drive you out of the area," she explained.

"The police?!" I bristled.

"Yes – undercover. Just in case."

I wondered how credible Dajuan's threat had been that meant undercover police had now been drafted in to vanish me off the radar. Lydia hurried me to a waiting, unmarked car. Two plainclothes, a man and a woman, helped slot my suitcases in the boot.

"Hi Danielle, are you OK?" the woman said.

I nodded. "Hi. Yeah, I'm cool."

They paced nearby, eager to hit the road, as me and Lydia said our goodbyes. Even in the high tension of my exit, the irony of the feds' involvement wasn't lost on me. All these years, we'd been on opposite sides of the law. Common enemies, cat-and-mousing it around the ends, in random towns OT, at roadside stop and searches. Honestly, I didn't feel they had any place in this. I was giving them nothing – but now I was having to accept their help. They were facilitating my rescue. I felt backed into a corner. But I had to see it through because I might never have the same chance again.

"Where am I going?" I asked Lydia.

"Lewisham. We're putting you up in a Travelodge – just for a couple of nights. Take this." Lydia handed me an old brick phone. "It's prepaid. Turn your iPhone off. Don't use it to call anyone. Don't take any calls on it."

"Will I see you again?"

"I'm not sure yet. I'll try and find a way." She looked choked as she told me, "You're the first girl I've helped in this way. I'm proud of you. Don't worry. It's going to be fine."

"Thank you, Lydia. For everything."

She gave me a tight hug and I got in the car, then waved goodbye as it pulled away and shunted into the traffic, heading east through Kensal Town and Maida Vale, skirting the edge of the Notting Hill Carnival route that had been the scene of so many good times. The two officers tried with the small talk, but I stayed quiet, trying to process what was happening to me. The drive felt long. I remember some dickhead driver tearing in and out of the lanes, executing a series of near misses as he careered around the cars beside us. My two chaperones just ignored him, leaving traffic duty to the more basic feds.

We landed at the Travelodge, a regular city hotel, and they helped me shift my luggage into reception.

"Good luck! Bye!" the woman said.

And then they were gone. I was on my own.

Alone in my room, I paced and fidgeted, turning my iPhone over in my hands, resisting the urge to turn it on. I tossed it down on the bed, paced some more and picked it up again. It was all I could do to stop myself running out of the place and jumping on the first train back to West London. I grabbed up the TV remote and flicked aimlessly through the channels, taking none of them in. Then I turned the TV off again and lay on the bed in near silence, with just the blood rush of my thudding heart in my ears.

Suddenly, the room phone rang. Shrill. Loud. Like a jolt of electricity. Marcia from Gang Exit was on the line.

"We're just checking in on you. Are you OK?"

"I'm OK. I think."

"Sure?"

"I'll be fine."

"OK, I'll call again in a bit. Ring us if you need anything."

"I will. Thanks."

And then I was on my own again, alone with my thoughts of exiting my exit and returning to what I knew. The back and forth in my head was relentless.

This is ridiculous. Just go home.

No! Stick it out.

You're betraying your friends.

You don't know yet what this might bring you.

I couldn't stand my own company any longer. I had to shut these voices down, distract myself from my dilemma. Stay or go. It was on a knife edge, and I was in danger of caving in and running west. In desperation I reached for my handbag, dug out a folded, dog-eared piece of paper I used as a little hand-written contact book and called one boy I knew.

"Hey! I'm in your ends."

"Oh really? What you saying?"

"Well, I dunno, you taking me out?"

"Yeah, sure. Tell me where you are, I'll come pick you up."

He was going to be a couple hours, so in the meantime I thought, *OK, let me just walk a while.* I plugged in my headphones and ventured outside. Walked up Deptford high street, up Lewisham high street. I stopped at one corner shop to grab a medicinal bottle of Hennessy. *I'm gonna have to get low-key tipsy,* I thought. That's how rattled I was. I didn't even drink, but I needed the numbing cognac to settle my jangling nerves.

The boy I'd called came by and took me for dinner. It was a distraction exercise, nothing more. We ate. Came back to the hotel. Chilled with the bottle of Hennessy for company. He didn't stay the night and I didn't sleep with him or nothing. After he'd left, I lay awake in the darkness for what felt like hours. And then I realised – I'd actually done it. I'd got through the first day.

The second, it was the same drill. More mind games. More pacing. Gang Exit checking in every couple hours to make sure I was sticking with the programme.

"We're moving you tomorrow," Marcia said.

"Where now?"

"It's still being finalised. But be ready for 10am. OK?"

"Sure."

Once again, I couldn't face spending the evening alone. I called the same boy. We ate out together, and for a few hours I forgot how my life had taken a turn towards the unknown.

The next morning, I met Marcia and her colleague, Chris, in the hotel reception as planned.

"So, where we heading?" I asked.

"The accommodation is Grays," Marcia said.

"Grays? Where's that?"

"Essex."

Chris caught the look of horror on my face. "It shouldn't be for long," he said. "Don't worry."

But I was worried. Essex had never been part of the plan.

I fell quiet on the walk to the railway station, my suitcase skittering over the paving slabs as I dragged it along behind me. What the fuck was going on? What were they sending me into?

Sat on the train, I tried to probe their plans and suss out what they had in store for me. "So, what's the process? What happens next?"

"Essex is just a stop-gap until we get you set up with something more permanent," said Marcia.

"How long for?"

"I don't know yet. But it won't be forever."

Discussing this with Lydia and Marcia, right from the outset, we'd talked about me going South London. I couldn't contemplate a future outside of the city. London was my home – albeit with certain limitations. North was off limits. Out east, my reputation preceded me, and some eastern ends had issues with mine. West – obviously – was a no-no because everyone there was gonna think I'd got rich and switched. The goal had always been south. Safe haven. Fresh start. I had a vague knowledge of the area. I knew the odd person there, but there was no danger because I wasn't well-known. And the area I had in mind – Streatham – was a spot my old lot would never venture. They had no business being there.

Essex though? The only bits of Essex I knew were night-club dancefloors.

"Am I gonna get to South London eventually?" I said.

"Yeah, yeah, of course," Marcia nodded.

I felt like everything was happening *to* me, that I wasn't in control. And after two nights with barely any sleep, I was exhausted. Too tired to battle the doubting voices in my head.

They were growing stronger, louder and I was already beginning to wonder how the hell I was going to get myself out of this.

'Grays' is about right, I thought to myself on the long walk to my new, temporary home. *Grays is what it says on the tin. This is nowhere land. There's nothing here.*

After the bustle, colour, noise and smells of Lewisham, Grays felt like viewing the world through damp fabric. It left me numb. The place was slow death.

We walked up to a fine-looking, brick-built detached house on a suburban cul-de-sac. A driveway led up to the front door.

This was it.

'Home'.

Marcia opened up and I followed her in, dragging my suitcase. Chris lifted the other one over the doorstep. The hall smelled vaguely damp and musty. Off to the side was a communal kitchen. Clocking its filth and cracked surfaces, I decided there and then never to cook in it.

"You're in here," said Marcia, slotting a key into a door on the ground floor. She pushed it open to reveal a double bed, headboard and mattress pressed flush against the walls on either side. It filled the whole room.

Marcia gave me a couple of keys and said, "Keep the phone on and try not to worry. I'll be checking in on you. I'm only a call away. OK?"

I nodded.

"This is the tenancy, if you could sign here," she said, handing me a pen.

I quickly scanned the page. "£900 a month?!" I said. "How am I going to pay that?"

"I'll be over next week and we'll sort out your benefits," Marcia reassured me.

And then they left. And I was on my own again.

Looking around the bare room, I wondered how many more lost and desperate souls had been marooned here, all for the princely sum of £900 a month.

Deep breath.

OK, I thought, *let me at least try and unpack some things.*

But first – a little spring clean. I hit up the Morrisons nearby for some cleaning products and set about disinfecting the place. I went to flip the mattress – and made a discovery that flipped my stomach instead. Stashed underneath was a bunch of used syringes, blackened foil and stained, sooty drug spoons.

The irony. Me – the newly-reformed drug dealer retching at the discovery of drug paraphernalia in her room.

It was the last straw.

Fuck it, I thought. *I can't do this. I've got to get out of here.*

To get out, I needed money. OK, I had my 12 bags in cash – but a girl can burn through that in no time. And that's not my mentality. I'm a hoarder. Remember that first £50 I got helping Trey sell weed? Saved it. That 50 spot was revered like some holy artefact.

I was a die-hard trapper, and there was only one way I knew to make money.

Selling drugs.

27

OUT OUT

My iPhone returned silently from the dead, white Apple logo blinking into being against the black. Thumbing through contacts, I found one boy I knew – Dwayne – from east. Walthamstow area. Back in the day, Dwayne had reached out to me, trying to poach me for his own operation.

Now I'd officially left the firm, he could have me.

"I'm in Essex," I told him. "What you saying? Can I come country?"

When Gang Exit works, it works brilliantly, and I'll always be grateful to them. But in that moment, I'd been manoeuvred out of one gang – potentially straight into the clutches of another. It just so happened that, luckily, this one boy had his own lone-wolf thing going.

He was happy to hear from me. "Perfect, come! I'm OT now. I'll pick you up tomorrow, sort out the details."

That night, I slept soundly for the first night in about a week. Still fully clothed, because I didn't have any clean bedsheets, and to me that place was a crack house. I dealt with it as I would any country trap.

The next morning, Dwayne met me at Stratford station and took me to the Westfield mall nearby to chat business over breakfast.

"Always wanted to work with you, D," he said.

"Here I am!"

"Do you know Ipswich?"

"Never been," I shrugged.

"No worries, you'll pick it up."

"I haven't got any food to bring to this," I told him. Fronting my own drugs was off the table.

"You'll help me flip mine," he said. "You OK with £600 a week to start? See how we go?"

"Sounds perfect. Let's go."

The way Dwayne's cunch spot worked, he rarely stayed OT. For the next three months, he'd pick me up at like five or six in the morning, we'd head up to Ipswich and hit the shots until around 1am. He operated a bit differently, in that he didn't like serving up out the window, so we'd always go in a house. But the shoots were the same as they were everywhere else – desperate people craving their drugs. We'd limp back down the A12 in the early hours to grab a few hours' sleep. Sometimes I'd stay at his place in East London, or at Haina's. If we were too tired for the drive, occasionally we'd crash in a cheap hotel OT. Net result was I spent less and less time in the emergency accommodation. And I never ate food there – I'd get takeaway, or eat on the road on the way home from country, or get Dwayne to take me out. All of which suited me fine.

Now, at least, I had a plan. I was selling drugs with an eye on an endgame – I couldn't stay in Essex, and I wasn't convinced Gang Exit would facilitate the move south. I wanted to put down enough savings to do it myself. Integrating with Dwayne or working with him long term was not on the agenda. Going back to my original block was out of the question.

In the meantime, I could also maintain my lifestyle. Going from big money to no money was scary. I'd become accustomed to having nice clothes, and selfishly I still wanted to live like I was living before. Going shopping. Buying designer. Getting my nails and hair done. I couldn't manage without my luxury necessities – and they cost money.

It didn't go unnoticed. Marcia visited me in Grays around once a week, and always clocked my flawless gel manicures, hair extensions and box-fresh trainers. Stratford Westfield had become my second home. "You've always got your nails done," she'd say. "Have you been to the salon again?"

I'd brush it away. Marcia wasn't stupid – she probably had an idea what I was on, but my probation appointments had been all but shelved for the time being until I got permanently settled. Lydia came to the Stratford office three or four times to check in on me, but no one was really digging deep into what I was up to. They tried. They really did. I was even offered counselling, but I pushed back, still not ready to fully commit or drop my guard. I was in survival mode.

"I'm grateful for your help getting me out," I told Marcia. "But there's nothing more you can do for me."

Back in the ends, people started to question my unexplained disappearance. I'd deactivated my Insta and Snapchat, and changed my phone number, so the old team had no way of reaching me directly. Instead, they bent Haina's ear, hoping she'd let something slip. I don't know if it was out of concern, or whether they were trying to track me down.

"Dajuan was asking after you," Haina told me.

"Asking how?"

"Like – have you heard from D? Is she OK? I just told him you'd gone off the radar and needed time."

No worries there. Haina was looking out for me.

I always knew I was gonna shake Dwayne at some point, and that moment came in December 2016. Whatever plan the council had in store regards re-housing me – it didn't seem to be happening. I decided to take matters into my own hands and found a privately rented flat in Herne Hill.

"You've got a deposit then?" Marcia asked me, surprised.

"Yeah, got it. I've been saving."

Don't know how she thought I'd managed that, but she didn't ask any questions. Three days before Christmas, I turned the key in the door to my new place and breathed a sigh of relief. It wasn't anything special – a top-floor, attic-conversion flat with sloping ceilings.

But it's mine, I thought.

The same day, I blocked Dwayne from calling or messaging me. He'd served his purpose – I'd made my money.

I hit up Ikea, bought clean bedsheets, got some snacks in and hunkered down for Christmas. Me, the TV and endless *Harry Potter* films. I was just happy to be safe and alive, and making a home for myself. It was brilliant. Finally, I was out.

Marcia stayed in contact. She gave it everything, phoning me regularly to make sure I was OK, travelling all over the place to come see me. I was ready to start living like a regular human being, which meant going back to the classroom. And finding a job.

"I don't know if I can do this," I sighed, staring blankly at the online university application form. I could sell drugs and backchat the police all day long, but I'd lost confidence in doing anything vaguely normal.

Marcia was sat beside me in the public library as my leg jackhammered with nerves below the table. I was all set to cut. "Don't worry, I'll help you," she said. "It's not as bad as it looks. Trust me."

We went through it together. I had my GCSEs, plus I'd scraped a couple of AS levels out of college before I'd left to have my baby. *Is it going to be enough?* I wondered.

Turns out, yeah. It was enough.

A few months later, I was astonished to get the green light. My personal statement swung it, I think. My life experience. The uni liked that. I enrolled on the same degree Marcia had done – Applied Social Science, Community Development and Youth Work.

The first day was another lesson in the definition of 'daunting'. I hadn't written an essay in maybe 10 years. Here I was, in a South London university, surrounded by South London girls, with years of lectures, tutor groups and exams ahead of me. And how was I ever going to find my place among all these student types?

But as it turned out, I instantly felt at home among the other girls on my course. One had been jail for importing drugs for a London gang. Another girl, Deon – now my best friend – was going through domestic violence with her good-for-nothing baby dad. There were loads of single mums. The course was full of girls like me, from working-class backgrounds. We all had fire in our bellies for social work. Not for the money, but because we cared.

I had a run of little jobs through uni – standard retail and hospitality stuff like WHSmith's, Costa and Vodafone. Later, I started volunteering at a specialist charity supporting women in the criminal justice system. Lydia had put me on to them for support while I was still living in Grays. It was only when I started uni that I stopped seeing my caseworker, Holly, as an inconvenience – and instead she became an inspiration. We'd meet every week, and Holly would bring her big-sister vibes. A rational big sister. She was the first independent person who, when I opened up about hood life, made me see it wasn't normal. Even Haina was biased to an extent – she'd come along with me for the ride. My people had become her friends.

Still, my past was never *that* far behind me, and certain people weren't going to let me forget it in a hurry. I was back on Instagram and was heading home from uni one day when Dajuan detonated my DMs.

Where are you? What's happened to you? I want to talk to you.
Boom!

A chill crept across my skin, the hairs on the back of my neck prickled, like a ghost had walked through me. Heart pounding, I searched the faces around me in the street, certain my new life was about to come crashing down. I felt like I was being watched. Then I bent back to my phone and blocked him without replying.

Another time – I still kick myself for this one – came when I went shopping up Westfield with an old friend from the ends. She'd never been in 'the gang', but she was trying to distance herself from the area all the same.

"You can't tell them lot we're talking," I told her.

"No, I wouldn't. I'm not in touch with them anyway."

"OK," I said. "Fancy meeting up? Go shopping?"

We set a date and I headed north over the Thames into my old stomping grounds. Everything was cool, I thought, apart from my friend spending an awful lot of time on her phone between shops. We were there all day and weren't long off saying our goodbyes when out of nowhere I sensed a blur of movement behind me and my temple exploded in pain. I hit the floor as my legs turned to jelly and folded beneath me. Two boys stood over me, raining kicks and punches, as I screamed for help. One of them pulled a knife and I just had time to think *'this is it'* before security piled in and the boys hightailed it off through the hordes of rubber-necking shoppers.

My 'friend' from the ends had set me up. Not with the old lot, bizarrely, but with Dwayne from east. Turned out he'd been robbed after I blocked him, and he was blaming me. I'd had no clue this girl even knew the boy. Stupid me. Never went back to Westfield again.

I stuck with the degree course for the duration, focusing on the learning and shunning the social side of student life. I'd go to lectures. Leave. Do my work. Being a 'student'? I wasn't on that. My campus was mostly art and drama for posh kids, which was not my bag.

Then, one morning in August 2020, I was woken at 6am by my phone bleating. It was results day, and Deon couldn't contain her excitement.

"We fucking did it!" she squealed.

"Oh my God!" I was screaming. I couldn't believe I'd actually completed a whole degree. Not only completed – I was one of only two students out of 24 to land a first-class honours. Finally, I really was Top Girl. In something that mattered.

When a job came up at the charity I'd been volunteering in for two years, I jumped at the chance. Right now, I'm employed as a young person's key worker. I work with girls aged 15 to 24 who, for whatever reason, have wound up in the criminal justice system. My caseload includes kids in and leaving care who've had some kind of engagement with criminal law enforcement. It might be something petty like a girl getting arrested for stealing from a shop, or it could be a far more serious crime like getting nicked for smuggling drugs to a prison boyfriend. Sometimes I'm just there for emotional support. Like Holly did for me, I fill that big-sister role. I can talk to kids about these things, because I've done it all. My learning's come full circle, too. Marcia inspired me to do the same degree as her, and one of my clients is now enrolled on the same course.

So, future – looking brighter. Past – where it belongs. I'm moving forward, but even as I'm writing this, part of me is still curled up – hollowed – on the old battlefields.

I still wake taut with anxiety from nightmares of being shot.

When I close my eyes, the faces of gaunt, harrowed addicts – open sores oozing pus – loom on the dark screen inside my head.

I see severed fingers falling to the ground and hear my son calling for me from the backseat of a stranger's car.

The stench of burning hair catches in my throat. I gag at the sensory memory of lavender tissues. In my mind, I rewind and replay the silent video identity parades of the boys who raped me. Turning to the left. Turning to the right. Facing forward.

People say to me sometimes, as I'm telling them stories about my old life, "It sounds like you don't care."

But I do care. I just don't *feel*.

I rarely cry. Emotion has been numbed out of me. Sometimes I feel nothing except anger and anxiety. I can't go into crowded places. I don't trust anyone. I can't stand touching raw meat – I've been told it's because I've seen so many wounds. I see police everywhere I go, and still feel like I'm gonna get nicked at any given moment, even though I'm doing absolutely nothing wrong. Until recently, I didn't know this had a name. It's called complex post-traumatic stress disorder. I'll be embarking on trauma therapy very soon.

Gang life is no place for a woman, and it's no place for a man either. It's no place for anyone. The dazzling Instagram facade might make it look fun and glamorous and easy.

It's not any of those things.

It's scary. It's dangerous. You can't sleep.

You might just get out of it alive, and you might even ride out a lucky streak and stay out of prison – but it will trash your mental health. Those photos of stacks of cash, smart cars and Balenciaga trainers are only part of the story.

You've heard the rest, and it's not pretty – right?

People sometimes ask me what I came out with after my five years shotting drugs. They reckon I must have a walk-in wardrobe stashed with designer clothes, and shoeboxes full of cash.

But no.

The designer is all gone, and I used every last penny of my life savings – all the cash I had from the road, plus a bit more – to find my son.

After two years, and six family court hearings, I was granted what's called a 'whereabouts order', which means I have to be told where Lloyd is living, what school he's in and his dad's phone number. On birthdays and at Christmas, I get photos. I write to Lloyd regularly and send him gifts. Money well spent.

That's what I came out with.

A piece of paper from the courts that says I can see my son.

He's 10 now. I've just got to hope that someday, he'll want to see me.

One step at a time.

EPILOGUE

MY SON

My son, I love you. I loved you from the moment I felt you squirm in my tummy. I loved you when I saw the black and white blurry image in the hospital and you were waving your hands. I looked at your daddy and I felt so happy. I was already so proud to be your mum. I dreamt of what you would look like. Every day that I got bigger was another day I got to care for you. Your dad looked after me, making me healthy meals, and we lay in bed together at night talking to you.

You arrived on your due date, which I've been told is kind of rare. It was such a blur, I couldn't move but I could hear you crying and I saw the nurse hand you to your dad to hold. We spent a week in hospital together and I hardly slept because I couldn't stop looking at you! Your hair was so long and curly, and you had fine down all over your body, so you felt so soft. Your skin was a beautiful, golden colour and your eyes were so dark brown they looked black. I remember thinking you looked like a Disney character. I named you after your dad.

I remember how your hands felt, and also how it felt to have your tiny little body tucked in next to me. Your eyelashes were so long they touched your eyebrows. You were so perfect.

We spent the next few months together, and you barely left my side. I took you to the park to play on the swings, and your little legs would kick out because you were so happy. We fed the ducks, went shopping in Westfield where I bought you so many toys and beautiful clothes, and to London Zoo. I treasure my photo of us by the lion cage, you in your buggy with a big smile on your face.

I'd do anything to go back in time and hold on to you tighter. But baby, I didn't see any of this coming – and then all of a sudden you were gone. I've never felt emptiness like it and I doubt I ever will again. When you went, you took half my heart and soul with you too. The pain of looking into my bedroom and not seeing you there was so intense, it felt like I was burning from the inside out.

I think about you all the time, I wonder what your voice sounds like now, I wonder what makes you laugh and what your friends are called. I wonder what your favourite food is. I wonder if you ever think of me.

I haven't written this letter to cause you hurt or upset – I want it to be a letter of love.

Always be kind, and always be strong, in whatever direction life takes you. Find happiness and remember you can be whoever you want to be. I may not be with you physically, but I'm here. Every time I miss you, I look into the sky and remember that we will forever be looking at the same sun or the same moon. I'm not too far away and I hope that in some way you can feel my presence.

Acknowledgements

Robin – and all the team at Mardle – thank you for believing in my story and giving me and other young girls a voice, thank you for putting up with my bad time keeping and for making me feel comfortable! Thank you for putting so much time, effort and dedication into making my story come alive.

Haina, you have been there since the beginning, we have laughed, and we have cried. Thank you for always being there for me no matter what the circumstances. You are the sister I never had. You made me feel strong when I felt weak, and I will forever be grateful.

Holly and Lydia, I have never met two more passionate women than both of you, you made me feel safe, you made me believe I was more than who I was, you took some of your courage and handed it to me. Thank you for not giving up on me, you restored my hope and gave me back the chance to dream and have aspirations. Holly, I am proud to work alongside you now and call you my friend.

Mama, I love you, I have no other words apart from I love you and I hope I have made you proud. You are a strong, beautiful, and fiercely passionate mum. It's only now I realise the sacrifices you made for me.

Dave, thank you for being the calm in the storm, thank you for taking care of mama.

B, you are the light I never expected to find, you have given me so much happiness, thank you for making me feel confident again and for making me feel safe. I am eternally grateful.

Deon, my sister, my right hand. You are without doubt the most resilient woman. Your children are so proud of you and so am I. You have never once let me give up, you motivate me every day. You are an amazing mother and friend and I can't wait to see you live your dreams, I love you.

About the authors

Danielle grew up in London with first generation immigrant parents, attending a nearby grammar school. During her school years she became involved with 'gangs' and crime. She was raped by four men at the age of 15, a crime which went unprosecuted by the police. She took a frontline role in county line drug dealing with a well-known London 'gang', which lasted for around 5 years, during which she witnessed serious gun and knife crime, as well as the more glamorous side of organised crime.

Assisted by probation services she was able to move away from the area for a fresh start. She enrolled at university and graduated with a first-class degree. She has since advocated for women in the criminal justice system, speaking to judges and law enforcement about the role of women in gangs. She began a Masters Degree in September 2021.

* * *

Robin Eveleigh is a freelance journalist with over 20 years' experience writing for national and digital titles, including Vice, The Guardian and the Daily Mirror.